Counselling in a Multicultural Society

EDITED BY
STEPHEN PALMER
AND
PITTU LAUNGANI

SAGE Publications
London • Thousand Oaks • New Delhi

Editorial arrangement and Introduction Stephen Palmer and
Pittu Laungani 1999
Chapter 1 © Don Rawson, Graham Whitehead and Mohan Luthra 1999
Chapter 2 © Pittu Laungani 1999
Chapter 3 © Fred Roach 1999
Chapter 4 © Waseem Alladin 1999
Chapter 5 © Zack Eleftheriadou 1999
Chapter 6 © Pittu Laungani 1999
Chapter 7 © Stephen Palmer 1999
Chapter 8 © Stephen Palmer 1999

First published 1999

SAGE Publications Ltd
6 Bonhill Street
London EC2A 4PU

SAGE Publications Inc.
2455 Teller Road
Thousand Oaks, California 91320

SAGE Publications India Pvt Ltd
32, M-Block Market
Greater Kailash – I
New Delhi 110 048

British Library Cataloguing in Publication data

A catalogue record for this book is available
from the British Library

ISBN 0 7619 5064 8
ISBN 0 7619 5065 6 (pbk)

Library of Congress catalog card number 98–75103

Typeset by Mayhew Typesetting, Rhayader, Powys
Printed and bound in Great Britain by Athenaeum Press, Gateshead

Counselling in a
Multicultural Society

To Maggie and Ann

CONTENTS

CONTRIBUTORS

Waseem Alladin is Chief Editor of *Counselling Psychology Quarterly: An International Journal of Theory, Research and Practice* and an Associate Member of the Institute of Directors. He is a consultant clinical and counselling psychologist with the East Yorkshire Community Healthcare Trust, Beverley, where he is the specialist in cognitive therapy. He is an Honorary Fellow in Clinical Psychology, PsyD Clinical Course, School of Medicine, University of Hull. He is also Director of the Centre for Couple, Marital and Sex Therapy. His current interests are in transcultural medicine, hypnosis, cognitive therapy for social dysfunction and forensic neuropsychology.

Zack Eleftheriadou, MSc, MA, Dip. Infant Mental Health, UKCP Reg. Psychotherapist, is a Chartered Counselling Psychologist and Psychotherapist. She works in private practice in North London entitled Noema Psychotherapy and Counselling Service. She is the coordinator of the Cross-Cultural Counselling and Psychotherapy course at Regent's College and course tutor for the Counselling for Refugees course at Birkbeck College, University of London. She has published widely, including the recent book *Transcultural Counselling*. She is currently completing a research project on children's representations of culture through drawings.

Pittu Laungani PhD is an Associate Professor in Psychology at South Bank University, London. His research interests are in the field of cross-cultural psychology, and over the years he has published more than 50 research papers in academic journals, contributed several book chapters on topics related to identity, mental illness, therapy, counselling, stress, death and bereavement, child abuse, health and illness – all of them from a cross-cultural perspective. He has also written and edited several books, including *Death and Bereavement Across Cultures*, published by Routledge in 1997, and a play entitled *The Strange Affliction of Hamlet, Prince of Denmark*, which was published by the British Psychological Society Division of Counselling Psychology in 1997. His book *India and England: a Psychocultural Analysis* is due out in 1998, and a new play, entitled 'Pillars of Society', had its world premiere in Melbourne in August 1998.

Mohan Luthra (Manmohan S. Luthra) has worked in local government for a number of years and has been a senior education officer. He has also been research fellow and principal lecturer at Brunel and South Bank Universities respectively. Currently he works at West London Leadership as Regeneration Manager.

Stephen Palmer PhD is Director of the Centre for Stress Management and the Centre for Multimodal Therapy in London, and is an Honorary Senior Clinical and Research Fellow at City University. He is a Chartered Psychologist (counselling and health), a UKCP registered psychotherapist and a health educator specializing in stress management and counselling. He is a Fellow of the British Association for Counselling and the Royal Society of Arts. During the period 1998–99 he is Chair of the Institute of Health Promotion and Education. He edits three book series in the field of stress counselling and psychotherapy, including the new *Brief Therapy* series (published by Sage).

Fred Roach, PhD, AFBPsS, CPsychol, is a Consultant Forensic Clinical Psychologist and Head of Psychology Specialty for Forensic Psychology Services within the Surrey Oaklands NHS Trust. He is also Head of Psychology Specialty for Alcohol and Substance Misuse Services and is a Listed Law Society Directory Expert Witness. His therapeutic interests include cognitive behavioural therapy, brief psychotherapy and hypnosis. Dr Roach also runs a private practice offering professional supervision, counselling, psychological assessment and treatment.

Don Rawson PhD is a Chartered Psychologist and is employed as a lecturer in Counselling Psychology at City University, London. He also maintains a small private practice. With a background in social psychology, he has a special interest in mind–body problems. His publications include an analysis of health promotion theory and development of models of interprofessional working.

Graham Whitehead MSc has been working in the field of student counselling since 1990, following completion of his training at Reading University. He is currently Senior Counsellor at South Bank University in London. He works from a humanistic integrative perspective with academic interests in transcultural and transpersonal counselling and psychotherapy.

INTRODUCTION: COUNSELLING IN A MULTICULTURAL SOCIETY

Stephen Palmer and Pittu Laungani

To use the well-worn cliché, the world has turned into a global village. Travel has become safe and easy, so much so, that many people live in one country and commute to work daily in another, thus adding a completely new dimension to the concept of work and travel. At the other end of this dimension, an increasing number of people in the West work from home. Those who work at home have little reason to feel deprived of the experiences enjoyed by those who travel. Multiple satellite transmissions make it possible for people to 'invite' the outside world into their homes. Moreover, by clicking their 'mouse' they are able to explore and surf through cyberspace and enjoy the exhilaration of virtual reality. It is clear that the outside world is catching up with the world inside our homes and our heads.

In the past decade people from different countries have come to Britain. There has been a steady flow of people from the European Union countries, from Eastern Europe, from the new Commonwealth countries, from Africa, from Hong Kong, and from countries in South East Asia. The persons coming to Britain have included a vast assortment of political refugees, asylum seekers, tourists and other types of 'settlers'. In addition to the newcomers, Britain, as a result of its past historical associations, has been the beneficiary of several groups of Asians (from India, Pakistan, Bangladesh, Sri Lanka, East Africa, South Africa), African-Caribbeans and Africans, most of whom emigrated to Britain soon after the Second World War to set up homes in Britain.

Some politicians in Britain have expressed concern over what they see as an influx of outsiders wishing to settle in Britain. There is among some politicians a belief, shared by many others in the country, that when people migrate to Britain they ought to jettison their cultural baggage. It is believed that such a course of action will assist greatly in the rapid process of assimilation to the norms of the host country. Such a belief is naïve, false and potentially dangerous. It is naïve because it is unworkable. It is potentially dangerous because a fiat of such a nature is in direct infringement of fundamental human rights. Such a belief also rests on the false assumption that the norms of the host country are the only ones that matter, and regardless of the kind of norms and values the outsiders might have imbibed in their own cultures, it is incumbent upon them to acquire the dominant norms of the host culture. No country or culture can claim to set up a 'gold standard' of norms and values, which the rest of the world is expected to follow.

What the proponents of the assimilationist policies keep forgetting is that people do not jettison their 'cultural baggage' when migrating to another country. What many politicians and indeed a host of other well-meaning individuals do not appreciate is that all of us are firmly rooted to our own culture. The roots run deep. They extend over several centuries. One can no more sever one's attachments to a culture than a tortoise can leave its shell. People bring with them not just their unique skills and qualifications and experiences. They bring with them their hopes, their aspirations, their ambitions, and of course their fears (known and unknown) and their uncertainties. Their own cultural beliefs and values, their traditions, their religious practices, their customs, their rites, rituals and ceremonies, their dietary practices, their family structures and, equally importantly, their own language(s) are an integral part of their upbringing. No immigrant in that sense ever travels light. No immigrant ever sheds his or her cultural legacies and acquisitions easily.

From a social psychological point of view, the mixture of cultures within the mainstream of British society provides exciting opportunities to academics, scholars, clinicians, doctors, health professionals and a host of other interested care-providers, for learning and acquiring insights into a variety of multicultural issues. For instance, several fundamental questions can be raised. How do people from different cultures bring up their own children? What constitutes child abuse in their culture? What are the parameters which they consider important in the socialization process? What are their attitudes and values towards women, towards the sick, the infirm and the elderly? What rules govern their family structures and kinship patterns? How do they grieve and mourn for their dead? How do they perceive members of the host culture, and vice versa? How do they attempt to relate to one another? To what extent do they succeed or fail to succeed in forming meaningful relationships with members of the host culture? What are the factors which lead to failures and successes? What effect do the dominant values of the host culture have on their own system of values? How far do their own values impinge upon the values of the host culture? In addition to clear psychological insights it also becomes possible to tease out the social, economic and political consequences which are likely to occur when people of different cultures, speaking different languages, imbibing different moral values, share and/or compete for available resources related to occupations, housing, medical care, and so on. What are the short-term and long-term consequences which are likely to occur in such a culturally diverse society?

It is beyond the scope of this book to address ourselves to all the issues raised above. This book is concerned with one important feature of the broad canvas that has been painted above. It deals with the very vital issue of considering the types of counselling and psychotherapeutic services which might be offered to people of different cultures living in Britain. What are their needs? What is the best way of meeting such needs?

A book of this nature could not be the creation of one or two persons. In planning this book, the Editors decided to call upon the expertise of people working in this area, inviting each of them to share their experiences in areas of counselling and a variety of related issues surrounding this difficult yet exciting field. They have all worked in the areas of multicultural, multiethnic counselling, and are intimately conversant with the major issues surrounding this delicate and sensitive area of work. The fact that more questions have been raised than have actually been answered, is in itself commendable. Given the delicate nature of counselling, it is certainly more desirable to raise intelligent and sensitive questions which at present may be difficult to answer than provide instant answers which, upon reflection, aided by one's experience, may turn out to be false. Several profound and thought-provoking questions have been raised throughout the book.

Even within an 'ideal' monocultural setting (what constitutes ideal, remains an open question), the field of counselling is beset with known and unknown difficulties. For instance, one is not always clear whether one is *actually* helping one's clients to determine their own life goals, or whether one's involvement as a counsellor or a therapist has had any positive effects upon the psyche and the eventual behaviour of the client. Sometimes it becomes inordinately difficult to define what one means by a positive outcome. One may find that one's definition is at total variance with those of other counsellors. Although one may formulate a set of interesting hypotheses, one may not be clear as to what it is about the counselling process that leads to a positive (or negative) outcome. One feels handicapped by one's inability objectively to test those hypotheses. What complicates the problem further is the fact that there isn't any one guiding theory of counselling to which all counsellors subscribe. There are several competing and complementary theories of counselling, each with its own traceable origins, and its own sets of assumptions, its own formulations and approaches, its own methods, and its own expected outcomes. Followers of a given theoretical approach often tend to ignore if not deride other theoretical approaches. This of course makes the task of evaluating the efficacy of theories an exciting but extremely difficult proposition.

But when it comes to counselling people from different ethnic and cultural backgrounds the above problems get compounded. Cross-cultural counselling is like venturing into uncharted psychic territories. One might find oneself moving into areas about which very little is known. For instance, one may be unfamiliar with the language of the client, one may have little knowledge of the cultural background of the client, one may find that the client's 'world view' is different from the counsellor's and so on. And moreover what may be known may not, upon reflection, turn out to be anything of any significance. There are several such issues, including the cultural and the racial setting within which counselling occurs, to which competent and informed counsellors would need to be sensitized. Many of these issues which, in a sense, are integral to cross-cultural counselling, have been addressed by the experts contributing to the making of this book.

The book contains eight chapters in all. The first, written by Don Rawson, Graham Whitehead and Mohan Luthra, considers the challenges of counselling in a multicultural society. Adopting a historical approach, the chapter offers valuable explanations and insights into important terms such as culture, race, ethnicity etc., and then goes on to examine the problems of counselling in a multicultural society. Written against the backdrop of contemporary British society, the chapter presents models that would help counsellors to understand cultural diversity. To highlight the issues involved in cross-cultural counselling, the authors offer a fascinating detailed case study as an Appendix to their chapter.

The second chapter, by Pittu Laungani, considers the notion of culture from several different theoretical perspectives, and examines the manner in which culture(s) influence and impact upon the acquisition of one's identity. The chapter presents a theoretical model which allows the reader to understand the fundamental differences and similarities between Asian (Indian) cultures and Western (British) cultures in terms of their salient beliefs and values, which exercise a powerful influence on their private and social behaviours. The chapter argues that an objective knowledge of the salient features of another culture can be a valuable asset in counselling.

Fred Roach, in the third chapter, examines the entire problem of cross-cultural counselling against the backdrop of racism: personal, societal and institutionalized. The chapter highlights the major racial problems which are likely to arise in cross-cultural counselling, and offers invaluable and sensitive insights into how counsellors might be trained to deal effectively with such problems.

In Chapter 4, Waseem Alladin highlights some of the Western models of counselling, examining in the process, the underlying theoretical assumptions of such models. He then considers the question of whether a transcultural model of counselling can be accommodated within the mainstream of Western counselling. He argues that some of the features of the indigenous models of counselling may not be compatible with Western models, and proposes a unique and yet workable solution to this dilemma.

The fifth chapter, written by Zack Eleftheriadou, outlines the specific counselling needs of those who come from different racial or cultural backgrounds. The chapter illustrates how a counsellor can take into account the client's cultural context. She is acutely aware of the dangers of generalizations that can occur in undertaking such an exercise, and offers rational approaches to dealing with this very important issue. She provides an excellent overview of the multicultural population of Britain from several different perspectives, which form the basis of the further development of her main thesis.

In the sixth chapter, Pittu Laungani discusses the suitability or the adaptability of the client centred model of counselling in relation to the ethnic minorities in Britain. After discussing the origins and the main features of the client centred model, he offers a sharp critique of the model, arguing that there are inherent limitations within it which would restrict its uses on Western clients. Moreover, when used with members of ethnic minorities, the client centred model is likely to be unworkable. He then offers a culture centred model (elaborated in Chapter 2) as a replacement for the client centred model.

In Chapter 7, Stephen Palmer is concerned with the extremely important problem related to effective counselling across cultures. He discusses a variety of issues which affect one's search for effective counselling. Several pertinent arguments are raised, several theoretical orientations and empirical approaches used by counsellors in Britain and in the United States are examined. He argues that the multimodal approach, with relevant modifications, would provide counsellors with a workable model which they could use with members of ethnic minorities.

The eighth chapter, also written by Stephen Palmer, describes the multimodal model in depth, and demonstrates how a multimodal perspective, first articulated by Arnold Lazarus, can be developed in individual counselling programmes. The versatility of this programme, which allows the counsellor to modify it to 'suit' the psychological and cultural needs of the client, make it eminently workable.

Each chapter includes four suggested discussion issues to help initiate further reflection and deliberation. Lecturers and trainers may also find suitable essay subjects in some of the discussion issues. The book also provides readers with the addresses of several organizations and agencies related to counselling in Britain (see Appendix 2). It needs to be emphasized that the book offers readers a clear insight into theoretical, practical, social and applied perspectives on multicultural counselling – set against the background of contemporary British society.

1

THE CHALLENGES OF COUNSELLING IN A MULTICULTURAL SOCIETY

Don Rawson, Graham Whitehead and Mohan Luthra

The practice of counselling has boomed in recent years. At the same time, counselling skills have been assimilated as an allied activity in many professions (such as social work, primary health care, education and even business consultancy). This has been attended by a proliferation of training courses offering a wide range of theoretical perspectives. Yet despite such expansion, there is cause for concern that counselling is set within a historically and culturally narrow structure. This is at odds with the increasingly multicultural society. The spread of training opportunities has evolved from a background of mostly psychodynamic, cognitive behavioural and humanistic traditions. Though these have much to offer, they are deeply embedded within a particular mono-cultural framework.

As McLeod (1996: 108) cogently summarizes, 'On the whole, the theory and practice of counselling and psychotherapy have served the dominant groups in society and largely ignored the problem of people who are disadvantaged against.'

Considerable demographic movement in the UK in the post-war years has resulted in transcultural communication being a necessity for many people using counselling skills. Multiculturalism demands the counselling profession expand its compass, and offer much more than is currently available.

Wrenn (1962) best describes the challenge, in positing that the transculturally competent counsellor needs to overcome 'cultural encapsulation'.

Terminology and contemporary discourses: the meaning of ethnicity, race and culture

The use of language is a sensitive area in cross-cultural studies. The term 'minority', for example, although frequently used to refer to some ethnic groups can be construed as insensitive by people living in areas where the term is statistically incorrect and inappropriately implies being outside the mainstream and hence of less social importance. Rack (1982) promotes the term 'cosmopolitan' to replace 'ethnic minority', which has now become a euphemism for a disadvantaged group in need of help.

Ethnicity can be a euphemism for race but is more commonly used to denote common origin. The concept thus overlaps with cultural and other identities. *Race* refers primarily to inherited physical character- istics. The biological basis for differences might have some evolutionary and health interest (for example, the function of skin pigmentation in adapting to climatic differences). Since, however, the concept reduces to gross appearance (skin colour, body shape, hair type etc.), its meaning is constrained by social and political values. Its pejorative derivative 'racism' amounts to a set of beliefs that one group who are identifiable by their physical characteristics are thereby of less value or inferior to another.

Culture has pedigree as a sociological and anthropological concept. It denotes how people live their lives through their particular beliefs and social practices, including religion and family customs. The *across cultures* epithet preferred in this volume currently retains positive con- notations. Sadly, however, where there is such a powerful set of social values, words can quickly cascade into negative associations. It may be that in a few years time, even the word 'culture' will be read as yet another outmoded euphemism for the same negative stereotyping.

Appropriate language selection is also an essential part of the trans- cultural process in counselling. This, however, is a tall order, and fear of using the wrong words, terminology and responses, no matter how well intentioned, can be all too easily misconstrued in cross-cultural com- munication. The reluctance of some practitioners to tackle culturally sensitive themes can no doubt be explained by this difficulty. Goldsborough (1996) asks why even the mention of equal opportunities reduces many to boredom, anger or anxiety, and concludes that awareness-raising exercises can, if badly handled, be attacking rather than challenging and supportive of change.

Terminology in this field has evolved considerably in recent years, with multiculturalism becoming a significant force in the development of academic debate and social policy. Pedersen (1996) argues that multi- cultural theory is a 'bottom up' social movement. That is, multicul- turalism has developed as social migrations have brought different cultures together which then highlight similarities and differences. Pedersen (1996) cautions, however, that the thinking behind the label multiculturalism has as much to do with defending social, economic and political colonization as with the desire to celebrate differences.

Different terms have become current in the debate surrounding cross- cultural counselling, with influential writers advocating particular phrases. They portray a distinct emphasis in the recognition of cultural difference. D'Ardenne and Mahtani (1989), for example, give preference for the active, reciprocal/relational and dynamic associations of *trans-cultural*. Others include *cross-cultural* (Pedersen, 1985), and *intercultural* (Kareem and Littlewood, 1992).

Subtle changes from major to minor

We are, of course, more context-bound than we think. Problems may arise where a minority cultural pattern is at variance with the dominant culture's time frame. Equally, it may offer legally sanctioned transitions which are at odds with the traditional mores of minority cultures.

Burnham (1986) also identifies problems inherent in time-related cultural patterns. For example, some of our customs are prescribed by law, such as children must attend school from the time they are 5 years old. Others, however, such as marriage and leaving home may be determined by other cultural forces. As Burnham (1986: 38) aptly summarizes, 'Such events signal cultural-specific rules.'

The greatest consequence for counsellors is to understand different practices in child rearing and the development of the family life cycle (Carter and McGoldrick, 1980). The literature on mid-life matters for different cultural groups, for example, is very sparse (Brown and Able Smith, 1996). This is significant given the advancing social demographic trend. Namely, a whole new ethnically diverse generation will soon be at the age where retirement becomes a major life transition.

Robbins (1996) reports that there is evidence that in many cultures the roles of men are changing and thus critically affecting help-seeking. The degree and pace of change, however, varies from culture to culture. Professional counselling is seen by Nigerian men as inappropriate where they support a large extended family. In Greece it is seen as an admission of weakness. This is also reflected in British regional and class differences. Northern working men are said to be similar in their attitudes to the Greeks. In the South, in contrast, middle-class men are more likely to accept the need for professional help.

Models to help counsellors understand cultural diversity

McGoldrick et al. (1982) published the first comprehensive attempt to map diverse ethnic groups in terms of cultural history, values and ethnically identifiable characteristics. In the USA a number of texts have since added to this stock of factual information on the cultural patterns of various ethnic minority groups. Little similar information has been collated in the UK (though Karmi, 1996, has been found useful, if somewhat brief). Krause and Miller (1995), however, are critical of this approach as almost being a travel guide for the counsellor to tour through the cultures of their clients.

In sounding cautions on the colonialism of psychological therapies and the implied racism of 'factual' stereotypes, Krause and Miller (1995) wish to challenge assumptions of cultural uniformity. Instead, a framework is suggested of 'good enough' transcultural understanding. As Krause and Miller express (1995: 155), 'We have no choice but to communicate with our clients through cultural codes.'

Fernando (1995) advocates a 'Relativistic multi-systemic approach' to problems of mental health and also emphasizes that culture is not fixed. Strong identification of ethnic diversity and cultural differences can lead to a view of culture as preset in a monolithic framework, whereas culture is constantly developing. Fernando (1995: 206) posits, 'culture of a group is something that "emerges" from society at large, including historical knowledge but by no means dominated by traditions.'

Most therapeutic models take little account of the complexity of relationships in the extended family. D'Ardenne and Mahtani (1989) contend that therapeutic models almost all have an emphasis on the self which undervalues the place of family and culture. The experience of clients brought up by many 'mothers' or other forms of collective child rearing practices may simply be beyond the explanatory reach of therapeutic models predicated on assumptions of dyadic parental units. Kareem (1988) describes the experience of a Nigerian client who was 'stuck' in accounting for his relationship to his mother. The client, however, had been fed by nine pairs of breasts. Cross-cultural counselling requires more than acceptance of differences, it demands knowledge and appreciation of divergent social structures and a sophisticated understanding of sociopsychological development.

In the Western world the dyadic relationship remains a significant social unit (Bubenzer and West, 1993). The nature of coupling, moreover, is voluntary, in contrast to the inherited ties and arranged alliances which sometimes characterize extended families. Against this, it should be said, some Western people, especially women, stay involuntarily in marriages because they fear the alternative; either social isolation following separation/divorce or financial disadvantage.

Models of the psychological functioning of black clients have been proposed with the aim of helping therapists improve the therapeutic process. Jones (1985), for example, proposes an interactive model for working with black clients which moves through the following stages:

1 Reactions to racial oppression.
2 Influence of the majority culture.
3 Influence of the client's culture.
4 Individual and family experiences and endowments.

Notice that the direction of exploration is opposite to the usual route of psychotherapeutic work (that is, from large macro influences towards more local influences of family). Other practical ways of engaging black clients at the early stages of therapy have been put forwards in order to build a treatment relationship (Jenkins, 1985).

The politics of identity

Erickson (1968) proposed that identity is a construct that represents a combination of individual uniqueness plus a striving for continuity of experience and group solidarity. He went on to hypothesize that the quality of an individual's psychological adjustment was dependent upon their personal identity (that is, one's feelings and attitudes towards oneself), their reference group orientation (that is, the extent to which one uses the value systems and culture of particular groups to guide one's feelings, thoughts and behaviours) and how they ascribe identity (that is, an individual's conscious affiliation or commitment to a particular group).

In colonial societies, identity is a central issue for people in a minority situation. The context they belong to is a matter of social and political empowerment as well as psychological wellbeing. Counsellors need to understand the psychological correlates of accepting an identity that has been conferred rather than being self-constructed.

Much postmodernist writing implies that identity can almost be chosen and that multidimensionality and fluidity of identities is a new phenomenon. In societies which have long been made of multiple ethnic and religious identities (pluralist societies), however, this has long been accepted as the social norm. Historically it has never been documented to be a source of psychological dysfunctioning. In any case, a number of forces from within ethnic communities and from the outside (such as Westernization and racism) shape the nature of identities of various ethnic groups in a British setting.

If the postmodern thinking about identity is to be believed, identity confusion is likely to be higher amongst the indigenous young people reared on a diet of rationalist certainties of modernism and very prone to the feeling of being alone in a culture much imbued with individualism and privacy. Hence, for many within the British Asian community the idea of being an Asian coexists (sometimes comfortably, sometimes not) with the idea of being a Muslim, another long distance identity without national identity. The Chinese also have a long distance affiliative non-nationalist identity. This is well known and owned by the various Chinese communities, aided further by the emerging economic culturalism which refers to *the Chinese way.*

Gilroy (1993) has attempted to establish the idea of a new distinct identity of being *Black Atlantic* for the African-Caribbean people, who are increasingly intermarrying into the indigenous white British population. For the growing number of children of mixed origin the experience of belonging to a black identity is a more important feature of their identity than skin colour. To this end Gilroy endeavours to develop a non-racialized identity whilst avoiding the pitfalls of ethnonationalism as well as Afrocentricism.

Struggles with dual identity are perhaps strongest in cases of transracial adoption (Jardine, 1996). Being manifestly part of one racial group on the outside and another adopting group on the inside, these people find themselves unable to voice their concerns about racism, unable to relate to their racial self and of being a stranger in that group. Jardine pleads for counsellors to take the cultural background of such clients into consideration, and acknowledge their experience of racism. The transculturally adopted have experiences synonymous with that of ethnic minority and black groups.

Cross (1971) provides a model of Black racial identity development entitled 'The negro-to-black-conversion-experience': This describes the attainment of positive identity via the following five stages:

1 Pre-encounter.
2 Encounter.
3 Immersion-emergence.
4 Internalization.
5 Internalization-commitment.

Gilroy (1993) adds another stage in which the individual does not see being an antiracist as the sole conception of their being.

The stages describe a shift from low self-esteem and acceptance of inferiority, through anger and guilt in becoming aware of oppression, through immersion in the world of 'blackness', to a developing sense of liberation. This culminates in a major psychological shift from negative to positive self-concept. The latter is said to be accompanied by realistic perceptions of individual position in society, and leads to challenges and activism.

The model, however, is not intended to be linear and applicable to every minority. It should not be assumed that all black and ethnic people start at the pre-encounter stages. Many young people have a positive sense of themselves and their racial identity from childhood. Furthermore, the extent to which a person is likely to start at the beginning will depend upon the extent to which they belong to a colonial experience of cultural imperialism.

Racism and transcultural counselling

Arguably, the responsibility of how and when to raise issues of racism rests with the counsellor, not with the client. D'Ardenne and Mahtani (1989) contend that transcultural counselling cannot, though, rectify racism and poverty, though d'Ardenne and Mahtani (1989) take a positive view of antiracism in their work and maintain that their position on culture is not neutral. Rather, they acknowledge the ethnocentricity of many practitioners and assert that counselling should be equally available to all cultural groups.

McLeod (1996: 150) is also critical of complacency in the mainstream. As he cogently describes, there is, 'no systematic attempt within humanistic therapy to assimilate the lessons of feminism or to confront the experience of racism and colonialism'.

Racism awareness training does not, however, enjoy a good reputation. If not handled sensitively, it can become a form of reverse racism, individually blaming white trainees who are made to feel personal guilt and responsibility for racism in society. The inevitable result is either disempowering of the trainee or a hardening and retrograde movement to a hidden racist position. Consequently, victims of such inept training become defensive. Ultimately this leads to Political Correctness (PC). As Goldsborough (1996: 11) aptly describes, PC is an 'Increasing reliance on taboo rather than debate [which] encourages anxiety in individuals and soon develops a veneer of adherence to a set of rules and correct language.'

Progress can be made, though, from a willingness to learn from mistakes. Negative criticism in contrast can frustrate progress leading counsellors to a tight-lipped reluctance to deal with cross-cultural issues. Clearly, an atmosphere of confidence is required, not a climate of fear.

The counselling relationship clearly demonstrates dynamics which point towards a power imbalance and hence the challenge to practitioners to give careful consideration to the possible expression either overtly or covertly of racial stereotypes. Again, this task is not an easy one for practitioners to approach and this question may be easily dismissed. Most practitioners will rightly insist that their intentions are strictly neutral, that they treat all their clients the same (meaning without favour or intentional prejudice). And no doubt this is true. The problem, however, is more shadowy.

Kareem (1988) notes that expectancy and dependency are always a part of the therapy process, and this is greatest when the client has a deprived background. Even the perceived need to have counselling can inadvertently reinforce stereotypes of inadequacy, that something is wrong with them because they are from a minority group. With sufficient repetition and indoctrination, victims of racism can come to believe it of themselves. Transcultural counselling, therefore, should have a liberating function, to help free clients from the sense of powerlessness which labelling reinforces.

Service provision and access

The post-war years have seen significant demographic shifts in the European communities. Practitioners are required to respond to a wider cultural client base. The significant question to arise is whether clients from minority groups receive a service that is culturally sensitive and responsive to their needs.

Providers of services have also to consider client utilization. Studies by Sattler (1977) and Sue (1977) show mental health services being underutilized. Sue and Zane (1987) state that therapists' inability to provide culturally responsive forms of treatment are the single most important reason for problems in service delivery. More recently, Tien and Johnson (1994) in their review of the literature found cultural sensitivity to be the major element contributing to successful therapy.

It is well documented that black and ethnic minority people are underrepresented in referral for verbal therapies. In addition, when black clients do enter therapy they tend to leave well before it is due to end (Sue, 1977). It is argued that rather than viewing black clients as untreatable by these means, changes in approaches are needed (Mays, 1985).

Active commitment of culturally appropriate services for black and ethnic minority clients will, however, require radical changes in practice (Nadirshaw, 1993). Only then is widespread trust likely to be gained, leading to better uptake of services. Whether it is a counselling service in a primary health care setting or staff counselling operation in a large multinational corporation, or even the use of counselling skills in a day care centre, the issues around service responsibility are similar.

The local context of the counselling organization is critical in a multi-cultural environment. Lago and Thompson (1996), for example, observe that in some cultures fear, shame and embarrassment at receiving counselling can all add to the original psychological distress. It may, therefore, be prudent to consider where the service is located and how it is described. Location is just one factor in service or agency strategy and cross-cultural sensitivity. Others include literature, availability of interpreters, languages spoken, and even the decorative style of waiting areas.

Service managers should build transcultural considerations into the basic economic equation of demand and supply. In particular, the following questions should be asked.

- Is there a clearly defined ethnic/cultural catchment client group for the service provision?
- Has this catchment group been surveyed?
- What distinctive cultural demands are there in this catchment?
- How can the service respond effectively to such groups?
- Does practitioner provision reflect the cultural diversity of the catchment group?
- Does the service monitor effectiveness of service provision with respect to cross-cultural sensitivity?

As in many other social services, there is little provision for language difficulties. Clearly, clients forced to use a second language cannot be expected to express themselves as fully as in their original tongue. More than this, some concepts do not translate so that cultural nuances may be missed. Fernando (1995) argues that interpreters could be used more broadly than merely translating speech. Rather, they should be regarded as 'cultural interpreters' to help inform the therapist about cultural and social codes and family structures. Interpreters thus will require further training in the therapeutic context.

Ethnic matching of counsellor and client

Doubts have been expressed that therapists from white middle class backgrounds are able to provide an effective therapeutic relationship for clients from minority groups (Vontress, 1971). Pedersen (1985) points out that there is considerable controversy as to whether counsellor and client should be culturally similar. Abramowitz and Murray (1983) provide evidence to suggest that minority clients have tended to prefer the same over opposite-race counsellors. Different conclusions, however, have perpetuated ambiguity on the issue. Tien and Johnson (1994) found that even though 60 per cent of their sample was made up of black people who preferred to see a black therapist, the major reasons for using the service depended upon the therapist's professional competence and attitudes, not just culture, race and linguistic compatibility. Similarly, Sue and Zane (1987) considered the ethnic match of practitioner and client should be more fully addressed.

Finding a match between counsellor and client is also beset with extensive practical difficulties, not least of which is the shortfall in the number of counsellors from ethnic minority groups. Whilst employing an ethnically matched counsellor can make the service more attractive to an ethnic group, counselling practitioners from different racial and ethnic backgrounds are unrepresented amongst the profession as a whole. Rectifying such an imbalance of supply and demand would require considerable determination and commitment from those with influence in recruitment and training of practitioners into professional bodies. The issue needs to be tackled at the societal level (for example, through the professional bodies). There are those who argue in favour of a period of positive discrimination in order to address the current imbalance. Lago and Thompson (1996) report increasing numbers of Black people are training in counselling and have formed the Association of Black Counsellors (ABC). Others, however, observe that counselling remains a very white middle class profession, and there are undoubtedly still not enough Black counsellors.

Lago and Thompson (1996) explored the implications for each pairing of black and white counsellor and client. On the neglected topic of black counsellors, they observe that black counsellors are most likely to be trained in the context of white middle class institutions and taught by members of the dominant cultural group. Ironically then, their training will have prepared them to deal with white not black clients. Lago and Thompson (1996) conclude that the black counsellor faces considerably greater professional demands than white practitioners and the shortage of black trainers and supervisors compounds the problem further.

Issues for white counsellors working with black clients include:

- Language differences.
- The client's experience of whites.
- The therapist's experience of blacks.
- Power and institutional problems.

The most recurrent motif in counselling with a cross-cultural element is, however, the problem of living in a multicultural society. Ramirez (1991) redefines the transcultural counsellor's task as being culturally flexible, to encourage the client to work in the best match of cultural behaviours.

Counselling clients who move between modern and traditional cultures may be especially problematic in the area of religion. Issues of fate and personal control, for example, are given powerfully different meanings by various religions. McLeod (1996) points out that counselling theory is predicated on largely Judeo-Christian religious traditions, though of course set in a humanistic and scientific framework. Traditional cultures contain their own 'counselling' systems of support and modes of helping people in crisis. Modern culture may come to supplant the traditional systems to make them effectively less available or perhaps conflict with them. It should, perhaps, be possible for the traditional and modern approaches to be complementary.

Some cultural groups may even need counselling to be labelled differently in order to be acceptable (perhaps, for example, 'discussions' for the Indian community; 'advice' for the African-Caribbean community). That is, there is a need to change the organizational aspects of the counselling process to fit the cross-cultural context. Different ways of working with extended family patterns of child rearing, family roles and responsibilities are also necessary.

Critical multiculturalism and critical psychology

The rapid expansion of multicultural society will inevitably disrupt the older understanding of social values. In Britain the law is not codified but based on case law. That is, the slow accumulating process of precedent forms the main touchstone of social values. The shock of new values inevitably leads to uncertainty and often to polarization. Political correctness might be seen as a reaction to this, as an expression of the need for clarity and codification.

Whilst society in the West can be seen to become materially multi-cultural (ethnic food etc. is popular), to what extent this trend is replicated in the spiritual, philosophical and the folk domain of life is a moot point. Whilst both the ethnic right and the white right have attacked multiculturalism, major questions remain unanswered. For instance, to what extent can the cultural practices of different ethnic groups be judged by universal human rights in terms of both mental and physical wellbeing when such practices are believed to cause illness or trauma (for example, circumcision, genital mutilations etc.)? Equally, it is important not to substitute one prejudice for another. It is all too possible for oppression within a cultural context to be ignored or effectively condoned because they are 'naturally' or intrinsically ethnic and should not be challenged.

Researchers concerned with culture have struggled with problems of trying to explain one culture from the perspective of another. Whilst much mainstream social research aims for universal explanations (that is to look for truths which apply across all cultures), it has become increasingly difficult to distinguish valid universals from cherished cultural values. The search for universals makes it possible to compare different cultures but can equally become a form of intellectual imperialism. There are also strong research traditions of cultural relativism, of claiming that each culture must have its own explanations in its own terms. Whilst this retains the richness of cultural diversity it can also logically reduce theory work to absurdity, of not being able to compare any cultural form with any other. The 'emic–etic' debate as this distinction is known remains an essentially contested problem (Alasuutari, 1995).

Much psychological theory reflects the predominant European and American cultural ideologies. Consequently, assumptions of institutionalized racism, ageism, sexism and other forms of cultural bias are all too often inherent in the application of psychological models. Parker (1989) reminds us that theories and models are not neutral. Each variant of psychology not only describes but creates reality and brings about the phenomenon being studied.

Littlewood and Lipsedge (1982) further observe that the dominant culture excludes non-members generating an out group of aliens. In turn, their diverse behaviours come to be seen as abnormal and deviant. Mental illness is itself a Western concept entailing mind–body dualism, and this social construction is arguably overdue for reappraisal. It may be that cross-cultural counselling can help promote a broader conception of mental health.

Black people are statistically overrepresented in the prison population and mental health settings, and are more likely to be sectioned under the Mental Health Act. Some groupings of black people are more likely to be given particular diagnoses (schizophrenia, for example). Research also shows that minorities are disadvantaged in their rights; racism and poverty together act to deprive them of legitimate rights (Cross, 1978).

Cross-culturalism is billed by Pedersen (1991) as a powerful fourth force in addition to the psychodynamic, behavioural and humanistic approaches. To be of practical relevance, however, cross-cultural studies need to highlight how the cultural context shapes and is shaped by counselling themes. Pedersen (1985) has documented several factors which contribute to the current limited perspective in this area.

- Cross-cultural counselling requires a collaborative, interdisciplinary approach which has not yet evolved.
- The complexity of cross-cultural issues means that it is easy to marginalize or avoid them completely.
- The links between counselling research and theory are tenuous.

The application of cross-cultural counselling theory into practice represents the greatest challenge facing practitioners at this stage of the development of the profession. It is also worth noting that much of the research in the area of transcultural counselling is of North American origin which inevitably influences both theory and practice. How this translates into the context of British culture is another (or meta) cross-cultural theme. In addition to assimilating American experience it is important that British counsellors contribute their own wisdom in the development of a transcultural approach.

Using current counselling models

Van Deuzen-Smith (1988) argues the existential phenomenological model is especially useful when applied to members of minority groups within a dominant culture, since it is said to suit people who perceive themselves as alienated from majority norms. The model explicitly values diversity of cultural and other identifications, and just as importantly, the concern with universal human experience provides a bridge for the counsellor (Spinelli, 1994). The existential approach also acknowledges a relativistic epistemology of perceived meanings. Eleftheriadou (1993) and Asmall (1994) further advocate its effectiveness for black communities.

Gilbert and Shmukler (1996) commend group work as a macrocosm of cultural issues since each member inevitably brings their own cultural heritage to bear. The resulting group culture is thus said to reflect whatever ethnic mix it contains and so provides through group processes the opportunity to challenge issues such as racism and other prejudices embedded in the British way of life.

Littlewood (1992) argues that family therapy has focused on belief systems rather than the deep structures affecting people. Ho (1987) contends the marginal impact of family therapy generally is precisely because of this narrow perspective. Norton (1978) insists that cultural family therapists need to be aware of the 'dual cultural perspective', especially of second generation ethnic minority clients.

Systemic thinking has been increasingly influential in counselling work in recent years, particularly as a means of addressing family difficulties. Proponents claim it expands counselling work to the broader social and cultural contexts (including gender, race and ethnicity, and historical political issues) which are seen to shape and interact with both the client's problems and the therapist's interventions (Bor et al., 1996).

Systemic family therapists focus on relationships systems. Families are by definition a system where family members are the elements and relationships are defined by operational interaction and feedback. The emphasis, however, is on social rather than necessarily biological family membership. Later systemic approaches also shifted the emphasis to one of the therapist not knowing (that is, not being expert about the family), but as someone who 'joins' the family system, co-constructing and co-evolving suitable interventions (Boscolo et al., 1987). Neutrality is said to come through curiosity rather than an external and epistemologically superior interpretive framework.

Systemic theorists have tried to move away from concepts of linear causality to circularity of explanations when dealing with interpersonal problems. Thus, for example, a person's anxiety may be seen to interact with family tensions rather than being caused by or causing them. Both may be self-sustaining as a system, each creating the conditions to bring about the other. This form of thinking is claimed to have brought about a significant shift in focus from individual to individual within context and a change to problem solving rather than analytical exploration. For psychotherapeutic counselling this amounts to an epistemological shift (Bor et al., 1996).

Liddle (1983) identifies two broad approaches of hypothesis generation used in systemic therapy which mirrors identically the emic–etic debate:

1 Universal dimensions of family functioning (Bowen, 1978). Since this implies a fixed frame of reference and observer neutrality/objectivity, it is essentially a positivist epistemology.
2 The family is its own frame of reference (Selvini-Palazzoli et al., 1980). This scheme explicitly rejects the idea of universal criteria and is therefore a relativist epistemology.

Bronfenbrenner (1976) distinguishes between two levels of system. The microsystem refers to the system parameters mapped by the family therapists. These are contained within the constellation of relationships between the person and their immediate environment (family, home and work settings etc). The macrosystem, in contrast, consists of the overarching cultural institutions including socioeconomic and legal-political infrastructure. Though usually considered to be outside the immediate scope of systems-based therapy, the wider system has an undoubted impact, and may be increasingly forcing its way through into the psychological microsystem. Campbell et al. (1991: 76) ask, 'Will people find increasingly that the meaning for their behaviours arises from the context outside their homes, such as . . . the political/social environment?'

The consequence for counsellors implies a role dilemma from therapy to social reform.

Training and development for transcultural counselling

The application of multicultural theories into transcultural therapeutic practice in Britain will be an ongoing process which will need reassessment and clarification to keep pace with cultural developments in this country. Distrust between minority and majority groups and the continuing blight of racial attacks can spread the same atmosphere of hostility and suspicion to the therapeutic environment. Transcultural training must therefore incorporate the relational aspect between the environment and the individual.

It may be useful to differentiate multicultural training which emphasizes the need for counsellors to be knowledgeable about different ethnic minority groups (the 'informed' model), from that which underlines the need for counsellors to expand their repertoire of communication skills (the 'sensitivity' model).

Sabnani et al. (1991) offer a comprehensive multicultural training model aimed at majority (white middle class) counselling trainees in the USA. The developmental training is promoted as improving on earlier stage models. This includes:

1 Pre-exposure/precontact.
2 Conflict.
3 Pro-minority/antiracism.
4 Retreat into white culture.
5 Redefinition and integration.

The model retains echoes of conversion experience and is interestingly comparable to the black racial identity model of Cross (1971) discussed earlier.

La Fromboise and Foster (1992) argue for specific training work within the scientist–practitioner model. The integration model draws cross-cultural content into all course material from general psychology to specializations in counselling psychology. The starting point is a basic understanding of cultural and political history of the main ethnic minority groups, which is claimed to be a prerequisite to understanding racism. 'Cultural synthesis' role play is recommended to simulate variation in client culture.

Transcultural training has shown promising developments in recent years. A number of courses have emerged in the past few years offering specialized/focused themes on cross-cultural counselling. A conference organized by UKCOSA (1996), for example, examined developments in cross-cultural theory and practice with respect to international education. The conference was organized to provide a forum in which UK participants had opportunity to reflect upon and reassess their own approaches to transcultural issues and to learn more about recent trends in cross-cultural theory and practice in North America.

The work of the RACE (Race and Cultural Education in Counselling) division of the British Association for Counselling is constantly pressing for greater inclusion of cross-cultural themes in counselling training. Similarly, the British Association of Inter-Cultural Therapists has begun to exert a positive influence. Kareem and Littlewood (1992) proposed to the UKCP (United Kingdom Council for Psychotherapy) that inter-cultural themes should be taken into consideration for training and practice.

The effect of training in transcultural themes

In an exploration of multicultural counselling competencies, Sue et al. (1992) suggest that inadequate training is the major reason for therapeutic ineffectiveness.

The link between practitioner training in transcultural themes and practitioner responsiveness to clients from different racial and cultural backgrounds is a central issue. Approaches to empirical research methodology, however, were questioned by Lefley and Urutia (1982), who conclude that attempts to evaluate cross-cultural training effectiveness had focused on theoretical frameworks of models rather than findings on efficacy.

Counselling theory and the degree of its effectiveness in the cross-cultural relationship was the focus of a recent study by Merta, Ponterotto and Brown (1992). This compared the effectiveness of two counselling styles, the authoritative and collaborative styles, as part of a study of academic counselling of international students. The results showed support for the general consensus that international students, at least, prefer directive over non-directive forms of counselling.

Training courses may address cross-cultural themes in detail, but how many practitioners receive relevant experience of working transculturally before embarking on their professional practice? The cross-cultural development of practitioners is an area hardly visited by research. There is considerable ambiguity regarding practitioner choice of training, the content and scope of training, and practitioner attitude following training.

Empirical approaches to research in transcultural counselling suggest that suitable strategies are still to be discovered and methodological advances are still at a premature stage. Very few research methodology textbooks incorporate cross-cultural dimensions, though there are a few notable exceptions (e.g. Alasuutari, 1995; Ponterotto and Casas, 1991; Triandis and Berry, 1980).

Developing sensitivity and beyond the anthropological counsellor

Whilst intercultural therapy is perhaps emerging as a discipline in its own right, the underlying assumption is that it is possible for a counsellor, in alliance with the client, to explore the client's inner self and so help them readjust. The difficult question is the extent to which a counsellor needs to be an anthropologist. That is, does the counsellor have to develop expertise in one or two cultures? Alternatively, is there a theory of intercultural intervention which allows the counsellor to transcend cultural barriers provided they have undergone a process of deconstruction (antiracist training) and self-analysis pertaining to culture (that is, to become epistemologically neutral)?

Clinical supervision is essential in allowing practitioners to explore cross-cultural themes further. Respectful, supportive supervision should facilitate the constructive questioning of a practitioner's attitude and expectancies of cross-cultural work. The need for appropriate training of supervisors is as pressing as it is with first-time counselling trainees.

As the counselling profession strives to respond in a professional culturally sensitive manner and to offer all things to all people, it must be remembered that the profession is still in its infancy and at times demonstrates impatience in the way it responds to cross-cultural themes. Pedersen (1985) considers the development of multicultural awareness not to be an end in itself, but rather a means towards personal empowerment in the multicultural context.

La Fromboise and Foster (1992) argue that cross-cultural sensitivity develops through practitioners' being involved in extensive fieldwork with ethnic minority communities. This could be taken as a process of immersion for the trainee to become culturally un-encapsulated, or as yet more missionary posturing by the dominant culture. On the other and, how else are counselling trainees from white middle class backgrounds, as the majority undoubtedly are, to be expected to acquire awareness, understanding and competence to work cross-culturally, if not through first hand contact?

D'Ardenne and Mahtani (1989) list various practical problems for counsellors in the process of cross-cultural work ranging from use of appropriate forms of address to acceptable patterns of non-verbal communication. More than this, they are argued to need sensitivity to their own attitudes. For clients too there can be cross-cultural hurdles to overcome. Not least of these may be the experience of being labelled and treated by white agencies which expect compliance to norms.

D'Ardenne and Mahtani (1989) ask counsellors to examine their own attitudes and expectations of transcultural work. In a training environment it is possible for fear to dominate and it can be easier for practitioners to say nothing rather than to actively allow themselves to challenge and be challenged.

Conclusions

The range of cultural possibilities clearly will or should shape specific therapeutic responses. There is no set formula or list of prescribed questions to ask. There are perhaps core issues which should be added to Carl Rogers's core conditions to reflect respect, interest and commitment to cultural differences. Embodying the principles in codes of professional conduct might further the agenda. Ultimately, though, cross-cultural counselling can only be realized through appropriate training. Continuous Professional Development is perhaps the key to unlock the profession from encapsulation in monocultural therapeutic approaches, to embrace the richness of cross-cultural diversity. Cross-cultural working need not only be seen as difficult but also as a means of enhancing professional and personal development. Therapeutic frameworks which evolve to embrace multicultural issues will also succeed in creating a more profound understanding of the human condition.

Counselling in a multicultural environment offers the greatest challenge. The importance of cross-cultural themes in counselling cannot be overstated. The demands of working in a multicultural environment are diverse, ranging from individual forms of practice to policy issues in service delivery and organizational factors which can only be addressed by the national bodies. The resources available to support practitioners in meeting this challenge are, however, still very limited. Training institutions have a significant part to play in shaping the attitudes, expectations and competencies of future practitioners. Practitioners for their part must face the challenge of developing their cross-cultural sensitivity. Finally, clients will determine whether the services on offer afford them the approaches and response they require. Counselling operates within a cultural context. Failure to respond sensitively will inevitably lead to a negative view of the profession. Through cross-cultural work, the counselling profession has the opportunity to take a significant part in leading British society towards a more integrated form of living in a multicultural society, not just to pick up the pieces when it goes wrong. This perhaps is its greatest challenge.

DISCUSSION ISSUES

What are the possible advantages and disadvantages of 'racism awareness training' for trainee counsellors?

What is your understanding of a multicultural society?

In your opinion will cross-culturalism become a powerful fourth force in the field of counselling in Britain?

Is it important for practitioners to receive relevant experience of working transculturally before embarking on their professional practice?

References

Abramowitz, S.I. and Murray, J. (1983) 'Race effects in psychotherapy', in J. Murray and P.R. Abramson (eds), *Bias in Psychotherapy*. New York: Praeger.

Alasuutari, P. (1995) *Researching Culture: Qualitative Methods and Cultural Studies*. London: Sage.

Asmall, I. (1994) 'Existential therapy in a non-Western context', Forum of the Society of Existential Analysis. June.

Bor, R., Legg, C. and Scher, I. (1996) 'The systems paradigm', in R. Woolfe and W. Dryden (eds), *Handbook of Counselling Psychology*. London: Sage.

Boscolo, L., Cecchin, G., Hoffman, L. and Penn, P. (1987) *Milan Systemic Family Therapy Conversation I: Theory and Practice*. New York: Basic Books.

Bowen, M. (1978) *Family Therapy in Clinical Practice*. New York: Jason Aronson.

Bronfenbrenner, U. (1976) *Reality and Research I: the Ecology of Human Development*. Master Lectures in Developmental Psychology. Washington, DC: American Psychological Association.

Brown, P. and Able Smith, A. (1996) 'Psychological counselling in mid-life issues', in R. Woolfe and W. Dryden (eds), *Handbook of Counselling Psychology*. London: Sage.

Bubenzer, D.L. and West, J.D. (1993) *Counselling Couples*. London: Sage.

Burnham, J.B. (1986) *Family Therapy*. London: Routledge.

Campbell, D., Draper, R. and Huttington, C. (1991) *Second Thoughts in the Theory and Practice of the Milan Approach to Family Therapy*. London: Karnac Books.

Carter, E.A. and McGoldrick, M. (1980) *The Family Life Cycle*. London: Gardner Press.

Cross, C. (1978) *Ethnic Minorities in the Innercity: the Ethnic Dimensions in Urban Deprivation in England*. London: Commission for Racial Equality.

Cross, W.E. (1971) 'The negro-to-black-conversion-experience: toward a psychology of black liberation', *Black World*, 20: 13–27.

D'Ardenne, P. and Mahtani, A. (1989) *Transcultural Counselling in Action*. London: Sage.

Eleftheriadou, Z. (1993) *Transcultural Counselling*. London: Central Book Publishing Company.

Erickson, E.H. (1968) *Identity, Youth and Crisis*. New York: Faber & Faber.

Fernando, S. (1995) 'The way forward', in S. Fernando (ed.), *Mental Health in a Multiethnic Society*. London: Routledge.

Gilbert, M. and Shmukler, D. (1996) 'Counselling psychology in groups', in R. Woolfe and W. Dryden (eds), *Handbook of Counselling Psychology*. London: Sage.

Gilroy, P. (1993) *Small Acts. Thoughts on the Politics of Black Cultures*. London: Serpents Tail.

Goldsborough, M. (1996) 'Equal opportunities: are you bored yet?', *Personal, Sexual, Relationship & Family Newsletter*, 5/2: 11–12 (British Association for Counselling).

Ho, M. (1987) *Family Therapy with Ethnic Minorities*. Newbury Park, CA: Sage.

Jardine, S. (1996) 'Transracial adoption: a personal experience', *Counselling*, 7 (2): 113–14.

Jenkins, A.H. (1985) 'Attending to the self-activity in the Afro-American client', *Psychotherapy*, 22: 335–41.

Jones, J. (1985) 'The sociopolitical context of clinical training in psychology: the ethnic minority case', *Psychotherapy*, 22: 453–6.

Kareem, J. (1988) 'Outside in – inside out: some considerations in inter-cultural therapy', *Journal of Social Work Practice*, 3 (3): 57–77.

Kareem, J. and Littlewood, R. (eds) (1992) *Intercultural Therapy: Themes, Interpretations and Practice*. Oxford: Blackwell Scientific.

Karmi, G. (1996) *The Ethnic Health Handbook*. London: Sage.

Krause, I.-B. and Miller, A.C. (1995) 'Culture and family therapy', in S. Fernando (ed.), *Mental Health in a Multiethnic Society*. London: Routledge.

La Fromboise, T.D. and Foster, S.L. (1992) 'Cross-cultural training: scientist–practitioner model and methods', *The Counseling Psychologist*, 20 (3): 472–89.

Lago, C. and Thompson, J. (1996) *Race, Culture and Counselling*. Buckingham: Open University Press.

Lefley, H. and Urutia, R. (1982) 'Cross cultural training for mental health personnel'. Final Report NIMH Training Grant No. 5. University of Miami School of Medicine.

Liddle, H.A. (1983) 'Diagnosis and assessment in family therapy: a comparative analysis of six schools of thought', in J. Hansen and B. Keeney (eds), *Diagnosis and Assessment in Family Therapy*. Rockville, MD: Aspen Systems.

Littlewood, R. (1992) 'How universal is something we can call therapy?', in J. Kareem and R. Littlewood (eds), *Intercultural Therapy: Themes, Interpretations and Practice*. Oxford: Blackwell Scientific.

Littlewood, R. and Lipsedge, M. (1982) *Aliens and Alienists*. Harmondsworth: Penguin.

Mays, M.V. (1985) 'The black American and psychotherapy: the dilemma', *Psychotherapy*, 22: 379–88.

McGoldrick, M., Pearce, J.K. and Giodorno, J. (eds) (1982) *Ethnicity and Family Therapy*. New York: Guilford Press.

McLeod, J. (1996) 'The humanistic paradigm', in R. Woolfe and W. Dryden (eds), *Handbook of Counselling Psychology*. London: Sage.

Merta, R.J., Ponterotto, J.G. and Brown, R.D. (1992) 'Comparing the effectiveness of two different styles in the academic counselling of foreign students', *Journal of Counseling Psychology*, 39 (2): 214–19.

Nadirshaw, Z. (1993) 'The implications of equal opportunities in training clinical psychologists: a realist's view', *Clinical Psychology Forum*, 54: 3–6.

Norton, D. (1978) 'Black family life patterns: the development of self and cognitive development of black children', in G. Powell, J. Yamamoto, A. Romero and A. Morales (eds), *The Psychosocial Development of Minority Group Children*. New York: Brunner/Mazel.

Parker, I. (1989) *The Crisis in Modern Social Psychology – and How to End It*. London: Routledge.

Pedersen, P.B. (ed.) (1985) *Handbook of Cross-Cultural Counselling and Psychotherapy*. New York: Praeger.

Pedersen, P.B. (1991) 'Introduction to the Special Issue on Multiculturalism as a Fourth Force in Counselling', *Journal of Counseling and Development*, 70: 4.

Pedersen, P.B. (1996) 'Recent trends and developments in cross-cultural theory', Seminar Report. London: UKCOSA.

Ponterotto, J.G. and Casas, J.M. (1991) *Handbook of Racial/Ethnic Minority Counselling Research*. Springfield, IL: Charles C. Thomas.

Rack, P. (1982) *Race, Culture and Mental Disorder*. London: Tavistock.

Ramirez, M. III (1991) *Psychotherapy and Counselling with Minorities: a Cognitive Approach to Individual and Cultural Differences*. Oxford: Pergamon Press.

Robbins, P. (1996) 'Psychology and the changing role of men: a multicultural perspective', *Counselling Psychology Review*, 11 (1): 45–7.

Sabnani, H.B., Ponterotto, J.G. and Borodovsy, L.G. (1991) 'White identity development and cross-cultural counsellor training: a stage model', *The Counseling Psychologist*, 19 (1): 76–102.

Sattler, J.M. (1977) 'The effects of therapist–client similarity', in A.J. Guraman and A.M. Razin (eds), *Effective Psychotherapy: a Handbook of Research*. New York: Pergamon Press.

Selvini-Palazzoli, M., Boscolo, L., Cecchin, G. and Prata, G. (1980) 'Hypothesizing–circularity–neutrality: three guidelines for the conductor of the session', *Family Process*, 19: 3–12.

Spinelli, E. (1994) *Demystifying Therapy*. London: Constable.

Sue, D.W. and Zane, N. (1987) 'The role of culture and cultural techniques in psychotherapy', *American Psychologist*, 42 (1): 37–45.

Sue, D.W., Arendondo, P. and McDivis, R.J. (1992) 'Multicultural counselling competencies and standard: a call to the profession', *Journal of Counseling and Development*, 70: 477–81.

Sue, S. (1977) 'Community mental health services to minority groups: some optimism, some pessimism', *American Psychologist*, 32: 616–28.

Tien, J.L. and Johnson, H.L. (1994) 'Black mental health client's preference for therapists: a look at an old issue', *International Journal of Social Psychiatry*, 31 (4): 258–66.

Triandis, H. and Berry, J. (eds) (1980) *Handbook of Cross-Cultural Psychology*. Boston, MA: Allyn & Bacon.

UKCOSA (United Kingdom Council for Overseas Student Affairs) (1996) 'Changing cultures: developments in cross cultural theory and practice'. Seminar Report (ed. S. Sharples). London: UKCOSA, 30 January.

Van Deuzen-Smith, E. (1988) *Existential Counselling in Practice*. London: Sage.

Vontress, C.E. (1971) 'The black male personality', *The Black Scholar*, 2: 10–16.

Wrenn, G. (1962) 'The culturally encapsulated counsellor', *Harvard Educational Review*, 32: 444–9.

Appendix to Chapter 1
Micro and Macro Perspectives on a Systemic Case Study: The Toulons

[*The names and some other identifying features of the clients have been disguised in this case study.*]

Psychotherapeutic counsellors are encouraged by systemic thinking to go beyond intrapsychic factors to the nature of family relationships. Circular and future oriented questions are central to the systemic approach generally (Penn, 1985). Information that makes a difference is sought. Circular questions are used to compare views and possibilities. Other major forms of systemic intervention include positive relabelling or reframing, paradoxical intervention and externalization.

Regarded here as an integrated field, systemic thinking refers to the approach and not to who is present in the consulting room (hence the possibility of systemic work with individuals alone). As Jenkins and Asen (1992: 1) aptly remark, 'Systems therapy is thus not a question of how many people are seen but refers to the theoretical framework which informs what the therapist does.'

Case Synopsis: The Toulons

A married couple (Mr and Mrs Toulon) were seen for eight sessions at my (Don Rawson's) private practice. The Toulons are an Asian couple in their mid thirties, both originally from Kenya in East Africa, where there is a thriving Asian community. Quietly spoken with a pleasant and genteel manner, they appeared to my eyes as a picture of an attractive and Westernized couple.

I commenced the first session by asking, 'Who would like to begin?' Khalid spoke to Belinda, 'You begin.' Then to me, 'It's her idea to come along here. I wouldn't have but . . .'

Belinda reported, still smiling, that they needed help to save their marriage. Khalid had been working for a few months in Kenya and she had stayed behind in England. Khalid had an affair with another woman in Kenya and eventually confessed to it in a telephone call to Belinda. Khalid looked unmoved by this account but shook his head in disapproval when Belinda recounted she had contacted his father for help. He had told Khalid to return to his wife in England to sort it out. Candy, the other woman, was however, still pursuing Khalid with telephone calls and letters, so the affair did not appear to be over. Belinda said she was prepared to forgive his affair but he had to make up his mind and make a go of the marriage.

I asked Khalid what he thought Belinda wanted from the therapy sessions. He replied, 'She needs to be strong. Needs confidence.'

To Belinda I enquired, 'What does Khalid want?' She replied, 'He's confused. He wants security – to be successful. He wants "chemistry" – a good physical side to the marriage.'

After the first session I listed the following questions in my notebook as a preliminary attempt at hypothesizing:

1 Power – who's on top?
2 Life cycle (vertical) – what stage is the relationship at now?
3 Horizontal (sociocultural issues) – how much push and pull is there between the two cultures?
4 What function does the problem supply – what is kept the same/held back from changing?
5 Process: how does counselling fit into this system?

Seeing a couple together has the advantage of not labelling any one individual (for example, as having a psychological problem or being weak). The focus is immediately and transparently on the system (that is, the marital relationship). Changes will thus also be jointly owned. In sharing this responsibility, it becomes 'our problem' rather than 'his/her problem'. Crowe (1995) adds that the goal is a reduction in labelling of the partner who is symptomatic.

In this particular case it is not immediately clear who was symptomatic. Belinda was clearly pressing for change and instigated the idea to attend therapy. Khalid appeared to have the 'problem' of the girlfriend and the uncertainty where his heart lay.

The following week (session 2), I suggested to them that the goals of therapy ought to be the reverse of their initial ideas. That is, Khalid is the one who needs to be strong, and Belinda is the one who needs security and success.

Paradox has a central place in strategic work. Haley (1976) posits that all therapeutic work is effectively paradoxical. Although this could be misrepresented as a 'fun and games approach' to therapeutic work, it has the serious intention of challenging the solutions which clients have become stuck with. The prevailing solution is seen by strategic systemic therapists as the principal problem to be solved. As expected, the clients were surprised by this formulation.

Khalid retorted: 'I was getting fat at home. Living in England is boring but secure. Kenya is different. There are possibilities.'

Belinda said she felt sorry for Khalid but didn't pity him. She saw marriage as a business.

The intervention had apparently helped to open up the problem. As will be seen, the issue of which country to live in and the expectations of marriage form a recurrent motif throughout the therapy.

The Systems Paradigm

Bor et al. (1996) identify systems thinking as both a school of therapy and a meta theory. Its distinguishing features compared to other therapeutic approaches are said to be:

1 There is no underlying motivational or personality theory.
2 Assessment and therapeutic process are integral to each other.
3 Change is a property of system functioning not individual characteristics.
4 Family and wider group issues are inherent and cannot be divorced.

The Milan approach early on developed characteristic methods which have been broadly influential in systemic approaches generally (Selvini-Palazzoli et al., 1978). Circular questioning, hypothesizing and neutrality are emphasized. The later Milan team also shifted the emphasis to one of the therapist not knowing (that is, not being expert about, the family), but as someone who joins the family system, co-constructing and co-evolving suitable interventions (Boscolo et al., 1987). Neutrality is said to come through curiosity rather than an external and epistemologically superior perspective.

For my own part I have adopted an uneasy, or perhaps delicately poised position between engaging my own sociocultural identity as part of the system under scrutiny and the view from the outside. I have to admit that the latter provides a ready retreat. This may be no bad thing as long as it serves the interests of the client and is not simply an expedient way of retaining therapist power. Either way, I have to confront my own epistemological position as well as my sociocultural heritage. Neither is easy to address without sounding pious or overdefensive.

In this case study I sometimes found myself presenting an (inauthentic) stance of naïve ignorance (I had in fact some first hand knowledge of Kenya), but appealing to my clients to fill the gaps. Whilst this may have facilitated their taking an active role and acknowledging their value as a resource, it also precludes my own. Clearly we need to work towards a shared understanding. The problem is that we all bring our own perceptual and cultural frameworks to bear. No one can be totally curious all the time. Perhaps we need most of all to be curious about our own way of thinking.

The sensitive therapist invites the family to educate him/her rather than invoking the expert role. This must help achieve a more egalitarian collaboration in the therapeutic process. Giving the expert role to clients is also a significant intervention in its own right, as a way of bringing cultural and ethnic issues to the fore without it being threatening. Manifestly too, it gives clients the role of therapeutic agency and is therefore empowering.

I took a Kenya travel guide into one therapy session and showed it to the Toulons who looked at it with great interest and started to expound on the Asian society. Belinda's version of the story explained, 'Marriage is easier in Kenya. The extended family is what counts, not just the person. Family would not accept marriage as failure – no therapy. Extended family is good when it goes right but intolerant when not.'

Shifting Perspectives

Hanna and Brown (1995) contend that the various systemic approaches can be organized along a continuum of micro–macro perspectives of family process. At the macro end, broad social factors (such as gender, ethnicity and culture) form issues intrinsic to the whole family system. At the other end of the continuum, the micro level of functioning, intergenerational and extended family patterns are 'external' influences to the nuclear family arrangement of the couple.

Hanna and Brown helpfully propose that it is possible for the counsellor to think of a zoom lens with which to view the continuum. The practitioner is argued to need a flexible viewpoint to see different levels of family process. The case study presented here, attempts to move the zoom from one end of the spectrum to the other.

In the strategic systemic school symptoms are frequently regarded as the attempted solution to a problem. Weakland et al. (1974) note that the family's attempted solution usually makes the problem worse. The therapist therefore has the task of redefining the problem. Consequently, great emphasis is placed on reframing in the strategic approach.

Like family systems generally, the marital couple is seen to develop and change over time. Haley (1973) contends problems in accomplishing developmental tasks lead to the need for therapy. The problem focuses attention on one party, not least because it is easier to focus on one person rather than the relationship. The family life cycle is emphasized and symptoms often show the family to be stuck at some stage of development as they attempt to adapt to a new stage.

Stages in the life cycle of couples are typically depicted thus:

- Growing independence of parents and need to communicate with each other.
- Establishing careers and having children.
- Increased commitment and maintenance of family pattern.
- Onwards to preparation for children leaving home etc. (Monte, 1989).

The pattern is, however, highly normative. It is squarely heterosexual in orientation and very Western in its implied aspirations of nuclear independence from family background.

In the Toulons case presented here, Khalid's behaviour is perhaps a metaphor for the difficulties they encounter in entering a new stage of the family life cycle. The stage, however, is ill-differentiated, or rather, confusingly so in the different sets of expectations from the two cultures, pulling and pushing the Toulons to be a 'modern' Western couple or a traditional part of the extended family.

The Toulons are both the same age and were married when nearly 30. Khalid said he thought he would settle down and that Belinda put no pressure on him. His mother and older sister, however, did.

Khalid revealed: 'The sex life started OK then the financial pressure started. I was always looking at the bank balance. I trained myself to stay at home. Belinda took control – she kept me at home.'

This account suggests a man struggling to reconcile both his dwindling financial resources and his ebbing sense of personal freedom. It also suggests a singular perspective. The wife is represented only as a constraining force, not as a partner in life's difficulties.

I instigated a role reversal task. Reverse role play is an especially useful technique to help increase empathy for the other, that is, to see things from the other's perspective. De-roleing afterwards is also a useful opportunity to reflect on how the opposite position made the actor feel. The players were instructed to exchange chairs and take turns answering my (circular) questions. These were (in their opposite roles), what dreams of the future did they have? Secondly, what did they imagine the other person wants out of life?

The couple took to the task eagerly. I had the impression they felt some therapeutic magic was being waved in front of them. Each, however, clearly found it difficult to stay in role. Each slipped seamlessly into their own persona and I had to remind them to stay in character. The principal issues to emerge concerned dimensions of domestic responsibility versus spontaneous, carefree fun.

The following week Belinda exhibited an air of serene acceptance. She reported being able to sleep at nights and had come to terms with the prospect of separation and divorce. She understood, she said, that there was no point pushing Khalid. He would have to make his mind up for himself. If he wanted her, she would be there, otherwise she would take a few months visiting her sister in Paris and get on with the rest of her life.

For Belinda, at least, the role reversal exercise may have facilitated therapeutic movement in this direction. Interestingly, Khalid had greater difficulty in adopted the other's position during the role play. As Bubenzer and West (1993) aptly remark, 'The energy of the couple is tied up in emotional conflict. Hope returns to the relationship when one or both parties can be coaxed into seeing things differently.'

Systemic counsellors focus on who interacts with whom, where and when. In the context of couple interaction, the pattern of who defers to whom is of particular importance. Lederer and Jackson (1968) describe two patterns of dyadic relationship. In the complementary style one partner is 'in charge' and the other follows. In the symmetrical style both compete for power. The characteristic style may range over issues from small scale domestic tasks (who does the washing up) to more profound decisions (where to live). The latter, of course, is pertinent to the Toulons.

Systemic counsellors also often ask family members to describe how they interact with regard to specific problem situations. My opportunity for this was given by the situation when Candy (the other woman) telephones. Belinda said Khalid was agitated when Candy rang. Khalid added he had asked her not to. They had last spoken three to four weeks ago and it was not pleasant. Belinda maintained she didn't care but thought Candy ringing was 'bad manners'.

Drawing triangles in the air I said, 'It seems there are two possibilities here:

1 Khalid is caught between two women – pulled from both sides – like piggy in the middle.
2 Khalid is in a powerful position in which he has two women chasing after him and he has power to decide.'

Khalid was quick to declare himself caught in the middle. Belinda thought he was in a powerful situation.

Minuchin (1974) talks of 'detouring' where concern for or about a third person replaces/masks conflict in a relationship. I hypothesized aloud that the triangular relationship was in some ways helpful to them both. For as long as Khalid couldn't decide between the women, he had to remain in England. For different reasons maybe they both preferred this option for now.

Khalid said he had taken a decision to separate but took it back when the couple were asked to look after his brother's children when they visited England for a few months. Family commitment had evidently countered his decision or maybe provided a way out of carrying through the decision.

The following week the Toulons reported that Khalid was going to Kenya at the end of the month and Belinda would follow. She would be like a tourist for four or five days, but, Khalid said, 'She is worrying about it.' Khalid would be working on the family enterprise, a new clothing factory with his father.

Belinda pondered, 'Kenya is a strange country to me. No family there' (Belinda's family all live in England or in other major Western countries). Khalid added there would be a clash of Belinda's Western ways with Khalid's family. Belinda's view was, 'I would be swallowed up. They are very strong.'

For Belinda there appears the prospect of having her Western idea of her marriage consumed without trace by Khalid's extended family. Perhaps too, there is an implied fear of loss of her individual identity. The alternative would be to resolutely hold to these principles but to live in disharmony. Attending the counselling sessions may well have been in Belinda's view a way of reinforcing the nuclear family, of strengthening that identity.

Belinda recounted, 'We have a letter from Khalid's mother this week. It is emotional blackmail.' And in a mocking voice, 'Give me some good news. I am 71 years old, life is ebbing away. Room is ready for you to return to Kenya.' Belinda added, 'In Kenya 71 is old. Married women are huge and fat.'

Khalid's story had a different focus. He began, 'In Kenya after work there is always something to do, someone to see – it's fulfilling. More space and room. Belinda is security emotionally. With Candy I was distracted and frustrated. I have to get work success out of my system – have to prove myself.'

The narrative lines hardly cross. Any prospect of therapeutic success for this couple would have to facilitate the two accounts to at least share common ground.

Hanna and Brown (1995) observe that women are more likely to seek therapy and wish for change in family relationships, particularly equality. Men, however, are typically disinterested in seeking therapy and wish to retain the status quo of traditional gender roles (in their favour). Accordingly, Belinda always paid for the therapy sessions (or at least took responsibility for handing money over).

Jacobson et al. (1989) also found men more likely to desire autonomy (freedom) for themselves whilst retaining a stable and secure home base, whereas women often want more closeness, and the husband's involvement in the family.

I asked how life would be for them as a couple living in Kenya. Belinda began, 'In Kenya often one side of the family doesn't approve unless there is an arranged marriage. I don't want kids until business is sorted out. But it's not a real pressure. Khalid's parents and sister will be our responsibility eventually. They are inviting us so as to look after them.' Khalid concluded. 'You're very English Belinda. We've got to do a bit of suffering – look after parents – clear debts.'

I felt I could only reflect back their different hopes and fears. Belinda feared problems of living with the extended family, Khalid felt he had to make his way in the family business and in return take on his responsibility in the extended family. The couple appeared to share a need to externalize the family whilst simultaneously attributing to it responsibility for initiating change.

The Toulons had negotiated, though, that the journey to Kenya would be a trial period. Khalid had agreed to stay with Belinda and to resolve his affair with Candy. After the initial foray, Khalid would return alone to begin working in the family business. As before, Belinda would remain in England until Khalid had made provision for a home in Kenya which, importantly, was separate from the extended family home. At the end of the sessions, I remarked that I was optimistic for their future. They replied that they had come a long way.

Hoffman (1983) is critical of systemic approaches which see family members as actors of their own system patterns and the therapist as the director of an unfolding play. In such a case the counsellor is compelled to maintain role distance and the language is necessarily adversarial. Epistemologically there is a subject–object split. At this juncture I felt the same distance, the same split but for reasons I couldn't easily follow. Somehow, moving the scenario to Kenya had left me and the therapeutic model behind. The joining process had been unjoined as the couple prepared psychologically for the cultural transition which the move to Kenya would bring. It felt as though my attempts at systemic intervention were being stretched beyond their range of convenience.

Goldner (1988) says gender is not a special topic for family therapy but central to theory since it influences the structure of the family. In a seminal paper on the subject Hare-Mustin (1978) questions whether women can model more egalitarian relationships and men reaffirm female strength. Hare-Mustin further asks whether family roles and communication styles disempower women in the family. I wondered how far Belinda felt Khalid's extended family did just that. Insofar as she was able to retain her marriage in the context of the Western nuclear family, I believe Belinda thought she had some prospects of independence and equality. Joining the extended family in Kenya would, from her perspective, consign her to a life governed by sociocultural rules she understood but did not wish to live by. Her husband, however, was already looking in that direction.

Cross-Cultural Challenges for Systemic Counselling

Bubenzer and West (1993: 163) astutely note, 'couple problems . . . can be conceptualised as a clash of derived world views'. Pedersen (1991) sees multicultural counselling as the fourth force in counselling. The need for cultural sensitivity extends to gender, sexual orientation, ethnicity, religion and disability among others. Reynolds and Pope (1991) caution, moreover, that people may have multiple identities and oppressions.

It is, though, too easy for counsellors to be overwhelmed by cultural diversity and retreat into the safety of mainstream therapeutic theory. Bubenzer and West (1993) draw attention to the goodness of fit between clients' and counsellors' sociocultural expectations and the fit between the two partners and their social context. The significant question, they say is 'Do couples view their cultural differences as a liability or an opportunity?' For the Toulons, it did not appear to be welcomed as an opportunity. With more time it may have been possible to explore along these lines.

For my clients, the Toulons, the shared sense of sociocultural identity was a source of marital conflict. Cultural identity manifests values and a sense of difference from other groups. This can be positive or negative. It is a major organizing principle in the development of family systems, either as pressure to conform to traditional values and customs or as something to rebel against.

Conclusions

The case of couple counselling described in this study was a part of, indeed it appears it could only exist in, the context of Western culture. For the three months' duration of the casework and the 60 minutes of each therapeutic session, the couple's problem belonged here in England. Khalid's father had sent him back to England, to his nuclear family, to sort out his Western problem of marital difficulties in a Western way, before returning to Kenya. Belinda sought therapy to the same ends, but also to reinforce the nuclear identity before, as she saw it, being drawn inexorably into the extended family. At the end of the sessions the couple appeared to have a clearer understanding of their dilemmas and had contracted with each other some measure of give and take.

At different parts of the study I have attempted to zoom between poles of micro and macro perspectives and have felt the expansion in the compass of my own ideas and working practices. I trust this has also been of benefit to my clients.

References

Bor, R., Legg, C. and Scher, I. (1996) 'The systems paradigm', in R. Woolfe and W. Dryden (eds), *Handbook of Counselling Psychology*. London. Sage.

Boscolo, L., Cecchin, G., Hoffman, L. and Penn, P. (1987) *Milan Systemic Family Therapy: Conversations in Theory and Practice*. New York: Basic Books.

Bowen, M. (1978) *Family Therapy in Clinical Practice*. New York: Jason Aronson.

Bubenzer, D.L. and West, J.D. (1993) *Counselling Couples*. London: Sage.

Crowe, M. (1995) 'How I assess in couple therapy', in C. Mace (ed.), *The Art and Science of Assessment in Psychotherapy*. London: Routledge.

Fernando, S. (1991) *Mental Health, Race and Culture*. London: Macmillan.

Fernando, S. (1995) 'The way forward', in S. Fernando (ed.), *Mental Health in a Multiethnic Society*. London: Routledge.

Goldner, V. (1988) 'Generation and gender: normality and covert hierarchies', *Family Process*, 27: 17–31.

Haley, J. (1973) *Uncommon Therapy: the Psychiatric Techniques of Milton Erikson MD*. New York: Norton.

Haley, J. (1976) *Problem Solving Therapy*. San Francisco: Jossey–Bass.

Hanna, S.M. and Brown, J.H. (1995) *The Practice of Family Therapy: Key Elements Across Models*. Pacific Grove, CA: Brooks/Cole.

Hare-Mustin, R. (1978) 'A feminist approach to family therapy', *Family Process*, 17: 181–94.

Hoffman, L. (1983) 'A co-evolutionary framework for systemic family therapy', in J. Hansen and B. Keeney (eds), *Diagnosis and Assessment in Family Therapy*. Rockville, MD: Aspen Systems.

Jacobson, N.S., Holtzworth-Monroe, A. and Schmaling, K.B. (1989) 'Marital therapy and spouse involvement in the treatment of depression, agoraphobia, and alcoholism', *Journal of Consulting and Clinical Psychology*, 57: 5–10.

Jenkins, H. and Asen, K. (1992) 'Family therapy without the family: a framework for systemic practice', *Journal of Family Therapy*, 14: 1–14.

Karmi, G. (1996) *The Ethnic Health Handbook*. Oxford: Blackwell Scientific.

Krause I.-B. and Miller, A.C. (1995) 'Culture and family therapy', in S. Fernando (ed.), *Mental Health in a Multiethnic Society*. London: Routledge.

Lederer, W.J. and Jackson, D.D. (1968) *The Mirages of Marriage*. New York: Norton.

Liddle, H.A. (1983) 'Diagnosis and assessment in family therapy: a comparative analysis of six schools of thought', in J. Hansen and B. Keeney (eds), *Diagnosis and Assessment in Family Therapy*. Rockville, MD: Aspen Systems.

Littlewood, R. (1992) 'How universal is something we can call therapy?', in J. Kareem and R. Littlewood (eds), *Intercultural Therapy: Themes, Interpretations and Practice*. Oxford: Blackwell Scientific.

McGoldrick, M., Pearce, J.K. and Giodorno, J. (eds) (1982) *Ethnicity and Family Therapy*. New York: Guilford.

Minuchin, S. (1974) *Families and Family Therapy*. Cambridge, MA: Harvard University Press.

Monte, E.P. (1989) 'The relationship life cycle', in G.R. Wecks (ed.), *Treating Couples: The Intersystem Model of the Marriage Council of Philadelphia*. New York: Brunner/Mazel.

Pedersen, P.B. (1991) 'Introduction to the special issue on multiculturalism as a fourth force in counselling', *Journal of Counseling and Development*, 70: 4.

Penn, P. (1985) 'Feed-forward: future questions, future maps', *Family Process*, 24: 299–310.

Reynolds, A.L. and Pope, R.C. (1991) 'The complexity of diversity: exploring multiple oppressions', *Journal of Counseling and Development*, 70: 174–80.

Selvini-Palazzoli, M., Boscolo, L., Cecchin, G. and Prata, G. (1978) *Paradox and Counterparadox*. New York: Jason Aronson.

Selvini-Palozzoli, M., Boscolo, L., Cecchin, G. and Prata, G. (1980) 'Hypothesizing–circularity–neutrality: three guidelines for the conductor of the session', *Family Process*, 19: 3–12.

Weakland, J., Fisch, R., Watzlawick, P. and Bodin, A. (1974) 'Brief therapy: focused problem resolution', *Family Process*, 13: 141–68.

White, M. (1989) *Selected Papers*. Adelaide: Dulwich Centre Publications.

White, M. and Epston, D. (1990) *Narrative Means to Therapeutic Ends*. New York: Norton.

Wilson, K. and James, J. (1991) 'Research in therapy with couples: an overview', in D. Hooper and W. Dryden (eds), *Couple Therapy: a Handbook*. Milton Keynes: Open University Press.

2

CULTURE AND IDENTITY: IMPLICATIONS FOR COUNSELLING

Pittu Laungani

In this chapter we shall delve into the problems of counselling in a multicultural society. At this stage, it would be useful to address ourselves to the question of culture, and what is meant by this ubiquitous term. We shall follow the major arguments, examine how it has been used by experts from different disciplines, and in so doing, hope that we shall arrive at a relatively satisfactory explanation of the word culture. We shall then consider the impact which cultural factors are likely to have on an individual's development of identity and personality.

Towards an understanding of culture

Like several other words which enjoy popular usage ('intelligence' would be one example), the word culture too is *so easy to misunderstand*. It has come to mean different things to different people. Everyone seems to know what the word means in a vague sort of way, but no one is quite sure as to its precise meaning. Let us consider some of its popular usages. People talk of a cultured person as one with impeccable manners, a person who is well-behaved, shows consideration, and is sensitive to the feelings and sentiments of others. On the other hand a person lacking in culture is seen as being uncouth, ill-mannered, coarse – hardly the kind of person one would wish to have at one's dinner table! In this sense, therefore, culture is seen in terms of an individual (or a group or a class of individuals) possessing certain types of social and behavioural attributes which are referred to as good manners.

In this context 'culture' carries a value judgement. Such a view of culture, although interesting, is rather limited in its usefulness. For one can, using Skinnerian methods of behaviour modification, train a monkey to behave impeccably! A person with impeccable manners may also turn out to be cruel and unkind. Thus while, as the saying has it, 'manners maketh the man [and woman]', manners alone do not make a cultured man (and woman). It is obvious therefore that the word culture carries with it more than a statement of good manners. Perhaps what is missing from the meanings associated with the word culture is the absence of learning and education.

A person of learning and education is often referred to as a cultured person. Thus culture is defined in terms of an individual possessing certain desirable attitudes and values which are a product of learning and education. But such a view of culture also runs into serious problems because by implication it rules out all those persons who have no formal learning and education. Every society, large or small, advanced or advancing, has within it a group of people (their percentage may vary from society to society) who, for one reason or another, have not had any formal learning and education. To this must be added several small-scale societies dotted round the world where people have had no formal education and learning. To refer to the people of such societies as being uncultured (assuming of course that the word uncultured is a connotatively appropriate opposite of the word cultured) is to lay oneself open to justifiable accusations of élitism and racism – a charge which was levelled against the anthropologists in the early part of this century. We shall return to this later.

We have seen therefore that good manners, learning and education, although considered to be desirable attributes, do not explain fully the meaning of the word culture. The word becomes even more difficult to grasp when it is used to form compounds such as *agriculture*, or *horti-culture*, or when a microbiologist studies and examines *cultures* (Eliot, 1948). Here culture carries a specific meaning, namely the pursuit of a given occupation or profession. For an objective and acceptable under-standing of the word culture one needs to turn away from value-laden and occupation centred or profession centred concepts.

What do the contemporary social science disciplines tell us about culture? Do they in any way help us to clarify the concept of culture? We will examine the concept here from three perspectives: anthropology, sociology and psychology.

Anthropology and culture

Our analysis must begin with the work of anthropologists who, in a sense, were pioneers in their studies of cultures (Singer, 1961). They used the term culture quite differently from historians, colonial admin-istrators, missionaries, travellers, soldiers of fortune, and more recently, sociologists, and latterly, psychologists.

Anthropology itself has had a chequered career. The early writings of anthropologists were speculative, naïve and even quite absurd (Harris, 1968). The anthropologists hardly ever visited the lands about whose people they wrote. In fact, Sir James Fraser, who wrote the twelve volumes of the classic The Golden Bough ([1932]1954), a study in magic, superstitions, rites and rituals, and religious practices across all societies in the world, boasted that he never met nor indeed visited any of the lands of the people of whom he wrote (Beattie, 1964)! Actually to visit the lands and live for extended periods with the peoples of those lands was considered to be a superfluous activity. The anthropologists' analyses of other societies were based largely on the available writings of colonial administrators, missionaries, historians and the like, which of course were based on their own preconceptions and stereotypes.

Anthropology, as Bock (1980), Harris (1968) and several others have pointed out, was also blatantly racist in its formulations. Differences between Negroes (as they were referred to then) and Europeans were often explained in terms of naïve and ill-founded theories. Darwin's theory of evolution had very little impact on these controversies. Even the publication of The Origin of Species in 1859 did little to contain the racial controversies. Non-European and non-white societies came to be judged as being backward, primitive and inferior, and white, Western societies as being enlightened and superior.

Such judgements are dangerous. Their dangers lie in their (occasionally) unintentional but (frequently) intentional promotion of appalling cruelty, savagery and, in extreme cases, genocide. The world has already witnessed several devastating consequences of such evaluations – the most traumatic being the horrors of the holocaust. It is therefore imperative that we pay heed to the wise words of George Santayana: 'those who do not learn from history are condemned to repeat it'. The recent massacres in Bosnia, Rwanda and Somalia, would lead us to believe that we have learnt virtually nothing from the past.

Although most of the pejorative evaluations concerning racial differences have currently fallen out of favour, from time to time they resurface in different guises; arguments related to racial differences in schizophrenia, in measured IQ etc., reappear in prestigious journals and books (see Herrnstein and Murray, 1994).

It was not until the early twentieth century that anthropology began to acquire some academic respectability. Anthropologists, led by the charismatic Franz Boaz (1911), started to undertake ethnographic field studies. Sensitive to the criticisms of ethnocentrism and racism with which the discipline had become tainted, Boaz paid special attention to research methodology. He insisted on maintaining the highest standards of scientific rigour, exhorting his colleagues to do the same. One of the ways by which this could be achieved was for the research worker to adopt a pure, non-judgemental attitude of scrupulous detachment and objectivity. All personal biases, subjective predilections, educated guesses, stereotypes etc., had to be jettisoned – before undertaking a voyage to another country. They had no place in Boaz's research methodology, for such factors impeded the pursuit of objective scientific goals. He was also opposed to any form of premature theorizing and eschewed the construction of theoretical models *before any facts had been painstakingly gathered*. Facts, he believed, ought to speak for themselves. In his zeal to rid anthropology of subjective biases and prejudices, Boaz threw the proverbial baby out with the bath water.

Constructing a theory *after* facts have been gathered is a form of inductive reasoning. This form of naïve inductivism to which Boaz was wedded is open to serious criticism (Chalmers, 1983). First, as Popper (1963, 1972) has pointed out, facts do not speak for themselves. They become meaningful only when interpreted, and any interpretation is always in the light of a theoretical or conceptual framework, however vague it might be. Facts, as has been pointed out elsewhere (Laungani, 1990), are used to test a theory, not to generate one.

Secondly, Boaz, as was mentioned above, insisted on the neutrality and purity of one's observations. This too, as it turns out, is a mistaken view. Neutral observations, as Popper (and several other philosophers) has painstakingly pointed out, are a contradiction in terms (1963). The notion of neutrality of perceptions can be traced back to the writings of Francis Bacon (1561–1626) and Descartes (1596–1650) in the sixteenth/seventeenth century. It is an interesting and seemingly attractive concept which has (mistakenly) remained in our psyche so to speak for over three centuries. But sadly, it is totally without foundation. Francis Bacon believed that Nature is an open book, and in order to read it, one needs to purge one's mind of all anticipations, or conjectures, or guesses or prejudices. Descartes, on the other hand, advocated that by the method of *systematic doubt* one could destroy all false prejudices of the mind, and consequently arrive at the unshakeable basis of *self-evident truth*. The religious underpinnings of these formulations will not have gone unnoticed by the readers, because we can see clearly that this form of epistemology – both Bacon's and Descartes' – remains essentially a religious doctrine in which the source of all knowledge (truth) is divine authority. But truth – however 'pure', innocent and unprejudiced the mind of the perceiver – is not self-evident. Popper (1963) argues that human perceptions are seldom or never 'neutral'. All our perceptions contain within them our hunches, guesses, intuitions, conjectures, prejudices and anticipations. From this it follows that all our perceptions are theory-laden and theory-saturated.

However, the greatness of Boaz lay in that he provided a much-needed paradigm shift, a new model. Armchair theorizing gave way to the systematic collection of ethnographic data. Field studies, using a variety of ethnomethodological techniques, came to be equated with anthropological research.

The influence of Boaz has not waned. Anthropologists in general, even to the present day, follow in his footsteps. The study of *whole* societies – describing a society in its totality – is still at the centre of their discipline. Their concern has been to *describe a system*. Conceptually and methodologically their discipline is more allied to psychiatry and psychoanalysis than to psychology (Jahoda, 1970; Klineberg, 1980). But with increasing collaboration the sharp dividing lines separating disciplines have blurred, and in recent years new specialisms such as psychological anthropology, cognitive anthropology, cultural psychology and so on, have emerged (Munroe and Munroe, 1980).

But the fundamental questions concerning the *validity* of anthropological formulations, to a large extent, *still remain unanswered*. Although the findings from anthropological studies are not without value, the question whether the study of anthropology leads to objective knowledge remains, for the moment, an open question. Such a state of affairs is unsatisfactory. It prevents us from ascertaining unequivocally the reality (or veridicality) of an observed and recorded significant social experience in a given society, for instance the precise individual and/or collective experience of grief following a loss in the family. One is not sure whether the observed experience(s) is representative of people of that society as a whole or an atypical, even deviant, response. Such unresolved issues prevent us from evaluating objectively the anthropological constructions of social reality.

Given the fact that anthropologists are concerned with describing whole systems, their definitions of culture too are all-embracing. To the anthropologists culture includes the 'total attainments and activities of any specific period and group of humans' (Triandis, 1980: 1). The concept is used as an umbrella term which incorporates within it all the distinctive human forms of adaptation and the distinctive ways in which different human populations arrange and organize their lives on earth (Levine, 1973). Thus, each culture is seen as having a structure and a pattern. And each part of the pattern, which includes, beliefs, attitudes, values, rules, laws, symbols, rites, rituals, taboos, patterns and networks of communications etc., coheres to form a *gestalt* possessing clarity and symmetry.

Sociology and culture

The sociologists in the 1940s and 1950s saw culture as an umbrella term – in that sense at least their formulations were not significantly different from those of the anthropologists. Kroeber and Klukhohn (1952) surveyed the literature on culture over the past hundred years and offered their own definition of culture, which to them, consists of explicit and implicit patterns of behaviour 'acquired by symbols . . . achievements of human groups . . .; the essential core of culture consists of traditional ideas and especially their attached values . . .' (1952: 181).

In recent years the diverse usages of the word culture have proliferated within sociology and cultural studies. Diverse inputs, instead of making the meaning any clearer have tended to cloud the concept even further. For instance, the term culture has been divided and sub-divided into other diverse terms. Sociologists have written about *popular* culture, *media* culture, *mass* culture, *minority* culture, *ethnic* culture, *aborigine* culture, *black* culture, *white* culture, *feminist* culture, *gay* culture, *lesbian* culture, *drug* culture, *colonial* culture, *modernist* and *postmodernist* culture, *Marxist* and *post-Marxist* culture, *high-brow*, *middle-brow*, *low-brow* culture, *techno-*culture, *organizational* culture, *managerial* and *executive* culture, culture *of complaint*, culture *of violence*, culture *of the classes*, the culture *of the underclasses* – the list is virtually endless. Some writers, for reasons which are not easy to understand, have felt it necessary to add further divisions into each of these concepts by adding the prefix 'sub' to the word culture. So now we have a sub-culture of violence, a sub-culture of drugs, etc. If one were being pedantic one could sub-divide a sub-culture into a sub-sub-culture, creating a meaningless fragmentation of the concept.

Eliot (1948) warns us that the very process of fragmentation of a culture into its sub-divisions is likely to lead to the disintegration of a culture. There is another difficulty which impedes our understanding of the term culture. The language used by the authors working in this area is by no means easy to understand. Often, the terms and concepts used in their writings are singularly idiosyncratic. As a result, the quality of clarity is further strained. Yet one might ask, is it possible to tease out from this myriad of writings a concept which would be of definite meaning to us, a concept on which there would be a high degree of consensus, and a concept which might be operationalized in order that systematic and meaningful research both within and between cultures might be undertaken? Sadly, no. Even their style of writing – lavishly sprinkled with jaw-breaking jargon – is virtually impossible to decipher. Read the following snippet, selected at random, from the book entitled *Cultural Studies*, edited by Grossberg, Nelson and Treichler (1992):

> This shift from the positivistic sense of rationality, as a possession of an a priori subject, to a mode of minimal rationality as the process of the activity of articulation, not only changes the concept of cultural value as pleasure and instruction but also alters the very subject of culture. It shifts the focus from the validity of judgment as causality, or the negative dialectics of the 'symptomatic reading' to an attention to the place and time of the enunciative agency. There is an emphasis on the relation between temporality and meaning in the present of utterance, in the performativity [sic] of the history of the present; in the political struggle around the 'true' (in the Foucaldian sense) rather than its pedagogical authenticity secured as an epistemological 'outside,' on the problematic level of a General Ideology. (Bhabha, 1992: 57)

On reading the above paragraph, one gets the feeling of being trapped in a pseudo-intellectual gas chamber. One feels suffocated; one's lungs long for the fresh air of clarity. Admittedly the author shows consummate virtuosity in stringing a long list of high-sounding words together to from sentences. But what do these sentences actually mean? What is the author trying to convey? Words, it needs to be realized, exercise a tyranny of their own. They seldom mean the same thing to all people. Nor do they always mean the same thing to the same person at different times. It is therefore absolutely essential to express words with great clarity, precision, simplicity and economy. Ambiguity is not an indication of profundity or erudition, as is mistakenly believed by some writers. It is a form of intellectual anorexia and the outpourings become a form of verbal bulimia.

Psychology and culture

Does psychology fare any better? It was in the late 1950s that cross-cultural psychology emerged as a discipline in its own right (Jahoda, 1970). Given that Britain had established a vast number of colonies all over the world, it is strange that British psychologists were initially unwilling to undertake cross-cultural research. The curious moratorium was lifted after the Second World War, and the 1950s saw a burst of sustained activity in the subject. What progress then has been achieved in the past 40 years of sustained research?

Cross-cultural psychology and anthropology have never enjoyed a good working partnership. They have usually gone their own separate ways. This is because of their differing approaches. Anthropologists, as was mentioned earlier, have been concerned about constructing social systems of the societies which they have set out to study. Their methods, on the whole, have implicitly or explicitly subscribed to an inductivist epistemology. And to a large extent, the theoretical basis of their work has been rooted in psychoanalytical formulations.

Mainstream academic psychology, on the other hand, has shied away from psychoanalytical theory. Psychologists tend to be guided by a hypothetico-deductive model in their research endeavours. They are more concerned about testing explicitly formulated hypotheses rather than constructing social systems on the basis of detailed observations. They therefore tend to treat societies as independent variables and examine the effects of those variables on relevant psychological phenomena. Like all disciplines, cross-cultural psychology is also guided by several interrelated assumptions. The one which is of concern to us is the belief in *cultural variation*.

The belief that societies vary along several important parameters is beyond dispute. One might, however, dispute the nature of the parameters, the number of parameters, and the methods by which they might be classified or categorized. As Triandis (1980) points out, societies vary with respect to their ecology, their subsistence system, the sociocultural system, the individual system and the interindividual system. Others (Murdock and Provost, 1973) have proposed different classification systems. Regardless of the lack of consensus on the number and type of parameters which would best define a culture, the necessity of a classification system cannot be denied. It allows us to understand the nature of variation in different societies and in so doing permits us to go beyond *a descriptive classificatory system* and *pose fundamental theoretical questions concerning the aetiology of such variations.*

For instance, the death of an elderly person in a Hindu family is not just a private family affair. It affects the family's immediate relatives (*the baradari*), their sub-caste (*jati*) and the local community of which the deceased was a part. Anyone who knew the deceased in any significant capacity is obliged to come to the funeral. Not to come to the funeral is more than a mere breach of social etiquette, it is an extremely serious social transgression. In contradistinction to a Hindu funeral, a typical middle-class Anglican funeral is often seen as a private family affair. Only those specifically invited may attend the funeral. A church service led by the vicar normally precedes the funeral itself. After the funeral the mourners, only if invited, may partake of the hospitality offered by the family of the deceased. Condolences are offered and gradually the mourners leave. The bereaved are left on their own. No further attempt is made to intrude into their grief, which is seen as being private and personal.

These are simple descriptive classificatory systems. They serve an important function in helping us to understand the manner in which social customs are performed in different societies. The aim of scientific research is to go beyond a descriptive level of analysis and attempt an *explanatory level of analysis.* Such a level of analysis would attempt to tease out how these differential social customs came into being, what functions, if any, they serve, the conditions under which they are likely to be perpetuated, or are modified, or disappear altogether.

We are now getting somewhere with our understanding of the word culture. The problem which concerns us is this. Do we understand culture with reference to a given individual, or with reference to a group (or a class) of people, or with reference to a given society, which would doubtless consist of several groups (or classes) of people? Secondly, what are the 'ingredients' which go towards making up a culture? In other words, what should a culture, any culture, consist of? Let us try to answer some of these questions.

We have already argued over the futility of trying to understand culture with reference to an individual. Nor does it make much sense to understand culture with reference to a group or a class of people. Given the fact that most larger-scale societies contain *several* groups or classes of people (the groups and classes being distinguished by rank, occupation, region and area of residence, linguistic and other vital differences), such an approach too is bound to be limited in its usefulness. For although such an approach may tell us something useful about a specific group, it tells us very little about other groups in the same society.

What about understanding culture with reference to large-scale societies, which may include countries and even nations? To understand the word culture with reference to large-scale societies seems a reasonable option despite the fact that large-scale societies may contain several disparate groups, separated by language, diet, mode of dress, climatic differences etc. For instance, compare the Punjabis who live in the State of Haryana in India with the South Indians (mainly Tamils) living in Tamilnadu. Even to an untrained eye, they seem so different. Despite the glaring differences, however, they form an integral part of Indian culture, and, to a large measure, share the fundamental value systems common to all Indians.

Let us continue with our discussion of culture with reference to India. Even at a popular level the word 'Indian' conjures up several images in the minds of people selected at random: Indian cuisine, music, clothes, crowds and crowds of people, slums, heat, dust, noise, chaos etc. Move these same people away from images to ideas and abstractions, and they will refer to poverty, overpopulation, overcrowding, malnutrition, hunger, illiteracy etc. These are popular stereotypes. *Stereotypes are the hooks on which people hang their initial impressions and observations.* They may have a grain of truth in them. But as Roger Brown (1987) points out, the actual and potential dangers of stereotyping far outweigh their advantages. Consequently, their usefulness in understanding culture is extremely limited.

Yet few people would deny the validity of the concept of Indian culture. What makes it so? For a group of people in a country or a nation to be defined as having a culture, several important considerations need to be taken into account. Many psychologists have emphasized several factors which constitute a culture: ecology, physical geography, climate, common language, dietary practices and so on (Leach, 1964; Murdock, 1964; Whiting, 1964). Others have focused on the value systems and the networks of communications as being the essential ingredients comprising a culture. Although it is not absolutely essential, it is desirable that the people one is referring to live within a legally and politically recognized geographical area. The reason why these conditions are not seen as being absolutely essential is because our definition of culture must also include those members who may have left that country and emigrated elsewhere, otherwise they would be excluded from the original culture.

So what constitutes a culture? It is suggested that all cultures possess a set of core (primary) features and a set of peripheral (secondary) features (Laungani, 1997). The core features constitute the essential requirements of any culture. The peripheral features, although important, may vary from culture to culture. The primary features of a culture are as follows:

1 A past history (recorded or oral).
2 A dominant, organized religion within which the salient beliefs and activities (rites, rituals, taboos and ceremonies) can be given meaning and legitimacy.

3 A set of core values and traditions to which the people of that society subscribe and which they attempt to perpetuate.
4 Regulated social systems, communication networks, including regulatory norms of personal, familial and social conduct.
5 Artefacts unique to that society, such as literature, works of art, paintings, music, dance, drama, religious texts, philosophical texts.

The secondary features of a culture are as follows:

1 Freedom from religious, political and social persecution.
2 It should, to a large measure, have a common language.
3 Internationally recognized common physical and geographical boundaries within which people of that particular society live.
4 Housing and other living arrangements.
5 Socially accepted dietary, health and medical practices.

It is clear from the above that cultures vary. Even a cursory observation reveals that cultures vary in terms of their political, social, economic and physical environments. In addition to physical and geographical differences, *it is clear that cultures also vary with respect to their value systems.*

The existing value systems have a significant bearing on the religious and social beliefs, the kinship patterns and the social arrangements of the people of that culture and on the development of individual and social identities (Kakar, [1979]1992; Roland, 1988). Values are best defined *as the currently held normative expectations underlying individual and social conduct* (Laungani, 1995).

Our salient belief systems concerning right and wrong, good and bad, normal and abnormal, appropriate and inappropriate, proper and improper, and the like, to a large measure are influenced by the values operative in our culture. When pressed as to why we hold such and such a belief, why this is important and that less so, we may be unable to offer plausible explanations. We might even be mystified as to why we hold certain beliefs dearly.

Yet values, like air, pervade our cultural atmosphere, and we imbibe them often without a conscious awareness of their origins. Values form the bases of social, political and religious order. They are often the result of past legacies: religious, political and philosophical. Since these beliefs are passed on over centuries, their roots get deeper and deeper. They cannot be easily severed. Values become an integral part of our psychological and existential being. We carry them as securely as a tortoise its shell. Although not entirely stable, values do remain so to a large extent. Over time, however, values may change. Several factors, for example, migration from one culture to another, political, religious, scientific and technological upheavals, may result in rapid changes in the personal evaluations of themselves, their behaviour and their value-systems.

Since certain values are culture-specific, it follows that certain behaviours, both private and public, are also likely to be culture-specific. Consequently, one would expect to find differences both within and between cultures on a variety of behavioural parameters, for example, the manner in which problems such as mental illness, depression, stress, child abuse, grief, work and relationships are conceptualized by people of a given culture, *and how and why* such conceptualizations differ from those of people of another culture.

We have discussed the concept of culture at some length. We have also accepted the view that cultures vary with respect to their value systems, which in turn influence the private and social behaviours of people in that culture. It is obvious therefore that one would expect to observe a variety of differences (and similarities) in values and behaviours between, say, the indigenous (native-born white) English, and Indians in India, and persons originating from the Indian sub-continent living in Britain. Objective knowledge of such similarities and differences, *and how and why they arise,* would be of immense value to teachers, educators, doctors, health workers, psychotherapists, counsellors – to name but a few.

Over the years, my colleagues and I have formulated a theoretical model which allows us to understand the similarities and differences between the white, native-born English and the Indians (in India) and persons originating from the Indian sub-continent (in Britain), in terms of their salient value systems, which influence the development of their respective cultural identities. The interested reader is invited to refer to Laungani (1990, 1991a,b,c, 1992, 1995, 1996, 1997a, 1998b; Laungani and Sookhoo, 1995; Sachdev, 1992; Sookhoo, 1995) for a detailed exposition of the theoretical model and the empirical studies that were carried out to test its validity.

Conceptual Model of Cultural Differences

It is suggested that there are four interrelated *core values* or *factors* which distinguish Western cultures from Eastern cultures, or more specifically, Indian approaches from British approaches to understanding the salient features of private and social behaviours of the two cultural groups. The proposed four theoretical constructs are:

- **Individualism . . . Communalism (Collectivism)**
- **Cognitivism . . . Emotionalism**
- **Free Will . . . Determinism**
- **Materialism . . . Spiritualism**

It should be noted that the two concepts underlying each factor are *not* dichotomous. They are to be understood as extending along a *continuum,* starting at, say, Individualism, at one end, and extending into Communalism at the other. A dichotomous approach, however, tends to classify people in 'either–or' terms. Such an approach is limited in its usefulness. In his critique of Individualism–Collectivism, Schwartz (1990: 140) argues that the acceptance of a dichotomous approach would lead to the belief 'that individualist and collectivist values form two coherent syndromes that are in polar opposition'. People seldom fit into neat theoretically formulated and/or empirically derived categories. The sheer complexity and variability of human behaviours and responses precludes serious attempts at such categorical classifications.

A dimensional approach on the other hand takes account of human variability. It has the advantage of allowing us to measure salient attitudes and behaviours at any given point in time and over time. It also enables us to hypothesize expected theoretical and empirical shifts in positions along the continuum both within and between cultural groups. Each of the hypothesized dimensions subsumes within it a variety of attitudes and behaviours which to a large extent are influenced by the norms and values operative within that culture.

Before discussing each factor it needs to be pointed out that the concepts to the *left* of each factor are applicable more to the British and to Western cultures in general, and those on the *right* to the Indians and to Eastern cultures in general. Let us now examine each concept briefly, and trace its relationship to the acquisition of identity and behaviours.

Individualism . . . Communalism (Collectivism)

Over the years, much has been written on the concept of Individualism and Collectivism (Hofstede, 1980, 1991; Hui and Triandis, 1986; Kim et al., 1992; Matsumoto, 1996; Triandis, 1994), and they have come to mean different things to different people. Many authors have construed the concepts in dichotomous terms, arguing that the sets of values related to each concept are in polar opposition (Schwartz, 1990).

INDIVIDUALISM   One of the distinguishing features of Western society is its increasing emphasis on individualism. At an abstract level the concept itself has come to acquire several different meanings: an ability to exercise a degree of control over one's life, the ability to cope with one's problems, an ability to change for the better, reliance upon oneself, being responsible for one's actions, self-fulfilment and self-realization of one's internal resources. As Triandis (1994) points out, individualism, in essence, is concerned with giving priority to one's personal goals over the goals of one's ingroup. Individualism has also been the subject of considerable debate among Western thinkers (Bellah, 1985; Lukes, 1973; Matsumoto, 1996; Riesman, 1954; Schwartz, 1990; Spence, 1985; Triandis, 1994; Waterman, 1981). Some writers have argued that the notions of individualism are incompatible, even antithetical with communal and collective interests. The 'dog-eat-dog' philosophy is seen as being divisive, inimical in terms of the promotion of communal goals, and in the long run, it alienates fellow-beings from one another. However, there are others – among them Sampson (1977) being the more outspoken of the defenders of individualism – who extol its virtues. Individualism, it is argued, is also in keeping with the philosophy of humanism. Individualism emphasizes, among other things, the notion of 'dignity of man', its disentanglement from theology and religion and its espousal of scientific enterprise as the fundamental bases for understanding the Universe (Cooper, 1996). In recent years, the increasing popularity of Individualism, as Sampson (1977) argues, can also be attributed to the Weberian spirit of capitalism and free enterprise. He believes that individualism can lead to a spirit of cooperation and coexistence.

How does the notion of Individualism affect our understanding of differences in social behaviours?

1 The philosophy of individualism has a strong bearing on the notion of identity. Identity, in Western society, is construed by psychologists and psychiatrists of virtually all theoretical persuasions, in developmental terms, which starts from infancy. And in the process of development, one's identity – according to received wisdom – passes through several critical stages in adolescence, into adulthood. To acquire an appropriate identity – which asserts one's strengths, which is located in reality, which separates the individual from others and is thereby kept distinct from those of others, which reflects one's true inner being and which leads to the fulfilment or the realization of one's potential – is by no means easy. If often results in conflict, which if unresolved leads to severe stress, and in extreme cases to an identity crisis (Erikson, 1963; Maslow, 1970, 1980; Rogers, 1961, 1970).

2 Individualism tends to create conditions *which do not permit an easy sharing of one's problems and worries with others.* As Albert Camus (1955) pointed out, individualism creates in people an *existential loneliness,* compounded by a sense of the absurd. The emphasis upon self-reliance, the inability to merge one's identity into those of others – familial or social – the expectation of being able to cope with one's problems, imposes severe stress upon the individual and may make the search for one's 'true' identity a life-long quest.

3 One of the dominant features of individualism is its recognition of and respect for an individual's physical and psychological space. People do not normally touch one another, for that is seen as an encroachment of one's physically defined boundaries. Secondly, physical contact, particularly between two males – an innocent holding of hands in public – may also be misconstrued; it arouses connotations of homosexuality. The taboos related to physical touch are so strong that even in times of grief they are not easily violated. Even eye-to-eye contacts between

two people are normally avoided. Several studies have shown that the effects of violating another person's physical space lead to severe stress and, in extreme cases, to neurosis (Greenberg and Firestone, 1977; Rohner, 1974).

4   Closely related to the concept of physical space is that of 'psychological space'. This is concerned with defining boundaries which separate the psychological self from others. It is an idea of immense value in the West, respected in all social situations. It comes into play in all social encounters, from the most casual to the most intimate. One hears of people feeling 'threatened', 'upset', 'angry', 'awkward', 'confused' etc., when they feel that their subjectively defined space is invaded. For instance, bereavement in the family is perceived largely as an individual problem, of sole concern to the affected family. One does not intrude, for fear of invading the other person's 'psychological' space. As has been pointed out elsewhere (Laungani, 1992), the notion of physical and psychological space is intertwined with the concept of *privacy*. Privacy implies a recognition of and respect for another person's individuality. Even the most casual encounters between people, both in social and familial situations, are dictated by a tacit recognition and acceptance of the other person's privacy. Several studies have demonstrated that the invasion of privacy leads to severe stress (Spielberger, 1979; Webb, 1978).

5   At a social level, individualism has also had an effect on the size of the British family structure, which from the post-war period onward has undergone a dramatic change (Eversley and Bonnnerjea, 1982). Although the nuclear family is still seen as the norm, it is by no means clear how a 'typical' British family shall be defined. With the gradual increase in one-parent families – at present around 14 per cent – combined with the fact that just under 25 per cent of the population live alone – the present nuclear family structure is likely to change even more dramatically. The changes in the size and the structure of families, combined with high levels of social and occupational mobility, may have 'destabilized' society, creating a sense of loss of community life, particularly in the urban metropolitan cities.

COMMUNALISM (OR COLLECTIVISM)   1   Indian society, on the other hand, has been and continues to be community-oriented (Kakar, 1981; Koller, 1982; Lannoy, 1976; Laungani, 1989; Mandelbaum, 1972; Sinari, 1984). Most Indians grow up and live in *extended family* networks. The structural and functional aspects of the extended family, the social and psychological consequences of living within it, have been discussed elsewhere (Laungani, 1989). Suffice it to say that Indian society cannot be seen other than in familial and communal terms. It is and has been for centuries a family-oriented and community-based society. In an Indian family life, one's individuality is subordinated to collective solidarity, and one's ego is submerged into the collective ego of the family and one's community. It may be of passing interest to note here that Indians often use the collective pronoun 'we' in their everyday speech. The use of the pronoun we or 'hum' (in Hindi) signifies the suppression of one's individual ego into the collective ego of one's family and community. Thus one speaks with the collective voice of others, and in so doing gains their approval. When a problem – financial, medical, psychiatric, or whatever – affects an individual, it affects the entire family. The problem becomes one of concern for the whole family. The problems are discussed within the inter-locking network of familial (hierarchical) relationships, and attempts are made to find a feasible solution.

2   A community in India is not just a collection of individuals gathered together for a common purpose. A community in the sense in which it is understood in India has several common features. People within a group are united by a common caste-rank, or *jati*, religious grouping and linguistic and geographical boundaries. The members within a community generally operate on a ranking or a hierarchical system. (A microcosm of such a ranking or hierarchical system may also be found within each extended family network.) Elders are accorded special status within the community and their important role is very clearly recognized. Elders, whether they come from rural areas or from large metropolitan cities, are generally deferred to. On important issues, the members of a community may meet and confer with one another, and any decisions taken are often binding on the rest of the members within the community.

However, it needs to be emphasized that for an individual to stay as an integral part of the family and of the community, it is expected that the individual will submit to familial and communal norms, and will not deviate to an extent where it becomes necessary for severe sanctions to be imposed on the deviant or, as an extreme measure, for the deviant to be ostracized. The pressure to conform to family norms and expectations can and does cause acute stress in individual members in the family, leading, in some instances, to psychotic disorders and hysteria (Channabasavanna and Bhatti, 1982; Sethi and Manchanda, 1978).

3   Identity in India, to a large extent, is *ascribed* and not *achieved*. By virtue of being born into a given caste (this applies mainly to the Hindus who comprise over 82 per cent of the total population of India) one's identity is *ascribed* at birth. There are advantages and disadvantages in such a traditional arrangement. On the one hand, the individual in an Indian family set-up does not have to pass through the critical stages in the process of developing an identity – as is normally the case with children within Individualistic cultures. On the other hand, an ascribed identity tends to restrict the choices open to the individual. While personal choice is central to an individualistic society, it is seen as an exception in a communalistic society.

4 Occupations are largely caste-dependent, and caste of course is hierarchical and determined by birth. While movement from the lower caste into a higher caste is virtually impossible, it is of course possible (as a result of certain 'caste-polluting' actions) to lose one's caste and drop from a higher into a lower caste. Although the pattern of caste-related occupations is beginning to undergo a transformation in the urban areas of India, there is little evidence of such changes in the rural areas of the country, which are inhabited by nearly 80 per cent of the Indian population. One has little choice even in terms of one's marriage partner. Marriages are arranged by the parents of the prospective spouses. Although the 'style' of arranged marriages has undergone a modest change within Indian society – particularly among the affluent members of society in the urban sectors of the country – they are still the norm.

One is born into one of the four given castes and is destined to remain in it until death. One's friends too are an integral part of one's extended family network; pressures from the elders and threats of ostracism ensure that one stays within the confines of one's caste and community and seldom or never strays away from it.

The major features of Individualism and Communalism may be summarized as in Table 2.1.

Table 2.1 *Cultural variations in attitudes and values in relation to Individualism . . . Communalism*

Individualism	Communalism
Emphasis on high degree of self-control	Such emphasis unnecessary; dependence on elders and other family members
Emphasis on personal responsibility	Emphasis on collective responsibility
Emphasis on self-achievement	Emphasis on collective achievement
Pressure on individuals to achieve an identity	Identity as ascribed at birth
Stress is related to the *acquisition* of identity	Stress is related to the 'imposition' of a familial and caste-related identity
Emphasis on nuclear families	Emphasis on extended families

With the exception of the caste system, which is a unique feature of Indian society, other collectivist cultures also share most of the features described above, including China, Taiwan, Korea, Hong Kong, Philippines, Thailand, Nepal, Pakistan, Iran, Turkey, Portugal, Mexico, Peru, Venezuela and Colombia, (Cheng, 1996; Gulerce, 1996; Hofstede, 1980; Jing and Wan, 1997; Kim, 1997; Matsumoto, 1996; Sinha et al., 1996; Ward and Kennedy, 1996; Yang, 1997). For instance, Kuo-Shu Yang (1997), in his excellent analysis of the traditional Chinese personality, refers to the tight, close-knit bond between the individual and his/her family. He points out that . . .

Chinese familism disposes the Chinese to subordinate their personal interests, goals, glory, and welfare to their family's interests, goals, glory, and welfare to the extent that the family is primary and its members secondary . . . (1997: 245)

Again, Kuo-Shu Yang (1997) points out that in order to attain harmony within the family it is essential for the individual to 'surrender or merge into his or her family, and as a result, lose his or her individuality and idiosyncrasies as an independent actor' (p. 245).

Cognitivism . . . Emotionalism

COGNITIVISM This is concerned with the way in which the British (the English in particular) construe their private and social worlds and the ways in which they form and sustain social relationships. In broad terms, it has been suggested by Pande (1968) that *British society is a work-and-activity centred* society, and in contradistinction, Indian society is relationship centred. It should be emphasized that these different constructions by British and Indians of their social worlds are not accidental cultural developments. They stem from their inheritance of their different philosophical legacies.

1 In a *work-and-activity centred* society, people are more likely to operate on a *cognitive* mode, where the emphasis is on *rationality, logic* and *control*. Public expression of feelings and emotions – particularly among the middle classes in England – is often frowned upon. The expression of negative feelings causes mutual embarrassment and is often construed as being vulgar. When negative feelings and emotions are expressed, this is done in a subtle and oblique manner.

2 In such a society, relationships are formed on the basis of *shared commonalities*. One is expected to 'work at a relationship' – in a marriage, in a family situation, with friends, with colleagues at work, and even with one's children. In a work-and-activity oriented society, one's identity, one's self-image and self-esteem grow out of one's work and one's attitude to work. Work defines one's sense of worth.

3 However, work and its relation to self-esteem acquire meaning only when seen against the background of time. Our conception of time is both objective and subjective. At an objective level time is seen in terms of an Einsteinian dimension, where each hour is divided into fixed moments of minutes, seconds and milliseconds. Each moment (at least on earth) expires at the same speed – an hour passes not a moment sooner, not a moment later. At a subjective level, however, there are variations in our perceptions of time. In a work-and-activity centred society, one's working life, including one's private life, is organized around time. To ensure the judicious use of time, one resorts to keeping appointments books, calenders, computer-assisted diaries;

one works to fixed time schedules, one sets deadlines; one tries to keep within one's time limits. One is constantly aware of the swift passage of time, and to fritter it away is often construed as an act of criminality. Time therefore comes to acquire a significant meaning in a work-and-activity centred society. McClelland (1961) has shown that people in general and high achievers in particular use metaphors such as 'a dashing waterfall', 'a speeding train' etc. to describe time. The fear of running out of time, the fear of not being able to accomplish one's short-term and long-term goals on time, is seen as one of the greatest stressors in Western society. Even casual encounters between friends, between colleagues at work, operate on covert agendas. Meeting people is seldom construed as an end in itself; it is a means to an end, with time playing a significant role. Even casual encounters are based on covert agendas.

EMOTIONALISM   1   This is not the case in non-Western societies in general, and in Indian society in particular. Although at an objective level time is construed in virtually the same way as it is in the West, at a subjective level time in India is seen in *more flexible and even relaxed terms*. Time, in Indian metaphysics, is not conceptualized in linear terms. A linear model of time, signifies a beginning, a middle and an end, or, in other words, a past, a present and a future. Time, in Indian philosophy, is conceptualized in circular terms, which means that time has no beginning (or its beginning remains unknown), no middle and no end. These differential conceptualizations have serious implications for our understanding the nature of private and social behaviours.

For instance, at a day-to-day observational level, one does not notice among Indians the same sense of urgency which appears to have become the hallmark of Western society. Time in India is often viewed as 'a quiet, motionless ocean', 'a vast expanse of sky'. It therefore comes as no surprise to learn that in Hindi there is only one word – *kal* – to stand for both yesterday and tomorrow! One gleans the meaning of the word from its context. The only exceptions to this flexible construction of time are to be found in those situations which are considered auspicious: undertaking an important journey, fixing the time of a christening, betrothals, weddings and funerals, etc. In these situations one is expected to consult the family Brahmin priest, who then consults an almanac from which he (Brahmin priests are male) calculates the most auspicious time for the commencement of that particular activity. Such events, because of their religious significance, are seldom left to chance; one seeks divine guidance in their planning and execution.

2   The close physical proximity in which people continuously live and share their lives with one another forces a *relationship centred society* to operate on an *emotional* mode. In such a society, feelings and emotions

are not easily repressed, and their expression in general is not frowned upon. Crying, dependence on others, excessive emotionality, volatility and verbal hostility, both in males and females, are not in any way considered as signs of weakness or ill-breeding. Since feelings and emotions – both positive and negative – are expressed easily, there is little danger of treading incautiously on others' sensibilities and vulnerabilities, such as might be the case in work-and-activity centred societies. Given the extended-family structure of relationships, emotional outbursts are, as it were, 'taken on board' by the family members. Quite often the emotional outbursts are of a symbolic nature – even highly stylized and ritualistic. Given the extreme closeness of life, the paucity of amenities, the absence of privacy, the inertia evoked by the overpowering heat and dust, the awesome feeling of claustrophobia, it is not at all surprising that families do often quarrel, fight and swear at one another and from time to time assault one another too. But their quarrels and outbursts are often of a symbolic nature – for otherwise such quarrels would lead to a permanent rift, the consequences of which would be far more traumatic than those of living together, There is in such outbursts a surrealistic quality, for at one level they are alarmingly real – the words and abuses hurled at one another, vicious and hurtful – yet at another, bewilderingly unreal. They serve an important function in terms of the relief which such 'cathartic' outbursts bring.

3   In a hierarchical family structure, each member within the family soon becomes aware of his or her own position within the hierarchy, and in the process of familial adjustment, learns the normative expressions of emotionality permissible to the person concerned. Even in such emotionally charged situations, the internalized familial norms often prevent the younger members of the family from openly expressing negative emotions towards their elders. In a relationship centred society, however, one is forced into relationships from which one cannot, or is unable to, opt out without severe sanctions being imposed upon the individual. Several studies have shown that one's inability to sever enforced relationships based on birth and caste often leads to severe stress and neurosis (Channabasavanna and Bhatti, 1982).

The major features of Cognitivism and Emotionalism, and the relative differences, are summarized in Table 2.2.

Table 2.2   *Cultural variations in attitudes and values in relation to Cognitivism . . . Emotionalism*

Cognitivism	Emotionalism
Emphasis on rationality and logic	Emphasis on feelings and intuition
Feelings and emotions kept in check	Feelings and emotions expressed freely
Emphasis on work-and-activity	Emphasis on relationships
Relations based on shared interests	Relations caste- and family-based

Free Will . . . Determinism

FREE WILL There does not appear to be a satisfactory end in sight to the philosophical and scientific wrangles concerning the nature of free will, predestination, determinism and indeterminism. Notwithstanding the unresolved debates in philosophy, there is a peculiar dualism in Western thinking concerning free will and determinism. Research in medicine, psychiatry, biology and other related disciplines, including psychology, is based on the acceptance of a deterministic framework – hence the concern with seeking causal explanations in accordance with rational, scientific procedures. Yet, at a commonsense level, there is a strong belief in the notion of free will, which manifests itself in the constant proverbs, homilies, poems and popular advice offered freely to children and adults – often by the very people who adopt a deterministic model in the course of their professional and scientific work (Laungani, 1992).

What do we mean by free will? Free will might be defined as a *non-causal, voluntary action*. However, at a commonsense level it is defined as exercising voluntary control over one's actions. Thus free will allows an individual to do what he/she wills, and in so doing, take 'credit' for his/her successes, and accept blame for his/her failures and mishaps. As a result, one is locked into the consequences of one's own actions. One is entrapped into one's own existential predicament, from which there does not appear to be an easy way out.

DETERMINISM Indians, by virtue of subscribing to a deterministic view of life, in a teleological sense at least, are prevented from taking final responsibility for their own actions. The notion of determinism plays an extremely crucial role in Indian thinking. The *law of karma*, which involves determinism and fatalism, has shaped the Indian view of life over centuries (Chapple, 1986; O'Flaherty, 1976, 1980; Reichenbach, 1990; Sinari, 1984; Weber, 1963). In its simplest form, the law of karma states that happiness or sorrow is the predetermined effect of actions committed by the person either in their present life or in one of their numerous past lives. Things do not happen because *we* make them happen: things happen because they were *destined* to happen. If one's present life is determined by one's actions in one's previous life, it follows that any problem that affects an individual was destined to happen. Reichenbach (1990) points out that the law of karma is not concerned with the *general* relation between actions and their consequences. It is usually held to apply to the moral sphere and is concerned with the moral quality of actions and their consequences. Thus according to the law of karma, we receive the results of our own actions and not another's. The sins of our fathers are not visited upon us. As von-Furer-Haimendorf (1974) pointed out, the theory of karma rests on the idea that the individual has the moral responsibility for each of his or her actions, and hence the freedom of moral choice.

One can see how the law of karma is invoked to explain not only the onset of mental illness, but all sorts of misfortunes which may befall an individual. If one's present life is determined by one's actions in one's previous life, it follows that any illness – mental or physical – that strikes an individual in a family was destined to happen. This idea is not as strange as it might appear at first sight. For in the West too, it is not uncommon to attribute the causes of psychiatric disorders to the patient's past experiences (namely, infantile traumatic episodes, faulty or maladaptive learning, hereditary predispositions, genetic abnormalities, and a variety of factors related to chemical imbalances). However, in India the notion of past is carried into one's previous life or lives.

The attribution of one's actions in one's previous birth to psychotic disorders takes away the sting and the stigma from suffering. No blame is apportioned to the afflicted individual; it was his or her karma. It was destined to happen. Determinism thus engenders in the Indian psyche a spirit of passive, if not resigned, acceptance. This prevents a person from plunging into an abyss of despair – a state from which the British, and indeed all individualistic societies, because of their fundamental belief in the doctrine of free will, cannot be protected. The main disadvantage of determinism lies in the fact that it often leads to a state of existential, and in certain instances, moral resignation, compounded by a profound sense of *inertia*. One takes no proactive measures; one merely accepts the vicissitudes of life without qualm. While this may prevent a person from experiencing anxiety it also prevents the person from overcoming the distressing condition.

Pandey, Srinivas and Muralidhar (1980), in a study of informants of psychiatric patients in India, found that the cause of psychotic disorders was most commonly attributed to sins and wrong deeds in the patient's previous and present life. These findings have been corroborated by Srinivasa and Trivedi (1982), who, in their study of 266 respondents selected from three villages in South India, found, among other factors, 'God's curse' (or 'the Will of Allah' among the Muslims) attributed as one of the most common causes of stress leading to mental disorders.

The major features of Free Will and Determinism are summarized in Table 2.3.

Materialism . . . Spiritualism

MATERIALISM Materialism refers to a belief in the existence of a material world, or a world composed of matter. What constitutes matter is itself

Table 2.3 *Cultural variations in attitudes and values in relation to Free Will . . . Determinism*

Free Will	Determinism
Emphasis on freedom of choice	Freedom of choice limited
Proactive	Reactive
Success or failure due largely to effort	Although effort is important, success or failure is related to one's *karma*
Self-blame or guilt is a residual consequence of failure	No guilt is attached to failure
Failure may lead to victim-blaming	No blame is attached to victim

debatable; the question has never been satisfactorily answered (Trefil, 1980). The notion of the solidity of matter was robustly debated by Heisenberg in his now famous research paper on indeterminacy in quantum theory in 1927 (Heisenberg, 1930). Such debates, however, are confined to journals of philosophy and science. At a practical, day-to-day level, however, aided by empiricism, one accepts the assumed solidity of the world which one inhabits – but not without paying a heavy price. For such an acceptance gives rise to the popular myth that all explanations of phenomena, ranging from lunar cycles to lunacy, need to be sought within the (assumed) materialist framework. This is evidenced by the profound reluctance among psychiatrists, medical practitioners and psychologists in general to entertain any explanations which are of a non-material or supernatural nature. Non-material explanations, which would include the acceptance of the supernatural, ESP, evil spirits, ghosts, and other supernatural 'forces', are treated at best with scepticism, and at worst with scorn.

A materialist philosophy also tends to engender in its subscribers the belief that our knowledge of the world is external to ourselves; reality is, as it were, 'out there', and it is only through objective scientific enterprise that one will acquire an understanding of the external world and, with it, an understanding of 'reality'.

The few psychiatrists and psychologists who have steered away from materialistic explanations, or have shown the willingness to consider alternative non-material explanations, comprise a very small minority. Most of them are only too aware that anyone offering such explanations of phenomena is in danger of incurring the wrath of the scientific community. Non-material explanations fall within the purview of the pre-scientific communities, or in other words, superstitious and backward societies, to be found mainly in underdeveloped countries (and by subtle implication, in collectivist societies).

Let us consider an example to illustrate such forms of thinking in Western society. For over two thousand years yogis in India have made claims about their abilities to alter their states of consciousness at will, thereby bringing their autonomic nervous states under voluntary control (Radhakrishnan, [1923]1989). In the *hathayoga*, yogic exercises – or *asanas* as they are called – were claimed to have therapeutic effects for a variety of physical and psychological disorders. Such claims were seldom taken seriously by Western scientists; they were dismissed as unsubstantiated exaggerations. It was not until 1969, when Neal Miller successfully trained his laboratory rats to lower and raise their blood pressure by selective reinforcement (Miller, 1969), that there began to dawn on the Western mind that there might after all be some substance in the claims made by yoga. Using a similar selective reinforcement strategy, Miller found that he could train his students to exercise voluntary control over their autonomic responses. Suddenly the claims made by the yogis began to acquire credibility. Miller's performing rats did the trick! Miller's findings opened the doors to yoga in American universities, and research into altered states of consciousness, followed by its applications into techniques of biofeedback, became respectable. It is therefore hardly an accident when one sees the importance given to yogic *asanas* in a variety of stress management exercises designed by Western experts.

SPIRITUALISM   In Indian thinking, the notion of materialism is a relatively unimportant concept. The external world to Indians is *not* composed of matter. It is seen as being *illusory*. It is *maya*. The concept of *maya*, as Zimmer ([1951]1989: 19) points out, 'holds a key position in Vedantic thought and teaching'. Since the external world is illusory, reality, or its perception, lies *within* the individual, and not, as Westerners believe, *outside* the individual. This, according to Zimmer, tends to make Indians more *inward looking* and Westerners more *outward looking*. Also, given the illusory nature of the external world, the Indian mind remains unfettered by materialistic boundaries. It resorts to explanations where material and spiritual, physical and metaphysical, natural and supernatural explanations of phenomena coexist with one another. To a Westerner, if A is A, A cannot then be not-A. If dysentery is caused by certain forms of bacteria, it cannot then be due to the influence of the 'evil-eye'. The two are logically and empirically incompatible. But contradictions to Indians are a way of life. A is not only A, but under certain conditions, A may be not-A.

Indian beliefs and values revolve round the notion of Spiritualism. The ultimate purpose of human existence is to transcend one's illusory physical existence, renounce the world of material aspirations, and attain a heightened state of spiritual awareness (Radhakrishnan, [1923] 1989; Zimmer, [1951] 1989). Any activity – particularly yoga – which is likely to promote such a state is to be encouraged.

The major features of Materialism and Spiritualism are shown in Table 2.4.

Table 2.4 *Cultural variations in attitudes and values in relation to Materialism . . . Spiritualism*

Materialism	Spiritualism
The world is 'real', physical	The world is illusory
Rejection of contradictory explanations of phenomena	Co-existence of contradictory explanations of phenomena
Reality is external to the individual	Reality is internal to the individual
Reality perceived through scientific enterprise	Reality perceived through contemplation and inner reflection

This chapter has highlighted the salient value systems of people in India and in England. Although India and England were singled out for a closer examination, it is clear that to a large measure the value systems described in this chapter are also applicable to other individualist and collectivist cultures. The chapter has also examined the influence of cultural values on a variety of private and public behaviours of the peoples of the two cultures.

The postulated conceptual model allowed us to describe each of the dominant value systems as extending along a continuum, thus *suggesting that the perceived differences in the behaviours of people may, more often than not, be a matter of degree and not of kind.* Such a formulation has one or two distinct advantages over a dichotomous formulation. First, it enables one to measure any changes in value systems which may occur in an individual due to migration from one culture to another (for example, a person moving from a collectivist to an individualistic culture, and vice versa). Secondly, it enables one to measure the influence of acculturation of second generation children of parents who have emigrated to another culture. To what extent do children imbibe the values of the new culture into which they are born, and to what extent do they internalize the values of the parents' culture? Thirdly, it enables one to hypothesize the source and types of variations in attitudes, values and behaviours which are more likely to be influenced by those living in another culture, for instance, do arranged marriages which, to a large measure are the norm in India, give way to 'love' marriages in England?

Before we turn to the last part of the title of this chapter – 'Implications for Counselling' – we need to address ourselves to one important issue. This is concerned with understanding the extent to which the attitudes, beliefs, values and behaviours described above are shared by Indians (or persons of Indian ancestry) living in Britain and in other Western countries, including America, Canada, Australia and elsewhere. It sounds a truism, but it needs to be stressed that when people emigrate from one culture to another, they are subjected to two, if not more, sets of cultural influences. It may turn out that the values of one may be significantly different and in some senses totally incompatible with those of the other. The issue is of even greater importance to the second generation children, for the children, as is inevitable, are socialized into two dominant cultural value systems: one at home, and the other outside, starting when they first go to school – or even earlier.

In using the term 'persons of Indian ancestry' I have deliberately avoided using the type of terminology which is fashionable, politically correct, and subscribes to what Popper (1963) refers to as *trendism*. I cannot bring myself to side with those social scientists who seem to spend an inordinate amount of time and energy worrying over the appropriate terms to use – whether it is desirable, appropriate and politically correct to use the word 'immigrant', or member of the 'ethnic minority', or 'black', 'brown', or 'Asian', 'Asian Indian', 'Asian Pakistani', 'Asian Bangladeshi', 'Sri Lankan Asian', 'East African Asian', 'South African Asian', 'Fijian Asian', 'Afghani Asian', 'Caribbean Asian', 'Black British', 'Brown British' etc. I should like to rise above such tedious and unprofitable debates, and so I hope will the readers. I shall merely content myself to refer to the persons around whom the chapter has been based as persons of Indian ancestry – which may be traced back by several centuries, when Pakistan, Sri Lanka (then known as Ceylon), Bangladesh and parts of Burma, were all an integral part of India. Over the years, hundreds of thousands of Indians have emigrated to several countries round the globe, including the USA, Europe, East Africa, West Africa, South Africa, the Middle East, West Indies, Fiji, Panama, South America, Australia and New Zealand, to name but a few. In fact, it would be difficult to find a country in which persons of Indian ancestry have not set up homes! What unites and brings all those diverse groups of people together is their common Indian ancestry and the dominant values (discussed above) shared by them all.

This, it must be admitted, is by no means a perfect formulation. But rather than create a category and thrust people into that category, it seems more sensible to let persons define for themselves their own cultural and/or religious, racial, ethnic or national origins. But the creation of arbitrary categories, although they may seem appropriate and politically correct at a given point in time, can lead to serious negative consequences for the persons concerned. One might, in this context, recall from the not too distant past the lamentations of R.D. Laing – the charismatic guru of the anti-psychiatry movement in Britain – when he pointed out that the application of a label such as schizophrenia led to serious consequences for the person so labelled. The person could then be incarcerated, invalidated out of society and subjected to forms of treatments which he or she neither understood nor over which he or she had any choice and control whatever. Categories, it cannot be stressed enough, can exercise their own implacable tyrannies. In fact, a good starting point in a counselling and/or therapeutic encounter would be to ascertain the manner in which clients define themselves, for their own perceptions of themselves may provide the sensitive counsellor with the necessary cues with which to explore their 'contractual' relationships further.

Let us now return to the question: how far do persons of Indian ancestry living in Britain share the attitudes, beliefs, values and behaviours of persons in India? A research project undertaken by Sachdev (1992) has provided a robust empirical validation of the four factors. In her research study, Sachdev (1992), by means of specifically designed questionnaires, compared the beliefs and values of British born Indian school children with those of Caucasian school children in West London. The two groups – although both born and socialized in a predominantly Western culture – showed marked preferences in terms of their favoured value systems. Her research also enabled her to predict the sets of conditions under which an individual's position is likely to shift – *in either direction* – along each continuum. Several sets of related hypotheses have also been subjected to rigorous empirical tests in India (Sachdev, 1992). The analyses of the data lend further support to the above model.

Further empirical validation of the theoretical model has also been provided by Laungani and Sookhoo (1995), Sookhoo (1995) and Laungani (1997b, 1998a). In their studies on coronary heart patients suffering from myocardial infarction, a set of questionnaires was administered to the two sample groups, one of which consisted of Asian (males and females of Indian ancestry) patients and the other of white Caucasian patients. The patients for the study were randomly drawn from the cardiology department of a medical ward in a hospital in East London. Analysis of the questionnaires revealed that the two groups showed significant preferences for their favoured value systems. In-depth, one-to-one interviews with each of the subjects revealed that the Asian subjects, to a large extent, conceptualized their myocardial infarction, its onset, aetiology, its course of treatment and its eventual prognosis in terms of Determinism and Spiritualism, whereas the Caucasian subjects saw their infarction in terms of Free Will. The close-knit family structures of the Asian subjects also enabled them to seek the comfort and security which they believed would assist them in the process of recovery. They were also able to express their feelings and emotions easily within the close-knit family structure. The Caucasian groups, on the other hand, either did not have the close-knit family structures, or preferred not to show any dependence on their family members.

It should be stressed that two confirmatory studies do not necessarily confirm the *total* validity of the theoretical model. More studies need to be done, fresh evidence needs to be gathered, different sets of hypotheses need to be tested. Several such studies are currently in progress (Laungani, 1998b; Sookhoo, 1998). It is hoped that the findings of the studies will provide greater support for the model.

Implications for counselling

The above exposition makes it clear that there are vast differences both within and between the two cultural groups, which extend along several parameters: language, food, religious practices, ethical beliefs, living arrangements, dietary practices, family structures, social networks, patterns of kinship, attitudes towards marriage, sex, work, leisure, achievement and success, personal growth and development, their relationships with their elders, their expressions of feelings and emotions, their beliefs concerning life, death and after-life, and so on. It is evident that the Indians and the English, notwithstanding the past historical ties which bind them, have differing conceptions of their own private, social and philosophical worlds.

Let us, at this juncture, try to visualize a counselling session between an Indian client and a white (male or female) counsellor. How does the counsellor enter the 'world' of a client of Indian (first generation) ancestry? How does he or she even begin to comprehend such a world? What would be the starting point of their relationship? What would be their meeting ground? What kinds of assumptions would each – the client and the counsellor – carry in their heads about the other? Neither of them is likely to proceed on the basis of a *tabula rasa*, because such a mental state (about which a lot has been written) is impossible to attain. Nor is it possible for each of them to maintain a stance of total neutrality in their encounters. Notwithstanding what the Rogerian counsellors advocate, it should be recognized that neither the client nor the counsellor is capable of perceiving the other in totally neutral terms. The so-called neutrality of perceptions, as has been discussed earlier, is a myth. Yet it is one of the dominant features in Rogerian counselling. Although it is a mistaken notion, lacking in any empirical foundation, the belief in the neutrality of perceptions persists among Rogerian adherents.

Even at their first meeting, both the counsellor and the client would have within their own heads a set of assumptions of the other. Initial questioning by the counsellor may result in the client disclosing information which the counsellor may be at a loss to appreciate fully. The counsellor and the client coming as they do from different cultural backgrounds would need more than a set of vague, ill-formed opinions in order to meet and establish a meaningful relationship which would lay the foundation for a productive counselling enterprise. Brief glimpses of each other's worlds, upon closer inspection, may turn out to be false, ephemeral and misleading. The vacuum created by the absence of any systematic, reliable and valid understanding of the other's cultural orientations would be filled by a set of popular cultural stereotypes which each would entertain of the other. While the use of stereotypes may initially help a person to anchor his or her immediate observations, they seldom or never lead to any deep systematic understanding of the individual or the group whose characteristics one is endeavouring to encapsulate. Therefore a reliance on stereotypes, which after all are exaggerated and distorted versions of 'reality', is in the long run bound to be counterproductive and even potentially harmful. One would need to go beyond the realm of stereotypes to arrive at a meaningful understanding of one another. But the question is, how? How can such a meaningful understanding be brought about? How can the counsellor and the client, coming as they do, each from a different culture, put their heads and hearts together?

In recent years, an argument has been advanced that for appropriate and productive intercultural counselling, there should be a process of cultural (and racial) matching of the client and the counsellor, namely that counsellors of a particular ethnic origin should counsel clients of the same ethnic origin. In other words, counsellors of Indian origin should counsel clients of Indian origin, and so on. The idea is based on the assumption that culture-matching is likely to lead to a positive thera-peutic and/or counselling outcome largely because of the familiarity which the counsellor possesses of the client's culture. The proposal carries within it the idea that only 'likes' can understand 'likes', and therefore likes should 'treat' likes.

On the surface this seems a reasonable argument. But there are two serious objections to this idea. First, it is not at all clear *how* this 'grand' aim shall be achieved. Nor is it in any way clear what constitutes counsellor–client matching. Would a Gujarati-speaking Jain counsellor from East Africa be seen as a good culture-match for a Punjabi-speaking Sikh client from Ludhiana? Remember neither speaks the other's language. Neither shares the other's food and dietary practices. Neither worships the other's Gods. What they share in common is their common Indian ancestry. Would a Bengali-speaking Hindu Brahmin from Calcutta be seen as a good culture-match for a Bengali-speaking Muslim from Sylhet in Bangladesh?

I was able to observe such an encounter in a London teaching hospital where a Bengali-speaking link worker was summoned to deal with a middle-aged Bangladeshi patient suffering from coronary heart disease. The Bengali link worker was a Hindu from Calcutta; the patient, a Muslim from Bangladesh. The two were divided by sex, religion, caste and education. The link worker was a highly qualified female, from a high caste Brahmin family, whereas the patient was an uneducated Muslim who came from a small village near Sylhet in Bangladesh. Both felt quite awkward in each other's company. The cardiologist asked questions in English, which were translated into Bengali. I noticed that the translations and counter-translations from English to Bengali to English which transpired were often inexact, cursory, trivial and occa-sionally quite meaningless. One could see that there were personal, unvoiced prejudices at play. The male patient resented being questioned by the female link worker. The link worker, conscious of her high caste and professional status, resented being summoned to talk to, what she referred to as a 'peasant' from Sylhet. Taking me into her confidence, she complained in Hindi (she chose to speak in Hindi because she was aware that neither the patient nor indeed the cardiologist understood the language) that her time could have been better spent in attending to more important matters instead of dealing with this peasant, who, she claimed, was unlikely to respond to any rehabilitation programmes in any case. This sad and unfortunate episode highlights the difficulties of counsellor–client matching. It also raises further questions: how far should the counsellor–client matching process go? Would the patient's health needs have been better served without the services of a link worker? Would a Muslim link worker from Bangladesh have had greater success than the Hindu link worker from Calcutta? Would a male link worker have been more appropriate? One can see that the whole process of counsellor–client matching can get more and more fragmented, reaching a point where it becomes an impossibility.

In fairness it should be pointed out that the above objection, upon close examination, does not stand up to scrutiny. It raises practical, resource-related issues. Given the present shortage of trained counsellors from different cultural backgrounds, it may not be possible to institute a desirable, if not perfect, counsellor–client match. Had that been the case, the unfortunate episode described above might have been avoided.

However, the second objection is a much more serious one. As has been pointed out above, the idea of counsellor–client match carries within it the assumption that only 'likes' can understand 'likes', and therefore only 'likes' should counsel 'likes'. When carried to its logical conclusion, the argument would advocate that only men ought to counsel men, women, women, blacks, blacks, whites, whites, and so on. The main weakness of such an argument lies, first, in its moral pre-scription, and secondly, in its conscious (or unconscious) espousal of a relativistic epistemology.

Defence of moral prescriptions has been and continues to be a contentious philosophical problem. How do moral prescriptions arise? On what grounds can they be defended? Merely to assert that such and such ought to be so, is not a good enough reason for its acceptance. Besides, how can one be sure that a particular moral prescription will lead to the intended consequences? Human actions, as is well known, also lead to unintended consequences, which might turn out to be the opposite of what one might have desired or intended. What compounds the problem even further is the unresolved dispute related to ethical relativism versus ethical universalism.

And this brings us to our second objection, namely that the proposal of a counsellor-client mix drops us into yet another contentious issue concerning relativism. Relativism in this context means that each culture develops its own conceptual system of rules which people subscribe to. Each culture devises its own internally consistent sets of rules. To understand, say, depression in another culture it is necessary to under-stand the system of rules and the assumptions which guide the private and social behaviours of people in that culture. It is assumed too that the adoption of a relativistic position would put an end to any form of pejorative (or racist) judgement of other cultures – because one would be attempting to understand a person (or client) from *within the culture's own consistent system of rules and not from the counsellor's cultural standpoint*. Thus there would be no need to 'order' cultures on a measurable scale of superiority or inferiority, civilized or primitive etc. The adoption of such an approach would also help to dilute, if not dissolve altogether, the oft-voiced accusations of scientific, educational and economic imperialism which have been levelled against Western countries by the developing countries. Is such optimism justified?

The acceptance of relativistic doctrines creates its own peculiar problems. How does one make sense of the rules of another culture? By what means does one attempt to understand the internal rules of another culture? One might learn the language, one might learn the rules of the cultural system, but that alone is not enough to guarantee a clear understanding of the principles underlying the rules of the culture. One of the main weaknesses of the relativistic principle, as Doyal and Harris (1986) point out, lies in the fact that in an attempt to understand the rules of the culture through translations, one would have to suspend judgements concerning whether a given rule was true or false, rational or irrational. If, for instance, one were to be told that the reason why a woman who had just been delivered of a baby was depressed (assuming one was able to understand the nuances of meanings associated with the word depression and find parallels to one's own understanding of depression in general and postnatal depression in particular) was because of the angry fluttering of birds in her stomach during her pregnancy, one would be totally bewildered by such information. It is obvious therefore that if the rules of the language of another culture do not have built into them canons of formal logic and conceptions of rationality, it becomes difficult, if not impossible, to interpret behaviours in any meaningful manner. No judgements of what constitutes positive health or illness would ever be possible.

Although one can see the value of adopting a relativistic position, it does not lend itself to a ready acceptance. It is hardly surprising that the value of relativism as a valid explanatory concept has come to be seriously questioned by several writers, including Bloom (1987), Doyal and Harris (1986), Feyerabend (1987), Gellner (1985), Musgrove (1982), Stace (1958) and Williams (1985). It has also been argued that relativism in recent years has come to acquire a variety of ideological connotations, and is often used as a gag to stifle any recognition of genuine differences in opinions, beliefs, values and behaviours. It is in that sense potentially dangerous, for its acceptance creates no room in it for any genuine understanding of cross-cultural differences in a variety of fields, including counselling. The uncritical acceptance of relativism, as Popper (1972, 1988) has demonstrated, leads to an epistemological *cul-de-sac*. Above all, it does not permit one to transcend one's cultural boundaries. One is forever trapped within the narrowly defined boundaries of one's culture.

Lest one be falsely accused of defending an inflexible universalistic position, it needs to be stated that a deep, systematic and objective knowledge of the culture of the client would be extremely helpful to the counsellor (who is not part of and does not share the client's culture) during the course of counselling sessions. *But it does not follow from this that the client and the counsellor, if they are to make any progress, must be culturally matched.*

For counselling to proceed effectively, it is important to bear in mind that counsellors do not need to imbibe or share the values of their clients. It is important that, to a large measure, they understand and, above all, respect the values of their clients. By the same token, it is necessary for counsellors to ensure that they do not wittingly or unwittingly transmit their own Western individualistic value systems to their clients, thereby achieving a *de facto* status quo in society.

What lessons can a counsellor learn from the brief glimpse we have had into the cultural differences between the English and the Indians in terms of their attitudes, values and behaviours, both private and public? The counsellor in relating to an Indian client might do well to remember the following general points.

1 Indians are family centred and community oriented (Kakar, 1981).
2 Indian families are hierarchically structured and members within the family generally defer to the head of the family (usually the patriarch), who plays a dominant role in decision making. Therefore consent of the head of the family may be necessary if a particular programme affecting any family member is to be successfully implemented (Laungani, 1996; Roland, 1988).
3 Indians often defer to figures of authority and persons in positions of power, seeking precise guidance and direction when in need (Roland, 1988). This would therefore suggest that a non-directive form of counselling is unlikely to lead to positive outcomes (Laungani, 1997a).
4 Indians often tend to adopt a pragmatic approach to illness. They will try out Western remedies, but will also subscribe to Ayurvedic, Unani, homoeopathic and other forms of treatment and folk remedies (Kakar, 1981).
5 Indians tend to feel more comfortable in a relationship which operates on a *personal* basis, rather than on an impersonal and/or contractual basis (Roland, 1988). A 'personalized' relationship sets into motion a set of rules which are not in any way different from those into which they have been socialized since infancy.
6 Indians tend to express their feelings and emotions relatively easily (Laungani, 1996).
7 They tend to respond quite favourably to *emotional* messages (Laungani, 1995; Roland, 1988).

What is essential for effective cross-cultural counselling is that the counsellor acquires a sound knowledge base of the major value systems of the client, and uses such knowledge to help with the process of counselling.

DISCUSSION ISSUES

What can impede our understanding of the term culture?

Discuss the dangers of stereotyping.

What constitutes a culture?

How does the notion of Individualism affect our understanding of differences in social behaviours?

References

Beattie, J. (1964) *Other Cultures: Aims, Methods, and Achievements in Social Anthropology.* London: Routledge & Kegan Paul.

Bellah, R.N. (1985) *Habits of the Heart: Individuation and Commitment in American Life.* Berkeley, CA: University of California Press.

Bhabha, H.K. (1992) 'Postcolonial authority and postmodern guilt', in L. Grossberg, C. Nelson and P. Treichler (eds), London: Routledge.

Bloom, A. (1987) *The Closing of the American Mind.* Harmondsworth: Penguin.

Boaz, F. (1911) *The Mind of Primitive Man.* New York: Macmillan.

Bock, P.K. (1980) *Continuities in Psychological Anthropology: a Historical Introduction.* San Francisco: W.H. Freeman.

Brown, R. (1987) *Social Psychology: The Second Edition.* London: Collier Macmillan.

Camus, A. (1955) *The Myth of Sisyphus.* London: Hamish Hamilton.

Chalmers, A.F. (1983) *What Is This Thing Called Science?*, 2nd edn. Milton Keynes: Open University Press.

Channabasavanna, S.M. and Bhatti, R.S. (1982) 'A study on interactional patterns and family typologies in families of mental patients', in A. Kiev and A.V. Rao (eds), *Readings in Transcultural Psychiatry.* Madras: Higginbothams. pp. 149–61.

Chapple, C. (1986) *Karma and Creativity.* Albany, NY: State University of New York Press.

Cheng, C.H.K. (1996) 'Towards a culturally relevant model of self-concept for the Hong Kong Chinese', in J. Pandey, D. Sinha and D.P.S. Bhawuk (eds), *Asian Contributions to Cross-Cultural Psychology.* New Delhi: Sage. pp. 235–54.

Cooper, D.E. (1996) *World Philosophies: an Historical Introduction.* Oxford: Blackwell.

Davies, P. (1990) *God and the New Physics.* Harmondsworth: Penguin Books.

Doyal, L. and Harris, R. (1986) *Empiricism, Explanation and Rationality: an Introduction to the Philosophy of the Social Sciences.* London: Routledge.

Eliot, T.S. (1948) *Notes Towards the Definition of Culture*. London: Faber & Faber.

Erikson, E. (1963) *Childhood and Society*, London: Penguin.

Eversley, D. and Bonnerjea, L. (1982) 'Social change and indicators of diversity', in R.N. Rapaport, M.P. Fogarty and R. Rapaport (eds), *Families in Britain*. London: Routledge & Kegan Paul. pp. 75–94.

Feyerabend, P. (1987) *Farewell to Reason*. London: Verso.

Fraser, J. ([1932] 1954) *The Golden Bough: a Study in Magic and Religion* (abridged edition). London: Macmillan.

Gellner, E. (1985) *Relativism and the Social Sciences*. Cambridge: Cambridge University Press.

Greenberg, C.I. and Firestone, I.J. (1977) 'Compensatory response to crowding: effects of personal space and privacy reduction', *Journal of Personality and Social Psychology*, 35 (9): 637–44.

Grossberg, L., Nelson, C. and Treichler, P. (eds) (1992) *Cultural Studies*. London: Routledge.

Gulerce, A. (1996) 'A family structure assessment device for Turkey', in J. Pandey, D. Sinha and D.P.S. Bhawuk (eds), *Asian Contributions to Cross-Cultural Psychology*. New Delhi: Sage. pp. 108–18.

Harris, M. (1968) *The Rise of Anthropological Theory. A History of Theories of Culture*. London: Routledge & Kegan Paul.

Herrnstein, R.J. and Murray, C. (1994) *The Bell Curve: Intelligence and Class Structure in American Life*. New York: Free Press.

Heisenberg, W. (1930) *The Physical Principles of the Quantum Theory*. Berkeley, CA: University of California Press.

Hofstede, G. (1980) *Culture's Consequences: International Differences in Work-related Values*. Beverly Hills, CA: Sage.

Hofstede, G. (1991) *Cultures and Organizations: Software of the Mind*. London: McGraw-Hill.

Hui, C.H. and Triandis, H.C. (1986) 'Individualism–Collectivism: a study of cross-cultural researchers', *Journal of Cross-Cultural Psychology*, 17: 222–48.

Jahoda, G. (1970) 'A cross-cultural perspective in psychology', *The Advancement of Science*, 27 (31): 57–70.

Jing, Q. and Wan, C. (1997) 'Socialization of Chinese children', in H.S.R. Kao and D. Sinha (eds), *Asian Perspectives on Psychology*. New Delhi: Sage. pp. 25–39.

Kakar, S. (ed.) ([1979] 1992) *Identity and Adulthood*. Delhi: Oxford India Paperbacks.

Kakar, S. (1981) *The Inner World – A Psychoanalytic Study of Children and Society in India*. Delhi: Oxford University Press.

Kim, U. (1997) 'Asian collectivism: an indigenous perspective', in H.S.R. Kao and D. Sinha (eds), *Asian Perspectives on Psychology*. New Delhi: Sage. pp. 147–63.

Kim, U., Triandis, H.C. and Yoon, G. (eds) (1992) *Individualism and Collectivism: Theoretical and Methodological Issues*: Newbury Park, CA: Sage.

Klineberg, O. (1980) 'Historical perspectives: cross-cultural psychology before 1960', in H.C. Triandis and W.W. Lambert (eds), *Handbook of Cross-Cultural Psychology*, vol. 1. Boston, MA: Allyn & Bacon. pp. 31–67.

Koller, J.M. (1982) *The Indian Way: Asian Perspectives*. London: Collier Macmillan.

Kroeber, A.L. and Kluckhohn, C. (1952) *Culture: a Critical Review of Concepts and Definitions*. Cambridge, MA: Peabody Museum, 47 (1).

Lannoy, R. (1976) *The Speaking Tree*. Oxford: Oxford University Press.

Laungani, P. (1989) 'Cultural influences on mental illness', *Political & Economic Weekly* (Bombay), 28 October, pp. 2427–30.

Laungani, P. (1990) 'Turning Eastward – an Asian view on child abuse', *Health & Hygiene*, 11 (1): 26–9.

Laungani, P. (1991a) 'Preventing child abuse and promoting child health across cultures'. Paper presented at The United Nations Conference on Action for Public Health, Sundsvall, Sweden, 9–15 June.

Laungani, P. (1991b) 'The nature and experience of learning. Cross-cultural perspectives'. Conference on Experiential Learning, University of Surrey, Guildford, 16–18 July.

Laungani, P. (1991c) 'Stress across cultures: a theoretical analysis'. Paper read at the Conference of the Society of Public Health on Stress and the Health Services at the Royal Society of Medicine, Wimpole Street, London, 25 July.

Laungani, P. (1992) 'Assessing child abuse through interviews of children and parents of children at risk', *Children and Society*, 6 (1): 3–11.

Laungani, P. (1995) 'Stress in Eastern and Western Cultures', in J. Brebner, E. Greenglass, P. Laungani and A. O'Roark (eds), *Stress and Emotion*, vol. 15. Washington, DC: Taylor & Francis. pp. 265–80.

Laungani, P. (1996) 'Research in cross-cultural settings: ethical considerations', in E. Miao (ed.), *Cross-Cultural Encounters*. Proceedings of the 53rd Annual Convention of International Council of Psychologists, Taipei, Taiwan (GIS). pp. 107–36.

Laungani, P. (1997a) 'Patterns of bereavement in Indian and English society', in J.D. Morgan (ed.), *Readings in Thanatology*. Amityville, NY: Baywood Publishing. pp. 67–76.

Laungani, P. (1997b) 'Cross-cultural investigations of stress, anger, and coronary heart disease', in *Rage and Stress*. Proceedings of the National 1996 Conference of the International Stress Management Association. London: ISMA Publications. pp. 16–50.

Laungani, P. (1998a) 'Coronary heart disease in India and England: conceptual considerations', *International Journal of Health Promotion and Education* (in press).

Laungani, P. (1998b) *India and England: A Psycho-cultural Analysis*. Amsterdam: Harwood Academic Publishers (in press).

Laungani, P. and Sookhoo, D. (1995) 'Myocardial infarction in British white and Asian adults: their health beliefs and health practices'. Paper read at the 4th European Congress of Psychology, Athens, Greece.

Leach, E. (1964) 'Comment on Naroll's "On ethnic unit classification"', *Current Anthropology*, 5 (4): 299.

Levine, R.A. (1973) *Culture, Behaviour and Personality*. Chicago, IL: Aldine.

Lukes, S. (1973) *Individualism*. Oxford: Basil Blackwell.

Mandelbaum, D.G. (1972) *Society in India*, vol. 2. Berkeley, CA: University of California Press.

Maslow, A. (1970) *Motivation and Personality*, 2nd edn. New York: Harper & Row.

Maslow, A. (1980) *The Farther Reaches of Human Nature*. New York: McGraw-Hill.

Matsumoto, D. (1996) *Culture and Psychology*. Monterey, CA: Brooks/Cole.

McClelland, D.C. (1961) *The Achieving Society*. Princeton, NJ: Van Nostrand.

Miller, N.E. (1969) 'Learning of visceral and glandular responses', *Science*, 163 (3866): 434–5.

Munroe, R.L. and Munroe, R.H. (1980) 'Perspectives suggested by anthropological data', in *Handbook of Cross-Cultural Psychology*, vol. 1. Boston, MA: Allyn & Bacon. pp. 253–317.

Murdock, G.P. (1964) 'Comment on Naroll's "On ethnic unit classification"', *Current Anthropology*, 5 (4): 301–2.

Murdock, G.P. and Provost, C. (1973) 'Measurement of cultural complexity', *Ethnology*, 12: 379–92.

Musgrove, F. (1982) *Education and Anthropology: Other Cultures and the Teacher*. Chichester: Wiley.

O'Flaherty, W.D. (1976) *The Origins of Evil in Hindu Mythology*. Berkeley, CA: University of California Press.

O'Flaherty, W.D. (1980) *Karma and Rebirth in Classical Indian Traditions*. Berkeley, CA: University of California Press.

Pande, S. (1968) 'The mystique of "Western" psychotherapy: an Eastern interpretation', *Journal of Nervous and Mental Disease*, 146: 425–32.

Pandey, R.S., Srinivas, K.N. and Muralidhar, D. (1980) 'Socio-cultural beliefs and treatment acceptance', *Indian Journal of Psychiatry*, 22: 161–6.

Popper, K. (1963) *Conjectures and Refutations*. London: Routledge & Kegan Paul.

Popper, K. (1972) *Objective Knowledge: an Evolutionary Approach*. Oxford: The Clarendon Press.

Popper, K. (1988) *The Open Universe: an Argument for Indeterminism*. London: Hutchinson.

Radhakrishnan, S. ([1923] 1989) *Indian Philosophy*, vol. 2. Centenary Edition. Delhi: Oxford University Press.

Reichenbach, B.R. (1990) *The Law of Karma: a Philosophical Study*. Honolulu: University of Hawaii Press.

Riesman, D. (1954) *Individualism Reconsidered*. New York: Doubleday Anchor Books.

Rogers, C. (1961) *On Becoming a Person*. Boston, MA: Houghton-Mifflin.

Rogers, C. (1970) *On Encounter Groups*. New York: HarperCollins.

Rohner, R.P. (1974) 'Proxemics and stress: an empirical study of the relationship between space and roommate turnover', *Human Relations*, 27 (7): 697–702.

Roland, A. (1988) *In Search of Self in India and Japan*. Princeton, NJ: Princeton University Press.

Sachdev, D. (1992) 'Effects of psychocultural factors on the socialisation of British born Indian children and indigenous British children living in England'. Unpublished PhD thesis, South Bank University, London.

Sampson, E.E. (1977) 'Psychology and the American ideal', *Journal of Personality and Social Psychology*, 15: 189–94.

Schwartz, S.H. (1990) 'Individualism–Collectivism: critique and proposed refinements', *Journal of Cross-Cultural Psychology*, 21 (2): 139–57.

Sethi, B.B. and Manchanda, R. (1978) 'Family structure and psychiatric disorders', *Indian Journal of Psychiatry*, 20: 283–8.

Sinari, R.A. (1984) *The Structure of Indian Thought*. Delhi: Oxford University Press.

Singer, M.A. (1961) 'A survey of personality theory and research', in B. Kaplan (ed.), *Studying Personality Cross-Culturally*. IL: Row, Peterson & Co.

Sinha, D., Mishra, R.C. and Berry, J.W. (1996) 'Some eco-cultural and accultura-tional factors in intermodal perception', in J. Pandey, D. Sinha and D.P.S. Bhawuk (eds), *Asian Contributions to Cross-Cultural Psychology*. New Delhi: Sage. pp. 151–64.

Sookhoo, D. (1995) '*A comparative study of the health beliefs and health practices of*

British whites and Asian adults with and without myocardial infarction'. Paper read at the 53rd Annual Convention of the International Council of Psychologists, Taipei, Taiwan.

Sookhoo, D. (1998) 'Coronary heart disease among Asians: cultural and psychological considerations', *International Psychologist*, 38 (1): 21–3.

Spence, J.T. (1985) 'Achievement American style: the rewards and costs of individualism', *American Psychologist*, 40: 1285–95.

Spielberger, C.D. (1979) *Understanding Stress and Anxiety*. London: Harper & Row.

Srinivasa, D.K. and Trivedi, S. (1982) 'Knowledge and attitude of mental diseases in a rural community of South India', *Social Science Medicine*, 16: 1635–9.

Stace, W.Y. (1958) 'Ethical relativity', in M.K. Muntz (ed.), *A Modern Introduction to Ethics*. Glencoe, IL: The Free Press.

Trefil, J. (1980) *From Atoms to Quarks: An Introduction to the Strange World of Particle Physics*. New York: Charles Scribner.

Triandis, H.C. (1980) 'Introduction' in H.C. Triandis and J.W. Berry (eds), *Handbook of Cross-Cultural Psychology*, vol. 2. Boston, MA: Allyn & Bacon.

Triandis, H.C. (1994) *Culture and Social Behaviour*. New York: McGraw-Hill.

von-Furer-Haimendorf, C. (1974) 'The sense of sin in cross-cultural perspective', *Man*, 9: 539–56.

Ward, C.A. and Kennedy, A. (1996) 'Crossing cultures: the relationship between psychological and socio-cultural dimensions of cross-cultural adjustment', in J. Pandey, D. Sinha and D.P.S. Bhawuk (eds), *Asian Contributions to Cross-Cultural Psychology*. New Delhi: Sage. pp. 289–306.

Waterman, A.A. (1981) 'Individualism and interdependence', *American Psychologist*, 36: 762–73.

Webb, S.D. (1978) 'Privacy and psychosomatic stress: an empirical analysis', *Social Behaviour and Personality*. 6 (2): 227–34.

Weber, M. (1963) *The Sociology of Religion*, 4th edn. London: Allen & Unwin.

Whiting, J.W.M. (1964) 'Comments on Naroll's "On ethnic unit classification', *Current Anthropology*, 5 (4): 305–6.

Williams, B. (1985) *Ethics and the Limits of Philosophy*. London: Fontana Press.

Yang, K.S. (1997) 'Theories and research in Chinese personality: an indigenous approach', in H.S.R. Kao and D. Sinha (eds), *Asian Perspectives on Psychology*. New Delhi: Sage.

Zimmer, H. ([1951] 1989) *Philosophies of India*. Bollingen Series XXVI. Princeton, NJ: Princeton University Press.

3

CULTURE, COUNSELLING AND RACIAL ISSUES

Fred Roach

The concept of culture has been discussed at length in Chapter 2. The author suggests that the word is value-laden and open to subjective analyses. There is an indication that any attempt to achieve objectivity in an explanation and understanding of what culture might be requires the enthusiastic enquirer to address and interpret the concept through various theoretical perspectives. Attention was drawn to three likely perspectives that might be employed in such a search, namely, the anthropological, sociological and psychological. Various interpretations that are usually embodied in each specific perspective were also explored. The author observed that the word culture becomes more difficult to grasp when it is added to different words, such as agriculture, horticulture etc., even within a suggested theoretical framework.

The present chapter explores an aspect of the complexity of the word by introducing 'counselling' and 'racial issues' into the discussion and considers aspects of the role of the counsellor in the context of racialism. It is known that counsellors operate from a set of assumptions that have an impact on their counselling. These assumptions may include the intentional or unintentional acceptance of racial stereotypes when dealing with clients who are racially different from them, and vice versa. An attempt will be made to suggest ways by which such stereotypes may become less influential in practice, or at most, be eradicated, so as to allow the counsellor to proceed with the skill of counselling the client on a premise of mutual understanding, acceptance and trust irrespective of colour or race.

Idealism, materialism and culture

As we have seen in Chapter 2, certain issues around culture surface despite our awareness. It can be said that similar issues and analyses can be drawn from alternative perspectives such as the idealist and the materialist. In brief, the idealistic perspective is concerned with creativity. It directs attention to the quality of one's thoughts and holds that culture is an autonomous product of the human mind. This is an elitist view of culture which focuses on the mind of great thinkers in relation to their creation of philosophical thought, literature and art. This view of culture revolves around a small group of eminently stratified people to whom high status is ascribed. As we know, each society produces its own eminent person who may in time become a historical figure, nationally or internationally known, who serves the society's culture idealistically. Examples of this are reflected through literature; for example, in the writings of Shakespeare or Chaucer; or in other areas of human activity such as academia, the philosophical thought of Aristotle or Plato; the music of Mozart or Beethoven; and in the artistic contribution of Dali or Rembrandt, to name but a few.

The materialist perspective on the other hand views culture as a product of society. It incorporates all aspects of society, including such things as education, law, politics, religion etc., and its way of life as identified within and across all groups.

The materialistic view is a reductionist one that reduces human beings to mere actors playing parts that are determined by others in society, including politicians, church leaders, teachers etc., and/or by the environment, including ecology, economic growth and technological development. Explanations from the materialistic perspective view Western societies as using occupation as a tool to stratify people into different social groups. The reliance on an established occupational typology, determined by occupational status, is all that is usually needed. However, in situations where idealism outweighs materialism and thinking about people of different races becomes an issue, there is an apparent tendency for black and ethnic minorities who may be readily stratified at an equitable level to their white counterparts to be subjectively ascribed to a lower stratified grouping despite the occupational typology. It is thus observed that although ethnicity is used as a high measure of culture in the context of race, it appears that very little attention is given to its relatively low status in the measurement of social stratification in terms of person-perception. The importance of these two perspectives in relation to culture and race is reflected in the general social arrangements of people in society and how people either see themselves or are seen by others in the said society.

The concept of culture is extremely complex. It cannot be readily reduced to commodity or lifestyle. Phillimore (1989) pointed out the falsity of emptying the concept of culture of its complexity and reducing it to lifestyle; and Sivanandan (1991) criticized the commodification of minority cultures. Sheldon and Parker (1992) hold that the use of these frozen and reductionist conceptualizations of culture leads writers into the trap of generalization and stereotyping as typified by Qureshi's

(1989) apparent guide to a range of cultures and racial stereotypes. Sheldon and Parker (1992) suggest that Qureshi's (1989, 1990) typification offers no more than a mosaic of assertions, prejudices, fragmentary facts and cultural stereotypes. There is no unified single position on the meaning of culture. Although there are those who might wish to adhere to the commodity view, others might consider ideals associated with philosophy, literature, art etc. to be more relevant determinants of culture.

Black (1984) drew attention to issues around the apparent pathologizing of minority groups or cultures. Such attempts appear to be more pronounced in the field of mental health, where it is said that African-Caribbeans and Asians have a much greater chance of being labelled mentally ill or schizophrenic (Bagley, 1971; Bebbington et al., 1981; Cochrane, 1977; Dean et al., 1981; Gordon, 1965), with few exceptions (Hemsi, 1967; Rwegellera, 1977), and who are generally overrepresented at the more severe end of the diagnostic classification spectrum (Grimsley and Bhat, 1988) and in compulsory admissions to mental hospitals (Harrison et al., 1984; Kiev, 1965; Pinsent, 1963); and who, as a consequence, are even more likely to remain in hospital for a much longer period than their white counterparts (Roach, 1992). Burke (1989) offers an explanation of the imbalance in the figures in terms of the severity of racism, and the racist bias in the diagnostic categories and methods used by psychiatrists has been supported by studies done in other countries (Sanua, 1969). The indication is that the apparent pathologizing of groups or cultures could have an institutional effect upon the groups so diagnosed.

Burke (1989) believes that the figures quoted over time only partially explain the severity of racism. He seems to suggest that such official statistics reflect the racist bias in the diagnostic categories and the methods used by psychiatrists who at times become involved in the counselling of their patients. The fact is that stereotypes of black and ethnic minority groups can be readily found in society (Lipsedge and Littlewood, 1982). Culture plays a part in this institutionalization process; it has a materialistic basis as well as a role for expressing and moulding ideas that constitute the social relations that people have with each other. It also recognizes the dynamic and historical character of the cultural forms through which social relations manifest themselves (Bujra, 1983). Thus, apart from the many other perspectives, any consideration of culture and race must therefore bring both the idealistic and materialistic perspectives together.

It is characteristic for various community policies to be developed under the sign of culture and for the masses to be socialized into that culture by way of the educational process. It is the view here that if racism is fundamentally embedded in every part of the institutions of a given society then strong, rigid attitudes about black and ethnic minorities would inevitably become incorporated in, and form part of, that socialization process. The fact is that strong rigid, attitudes may be assimilated by the individual who developed in that society from childhood through adulthood and may be either covertly or overtly expressed in what that person does. It is known that assimilation into a national culture and way of life does become the preoccupation of the educational establishment. It therefore seems inevitable that the training and subsequent practice of counsellors might also be affected by some strong, rigid attitudes and values towards black and ethnic minorities. This is one of the major problems counsellors face. The fact is that personal assimilation into a culture of helping means becoming a host to the underlying principles of the theory and educational grounding of the society within which the practice takes place. Culture and society are distinct though not separate because the way people relate to each other and how they come to relate in such ways forms part of the socialization process.

Underlying assumptions and racial stereotypes

On a world population basis, the white population constitutes the ethnic minority. However, on a European nation population basis, it is generally the black population which is perceived as being an ethnic minority. This limited view has tended to be sustained within the various institutions through the socialization process. Thus, black people who make up many of the world's very mixed societies find themselves being labelled as ethnic minority. Arising from this is a persistent view of black people as constituting only a small part of a larger world-wide white population. The problem is historical. As a result of this, certain assumptions have traditionally been made about the lives of black people of African origin, or Asian or other origin: assumptions about how they live, and even about how they might be treated. The dangers associated with an unquestioning adherence to these assumptions can be reflected in questionable decision making and insensitive therapeutic practice by some professionals, including those who might counsel black or ethnic minority clients.

Lago and Thompson (1997) hold that white people are already rooted in white culture. International reflections of a number of racially linked occurrences, or outcomes, might be quoted that indicate the influence of this culture in expressions of strong, rigid attitudes and values around race. In relation to opportunities, some British research has suggested that members of the black and ethnic minority population do not have equal access to the opportunities and provisions that become available (Coard, 1971; Dummett, 1980; Hartmann et al., 1974; Jowell et al., 1984; Jumaa, 1993; Skellington and Morris, 1992; Smith, 1977). There is also some evidence of a number of underlying assumptions. Cashmore and Troyna (1982) were criticized for accusing 'black youth' of being 'arrogant, rumbustious and contemptuous' and have 'a certain fascination for violence'. Both men and women are affected by such pejorative labels.

There is an assumption that the Asian culture is tightly knit and that the family acts as a cultural agent providing a key influence in producing high educational achievements (Swann Report, 1985). However, it should be understood that individuality is an important factor in understanding differences among people, and that all those people who form part of a group of individuals whose origins are geographically shared, or otherwise, cannot be generally ascribed labels. Rex (1982) suggested that mental health breakdown would occur when he contrasted the 'altruistic solidarity' of Asian culture, that is, the idea of being a good Indian, with the Western 'middle class' culture of 'individualism' and 'competition', such as being a successful middle class student. This view assumes that certain deterministic and invariable cultural patterns are responsible for producing inevitable individual responses. Account ought to be taken, however, of individual responses to situations in society since no two people who share the same culture would necessarily react in the same way to the same situation.

More recently, Asian woman tends to be the subject of contradictory and ambivalent stereotyping. On the one hand, she is seen as the symbol and chief bearer of the strong, tightly knit family, and on the other, as the oppressed subject of traditional Asian patriarchal practices. The argument is then posited in the framework of cultural racism with a view that problems arise because of the Asian woman's failure to learn the nation's local language and customs that might allow a smoother integration of her community and children into the local way of life. Other stereotypifications are observed. African-Caribbean women are often seen as being crushed under the weight of a triple oppression of class, gender and racism. This image, however, is overlain with images of the strong black woman, the single mother, holding the family together in the face of irresponsible black males, whether they be husbands or disruptive youth. Lago and Thompson (1997) suggest that where there is a racial difference in any counselling relationship the existence of aspects of racism must be assumed and might also require focused attention. Counsellors are part of this culturally determined issue and ought therefore to attend to the dilemma this poses in the process of counselling.

Counselling

What is counselling?

Counselling can simply mean listening attentively to disciplinary censure. What is involved in this process may vary in terms of perspectives and the degree of intervention. Some basic communication skills may be all that are necessary; however, it is known that counselling in the health field is more about 'helping' someone who needs help. It is useful to add to this the view that effective helping involves a willingness on the part of the person to be helped. Thus for someone to assume responsibility for counselling the counsellor must have certain qualities and abilities necessary for the task of helping people (Davis and Fallowfield, 1991), irrespective of the person's race, culture or ethnicity.

Counselling also involves a cooperative interface between the person seeking help and the person giving that help. If the counsellor experiences some personal difficulty helping black or ethnic minority people in society, he or she will also have difficulty counselling those who ask for help for a problem. The process of counselling involves giving some advice, giving information, decision making, helping the person to clarify their own problems or to facilitate the development of their own solutions (Davis and Fallowfield, 1991). The counsellor should be able to listen and enable people to describe their problem and grasp the meaning of terms used. The counsellor ought to be able to offer advice that is understandable and accessible to the client. It is desirable for counsellors to be aware that counselling may prove ineffective if attention is not given to the triangulatory effects of race, culture and the language of the client. Bennett and Hobbs (1991) suggest that the information offered to the client is not effective if it is not tailored to the individual's needs. One of the central tasks of the counsellor therefore is to listen and understand the other person's experience and feelings sensitively and accurately as they are revealed in the moment-to-moment interaction during the counselling session.

The influence of a theoretical approach

There are several approaches to counselling. However, the temptation slavishly to practise one particular approach in helping someone who asks for help without taking account of the possibility of certain institutionalized racist adaptations of the approach would be to fall into the continuing trap of stereotyping those clients who are different, that is, black or ethnic minority, merely for the purpose of theoretical emphasis.

The world is bountiful on the experiences of black and ethnic minority people who, from time to time, are in need of help for problems that they experience in the society in which they live. Counsellors may be exposed to such experiences in a very uncritical way and as a result may come to the situation with some set or preconceived institutionally determined ideas about black and ethnic minority people and about how they should work with them rather than how to help them. Counsellors should therefore seek to rid themselves of any set or preconceived ideas about black and ethnic minority people and address the structure of their own attitudes towards black and ethnic minorities as a prerequisite to determining the counselling needs of the people who made up these groups in society.

Cultural influences

When a person seeks help for an emotional or behavioural problem there is an expectation that the counsellor will understand the person's problem and will show some awareness of the cultural factors that have shaped the problem. This means that a strong adherence to a particular approach, though fundamental to practice, is not all that the counsellor needs to do when counselling people from the black or ethnic minority population. It is desirable for the counsellor to be aware that people from cultures other than their own may present problems in different ways. This has been observed when looking at clients from differing cultures, such as China (Kleinman, 1977), Saudi Arabia (Racy, 1980) and India (Teja et al., 1971). Psychological problems may be presented in terms of somatic symptoms and the extent of somatization may vary between groups within a culture (Hollingshead and Redlich, 1958). Fitzpatrick (1983) holds the view that explanations of somatization vary and illustrate some of the complexities of interpreting the cultural component in the experience of problems. He also noted that in cultures where emotional problems are highly stigmatized, physical complaints are considered as 'legitimate metaphors whereby personal problems may be expressed'.

Another factor that ought to be borne in mind is that the recently migrated black or ethnic minority person may feel displaced in the new environment, both materialistically and idealistically, from membership of their own black or ethnic group. This is likely to give rise to what Lipsedge and Littlewood (1982) observed as being the development of culture-bound syndromes, which frequently follows a triphasic pattern involving:

1   the dislocation of the individual as a representative of a particular group;
2   emergence of symptoms as a symbolic and exaggerated representation of this; followed by
3   the restitution of the individual.

It therefore seems useful for the counsellor to take account of the importance of culture-bound syndromes in the development of their counselling skills. Littlewood (1985) suggests that rapid culture change and migration have usually been regarded as the cause of pathology. There is also the possibility of the migration of syndromes (Littlewood and Lipsedge, 1981; Rawsley and London, 1964). However, these culture-bound syndromes are frequently variants of more normative roles and principles (Kiev, 1961; Teoh, 1972), which may become less socially adaptive and more pathological during migration or 'through contact with European expansion' (Littlewood, 1985). The black or ethnic minority person may have found it difficult to adjust to the changes in their lives that generally follow geographical or social mobility. In such cases the counsellor ought to be aware of measures that would help the client come to terms with the changes in their lives and to find satisfactory ways of adjusting to change.

Counselling involves human judgement and, as a consequence, counsellors have a duty to be well informed and should refrain from casting blame on the black and ethnic population. The counsellor who works with clients from different cultures ought to be aware that one of the most important assets is themselves. Knowledge and skills, though essential, are now always enough for establishing and maintaining effective therapeutic multicultural relationships.

Is there a solution for the counsellor?

It is important that we accept that there is no right way of therapy and that wide variations in approach can be effective (Corey, 1991). However, just as counsellors in training need to be cautioned about the tendency to mimic the style of their supervisor, they also need to be cautioned about adopting strong, rigid attitudes that may be inherent in the institution of their training through their socialization into the profession or through policy associated with the institution in which they have been trained. This has been reflected by Alladin (1992), who observed that concerns about racism against ethnic minorities have highlighted Eurocentric conceptualizations of academic and applied psychology that are anchored in white middle class norms. The same may be said about counselling and counsellors. Ibrahim and Arredondo (1986) put forward the view that professional codes of ethics should address multicultural perspectives and that these should be reflected in the counselling activity, the selection and use of culturally appropriate assessment tools and the conducting of culturally appropriate research. Counsellors who depend entirely on their own internalized value system about what constitutes a state of wellbeing for an individual who asks for help for a problem may come to rely on stereotypes in making decisions about their clients who are drawn from different cultural groups. Thus it becomes dangerous for counsellors to ignore any perceived cultural differences among clients and proceed to define reality in terms of one set of cultural assumptions (Pedersen, 1988), values, or in terms of one theoretical principle or set of principles, without acknowledging the importance of differences. Such may be the narrowness, and personal failure, of the counsellor in not challenging their rigid beliefs and questionable behaviour towards black and ethnic minority clients. Culturally mixed populations may bring culturally mixed values to the counselling situation and counsellors ought to take note of the impact of culture upon them and their clients and be aware of the influence of their own attitudes and values upon the therapeutic process.

There has been a tendency to concentrate on the adequacy or inadequacy of the client's language skills in making decisions about counselling people from different cultural groups. Until recently there has been little questioning of the language and communication skills of the counsellor. Counsellors, however, ought to become more aware of their own use of language because failure in understanding can lead to subsequent breakdown in communication between client and counsellor. The black and ethnic minority person has been perceived as having a ready-made language problem. This has often led to the view of difference as a deficit (Karseras and Hopkins, 1987; McAvoy and Sayeed, 1990). Clients of black or ethnic minority groupings therefore may not be given the opportunity freely to express themselves or their feelings. They may not be listened to nor given the opportunity to comment upon the counsellor's understanding of the problem and subsequent advice. The risk to the client is that he or she may receive unsatisfactory or totally inappropriate help or support for the situation for which help was sought. This would seem to imply that counsellors ought to become more lingual or linguistic in the delivery of a counselling service within a multicultural society. Fitzpatrick (1983) argues that many non-Western societies lack a vocabulary whereby mental feeling states can be expressed. In such situations, physical and mental illness is less sharply distinguished and consequently not regarded as stigmatizing. Thus, the counsellor ought to avoid repeating some earlier misconceptions which assume that black and ethnic minorities are not capable of experiencing the pathological emotions that are often associated with European culture.

Poor communication could affect treatment outcome and failure to elicit relevant information about symptoms and concerns can result in inaccurate diagnosis, inappropriate treatment and unsound advice. It has been shown that some 50 per cent of patients overall have expressed dissatisfaction with medical care due to poor communication (Ley, 1983). Counsellors need to be aware of this finding and try to avoid any attempt to become too firmly attached to the language of theoretical models or indeed to the language of their own culture. Lago and Thompson (1997) suggest that words and phrases can be loaded with connotative and ideological meanings. Counsellors need to understand the client's culture and use of language within that culture in order to maintain the importance and effectiveness of their communication. The inaccurate exchange of information, its misunderstanding or misinterpretation can also lead to limited intervention and ineffectiveness in terms of counselling outcomes. Irrespective of the client's origins or background, the counsellor will need to communicate at an appropriate level of understanding and give consideration to what the client needs to do to feel better or to get over the problem for which help had been sought. Attention will also need to be given to the appropriateness of the therapeutic theoretical approach and consideration to how the psychological theory needs to be interpreted in terms of helping the black and ethnic minority population within a multicultural society.

The counsellor should be familiar with relevant ethnic data sets that report on health-related data as well as on outcomes. Ahmad et al. (1989) pointed out that in considering the health of British Asians few researchers have attempted to interpret their findings against their disadvantaged background and, as a consequence, implied that differences in health are due to linguistic and cultural factors alone. The counsellor needs to be aware that some differences that might be identified as being racial (for example, commodities, living conditions, occupation) are in fact social in origin and may be a product of the materialistic social conditions in which the black or ethnic minority person finds him- or herself.

There might also be a need for the counsellor to reflect on the role of institutions in maintaining strong rigid attitudes about black and ethnic minorities within the society. Questions such as from whom, or from where, do people get their ideas? could be addressed. Apart from a clear focus on the anthropological, sociological or psychological perspectives, an awareness of the idealistic and materialistic perspectives might be useful for the counsellor to consider because counsellors ought to be aware of the social stratification structure within society and its impact upon the black and ethnic minority population. How a vertical stratification system of power and domination affects the client should be acknowledged in terms of the materialistic and the idealistic perspectives. The counsellor needs to be aware that effect can become cause and that this can often lead to a way of legitimizing inequalities. Townsend (1987) points out that care must be taken not to treat ethnicity as the cause of the phenomenon. Counsellors are generally at risk of accepting this view as reality and thus fall into the trap of perceiving the problem in terms of the client's race or ethnicity.

Potential negative counsellor attitudes towards black or ethnic minority clients

There is no such thing as a culture-free state; counsellors ought to be aware that as a consequence they are not operating from a culture-free stance. The counsellor ought to accept that they are able to change their own personal views rather than settling for an institutionalized racist attitude as a basis for their practice. But if they work solely with this premise, it may lead to the view that black and ethnic minority clients have different cultures because of differences in appearance or skin colour. Sheldon and Parker (1992) point out that the racialization of national origin may give rise to a victim-blaming understanding of problems. The potential tendency to see black and ethnic minorities as being the problem and being responsible for their presenting problem should not be minimized. Such a tendency may be sustained if there is a strong concentration on illnesses or diseases that are more likely to affect certain black or ethnic minority groups. For example, rickets, which was once referred to as the British disease, has been transformed into Asian rickets and often this concentration is blamed on culture (Sheldon and Parker, 1992). The general tendency has been to refer to the special needs of these groups rather than to a health service that adequately responds to the population (Donovan, 1984).

The counsellor ought to respect and appreciate people whose race or culture is different from their own. The objective must be to help the person not the culture of the person. It is desirable for counsellors to seek a better understanding of how black and ethnic minorities respond to life events. They ought not to isolate themselves from members of the perceived black or ethnic community because such type of asocial behaviour is likely to equip the counsellor with a false view of power. The powerful use of counselling skills should never lead counsellors to abuse their power as counsellors. They should recognize the dangers associated with the misuse of power and the vulnerability of black and ethnic minorities and therefore allow their black and ethnic clients to feel empowered and powerful with them. Thus more energy needs to be invested in reality oriented tasks rather than defensive tactics to hide strong, rigid attitudes. They ought to trust their intuitive judgements and willingness to understand ideas and beliefs that differ from their own. They need to develop self-trust and to help the black and ethnic minority client to understand their willingness to help and see them as trustworthy.

The counsellors need to examine their own philosophy of life and their own counselling approach and style. This would help counsellors to avoid a mechanical imitation of theoretical perspective or style and adherence to an approach without taking into account the cultural and racial differences of the client. They should try to experience the world of the patient and develop a frame of reference for identifying the problems that are presented. They should also have respect for the diversity of cultures and show some sensitivity to the unique differences arising out of status or socially stratified groups.

Conclusions

The practising counsellor is subject to the law of the land and ought to abide by and work within the law. The British Association for Counselling states that the overall aim of counselling is to provide an opportunity for the client to work towards living in a more satisfying and resourceful way (BAC, 1992). The literature is full of examples of widespread ineffectiveness of traditional counselling approaches and techniques when applied to racial and ethnic minority populations (Bernal and Padilla, 1982; Casas, 1982; Casas et al., 1986; Ibrahim and Arredondo, 1986; President's Commission on Mental Health, 1980; Smith, 1982; Sue, 1990; Sue and Sue, 1990; Sue et al., 1982). Inadequate training has been blamed for the therapeutic ineffectiveness (Sue et al., 1985). The Code of Ethics and Practice for Counsellors (BAC, 1992) sets out the standards of practice required to fulfil the ethical principles for those counsellors who are members of the British Association for Counselling and reminds both counsellor and client of certain basic legal principles.

The Code of Ethics and Practice may vary from country to country as appropriate to the country's established law. The counsellor should take all reasonable steps to be aware of current legislation affecting his or her work as a counsellor and be aware of, and practice within, the framework of the legal system and relevant Code of Ethics and Practice for Counsellors, as appropriately established in the country in which they are engaged in practice (for example, for England and Wales, BAC, 1992; for USA, APA, 1981). Neither a client's nor counsellor's ignorance of the law is a defence against legal liability or penalty; as citizens they are both subject to the law throughout the counselling relationship. In this context the counsellor should be knowledgeable of any specific law that has a bearing on relationships with respect to black and ethnic minorities and should value integrity, impartiality, safety and respect for the individual.

The idea of a matched counsellor (black-on-black, Asian-on-Asian, etc.) is not supported universally. Kareem and Littlewood (1992) suggest that a psychotherapeutic process that does not take into account the individual's whole life experience or that denies consideration of race, culture, gender or social values can only fragment that individual. On the other hand, Pearson (1986) holds that by concentrating on individual differences the centrality of racism in structuring black or ethnic minority peoples' experience is often denied. It is felt that denial of such experiences may lead to some potential psychological harm to the individual.

Lago and Thompson (1997) made reference to two opposing views on the extent to which counsellors require specialist knowledge of and sensitivity to race in order to counsel. Other issues have also been tackled (Lago and Thompson, 1996; Lee and Richardson, 1991). There is the view that the knowledge and skills of counselling are all that is required to counsel any client. The alternative view is that an understanding of relationships between black and white people requires a historical knowledge of the differences between racial groups. Irrespective of the counsellor's position, it is desirable for the counsellor to take all reasonable steps to ensure that the client suffers neither physical nor psychological harm during counselling. Farley (1995) suggests that the reality of the presenting situation is often such that the client has limited choice in determining the cultural sensitivity of the counsellor and therefore looks for competency rather than matching variables as a central factor in the counsellor's repertoire of skills. This suggests that counsellors ought to strengthen their competency and ensure that the monitoring of their competence as a counsellor is continual through supervision and appropriate consultative support. Such consultative support, when necessary, should be drawn from responsible black or ethnic minority persons in order to ensure that reasonable conclusions are determined which are culturally sensitive.

Counsellors have a responsibility to themselves and their clients to maintain their own effectiveness, resilience and ability to help clients. The Code of Practice suggests that they are expected to monitor their own personal functioning and to seek help and/or to withdraw from counselling, whether temporarily or permanently, when their personal resources are sufficiently depleted to require this action. It is note-worthy that counsellors do not normally give advice; they should be aware that race can be used to inform and explain rather than to obfuscate and oppress. They should work in ways that promote the person's control over his or her own life, and respect the client's ability to make decisions and change in the light of his or her own beliefs and values, irrespective of race. Korman (1974) suggested that the provision of professional services to persons of culturally diverse backgrounds by persons not competent in understanding and providing professional services to such groups should be considered unethical. Ethical guide-lines have been published in the USA making training on cultural differences imperative for counsellors and therapists (AACD, 1981; APA, 1981).

The counsellor needs to take reasonable steps during the counselling process to ensure that the client is able to review the terms on which counselling is being provided and the methods of counselling being used. It is often felt that the experience of discrimination is a risk factor in counselling, because this might take place without challenging existing structures and theoretical frameworks. Despite the use by the counsellor of varying counselling perspectives, there might be a concen-tration on some stereotypes. Counsellors need to use race uncritically as a natural variable. This would aid the racialization of society (Phizacklea, 1984) and impact on the racialization of the counselling process. It has been suggested that the possibility ought to be considered more seriously that the locus of those forces that restore and ameliorate the client of psychotherapy resides more within the client, and less within the therapist or the therapist's actions. But counsellors should have both responsibility for and maturity to understand these forces, since it is known that little distinction is made among counsellors between basic counselling and in-depth counselling/psychotherapy. Health care ought to be age, gender, race and colour blind. Dudley and

Rawlins (1985) suggest that the counselling of ethnic minorities is often defined by two processes expressed in terms of the personal and institutional racism within psychology itself. The future counsellor therefore needs to be far more aware of the impact of social relations and structures on minorities.

There seems to be little evidence to suggest that counsellors are becoming more aware of the value-laden word 'culture' and the apparent difficulties that arise when it is linked to race. The counsellor need is to be mindful that the application of such terms as black, white or ethnic minority to culture and to the process of counselling is likely to interfere with the counselling process itself and confound the development of a more objective approach to helping the black and ethnic minority person who asks for help for a problem. Careful consideration must also be given to the factors influencing the use of such variables as ethnicity and race (Zwi, 1991). Sue and Sue (1990) suggest that counselling professionals need to recognize that race, culture and ethnicity are functions of each and every one of us and not limited to 'just minorities'. It is the view here that by rejecting the notion of ethnicity in the counselling process there is an opportunity for counsellors to address the multi-racialization of the helping process. The need is for counsellors to be trained in this colour blind skill. Much more training and research is therefore needed to help counsellors think about the conceptual, methodological and political issues surrounding these terms prior to embarking on counselling people who consider themselves to be black or ethnic minority, or indeed, those who are considered by others to be members of this population group.

Key points

- Counsellors operate from a set of assumptions that have an impact on their counselling. These assumptions may include the intentional or unintentional acceptance of racial stereotypes.
- Certain issues and concerns can be drawn from alternative perspectives on culture. For example, the idealist perspective is concerned with creativity whereas the materialist perspective views culture as a product of society.
- Strong, rigid attitudes about black and ethnic minorities may be assimilated by the counsellor from childhood and may be either covertly or overtly expressed in practice.
- On a world population basis the white population constitutes the ethnic minority. Where there is a racial difference in any counselling relationship the existence of aspects of racism must be assumed and might also require focused attention.
- To assume responsibility for counselling the counsellor must have certain qualities and abilities necessary for the task of helping people. It is desirable for counsellors to be aware that counselling

may prove ineffective if attention is not given to the triangulatory effects of race, culture and language.

- There is no right way of therapy in relation to counselling black or ethnic minority clients; wide variations in approach can be effective. Counsellors who depend entirely on their own internalized value system about what constitutes a state of wellbeing for a client may come to rely on stereotypes in making decisions about their black and ethnic minority clients.
- The counsellor ought to respect and appreciate people whose race or culture is different from their own. The objective must be to help the person not the culture of the person.
- The counsellor needs to be mindful that the application of such terms as black, white or ethnic minority to culture and to the process of counselling is likely to interfere with the counselling process itself and confound the development of a more objective approach to helping the black and ethnic minority person who asks for help for a problem.

DISCUSSION ISSUES

What assumptions do you make about different cultures?

How could you avoid stereotyping your clients?

Counsellors should become more lingual or linguistic in the delivery of a counselling service within a multicultural society. Discuss.

Why is the idea of a 'matched counsellor' not supported universally?

References

AACD (American Association for Counseling and Development) (1981) *Ethical Principles*. Alexandria, VA: AACD.

Ahmad, W.I.U., Kernohan, E.E.M and Baker, M.R.I. (1989) 'Health of British Asians: a research review', *Community Medicine*, 11: 49–56.

Alladin, W.J. (1992) 'Clinical psychology provision: models, policies and prospects', in W.I.U. Ahmad (ed.), *The Politics of Race and Health*. Bradford: University of Bradford.

APA (American Psychological Association) (1981) 'Ethical principles of psychologists', *American Psychologist*, 36: 633–81.

BAC (British Association for Counselling) (1992) *Code of Ethics and Practice for Counsellors*. Rugby: BAC.

Bagley, C. (1971) 'Mental illness in immigrant minorities in London', *Journal of Biological Science*, 3: 449–59.

Bebbington, P.E., Hurry, J. and Tennant, C. (1981) 'Psychiatric disorder in selected immigrant groups in Camberwell', *Social Psychiatry*, 16: 43–51.

Bennett, P. and Hobbs, T. (1991) 'Counselling in heart disease', in H. Davis and L. Fallowfield (eds), *Counselling and Communication in Health Care*. Chichester: Wiley.

Bernal, M.E. and Padilla, A.M. (1982) 'Status of minority curricula and training in clinical psychology', *American Psychologist*, 37: 780–7.

Black, J. (1984) 'Afro-Caribbean and African families', *British Medical Journal*, 290: 984–8.

Bujra, J. (1983) *Cultural and Social Diversity: a Third World in the Making*. Milton Keynes: Third World Studies, Open University Press.

Burke, A. (1989) in J. Cruickshank and D. Beevers (eds), *Ethnic Factors in Health Disease*. Oxford: Butterworth.

Casas, J.M. (1982) 'Counseling psychology in the market place: the status of ethnic minorities', *The Counseling Psychologist*, 37: 780–7.

Casas, J.M., Ponterotto, J.G. and Gutierrez, J.M. (1986) 'An ethical indictment of counseling research and training: the cross-cultural perspective', *Journal of Counseling and Development*, 64: 347–9.

Cashmore, E. and Troyna, B. (1982) 'Black youth in crisis', in E. Cashmore and B. Troyna (eds), *Black Youth in Crisis*. London: Allen and Unwin.

Coard, B. (1971) *How the West Indian Child is Made Educationally Subnormal in the British School System*. London: New Beacon Books.

Cochrane, R. (1977) 'Mental illness in immigrants to England and Wales: an analysis of mental hospital admissions, 1971', *Social Psychiatry*, 12: 25–35.

Corey, G. (1991) *Theory and Practice of Counseling and Psychotherapy*, 4th edn. Monterey, CA: Brooks/Cole.

Davis, H. and Fallowfield, L. (1991) 'Counselling theory', in H. Davis and L. Fallowfield (eds), *Counselling and Communication in Health Care*. Chichester: Wiley.

Dean, G., Walsh, D., Downing, H. and Shelley, E. (1981) 'First admissions of native-born and immigrants to psychiatric hospitals in South East England, 1976', *British Journal of Psychiatry*, 139: 506–12.

Donald, J. and Rattansi, A. (1992) *Race, Culture and Difference*. London: Sage/Open University.

Donovan, J. (1984) 'Ethnicity and health: a research review', *Social Science and Medicine*, Vol. 19.

Dudley, G.R. and Rawlins, M.L. (1985) 'Psychotherapy with ethnic minorities', *Psychotherapy: Theory, Research, Practice, Training*, 22 (2).

Dummett, A. (1980) 'Nationality and citizenship', in Conference in Support of Further Education in Ethnic Minorities. London: National Association for Teachers in Higher Education.

Farley, N. (1995) 'Patient's preference for therapist – a preliminary investigation into patients with sexual dysfunction preference for therapists'. Unpublished MSc Thesis, University of London.

Fitzpatrick, R.M. (1983) 'Cultural aspects of psychiatry', in M. Weller (ed.), *The Scientific Basis of Psychiatry*. London: Bailliere Tindall.

Gordon, E.B. (1965) 'Mental illness in West Indian migrants', *British Journal of Psychiatry*, 111: 877–87.

Grimsley, M. and Bhat, A. (1988) 'Health', in A. Bhat, R. Carr-Hill and S. Ohri (eds), *Britain's Black Population*, 2nd edn. Aldershot: Gower.

Harrison, G. Ineichen, B., Smith, J. and Morgan, H.G. (1984) 'Psychiatric hospital admissions in Bristol, 11: Social and clinical aspects of compulsory admission', *British Journal of Psychiatry*, 145: 605–11.

Hartmann, P., Husband, C. and Clark, J. (1974) *Races as News*. Paris: UNESCO Press.

Hemsi, L.K. (1967) 'Psychiatric morbidity of West Indian immigrants: a study of first admissions in London', *Social Psychiatry*, 2: 95–100.

Hollingshead, A.B. and Redlich, F.C. (1958) *Social Class and Mental Illness*. New York: Wiley.

Ibrahim, F.A. and Arredondo, P.M. (1986) 'Ethical standards for cross-cultural counseling: counselor preparation, practice, assessment and research', *Journal of Counseling and Development*, 64: 349–52.

Jowell, R., Witherspoon, S. and Brook, L. (1984) *British Social Attitudes: the 1984 Report*. Aldershot: Gower/Social and Community Planning Research.

Jumaa, M. (1993) 'From the chair', *Race Newsletter*, December, No. 3 (Rugby: BAC).

Kareem, J. and Littlewood, R. (eds) (1992) *Intercultural Therapy. Themes, Interpretations and Practice*. Oxford: Blackwell Scientific.

Kaseras, P. and Hopkins, E. (1987) *British Asians Health in the Community*. Chichester: Wiley.

Kiev, A. (1961) 'Suicide and risk taking in Tikopia society', *Psychiatry*, 23: 1–17.

Kiev, A. (1965) 'Psychiatric morbidity of West Indian immigrants in an urban group practice', *British Journal of Psychiatry*, 111: 51–6.

Kleinman, A. (1977) 'Depression, somatisation and the new cross-cultural psychiatry', *Social Science and Medicine*, 11: 3–10.

Korman, M. (1974) 'National conference on levels and patterns of professional training in psychology: major themes', *American Psychologist*, 29: 301–13.

Lago, C.O. and Thompson, J. (1996) *Race, Culture and Counselling*. Buckingham: Open University Press.

Lago, C. and Thompson, J. (1997) 'Counselling and race', in S. Palmer and G. McMahon (eds), *Handbook of Counselling*, 2nd edn. London: Routledge.

Lee, C.C. and Richardson, B.L. (1991) *Multicultural Issues in Counseling: New Approaches to Diversity*. Alexandria, VA: American Association for Counseling and Development.

Ley, P. (1983) 'Patients' understanding and recall in clinical communication failure', in D. Pendleton and J. Hasler (eds), *Doctor–Patient Communication*. London: Academic Press.

Lipsedge, M. and Littlewood, R. (1982) 'Private pathology and public performance'. Personal Meanings Symposium, London University.

Littlewood, R. (1985) 'The migration of culture-bound syndromes', *Bulletin of the Transcultural Psychiatry Society (UK)*. No. 7 (May): 12–15.

Littlewood, R. and Lipsedge, M. (1981) 'Acute psychotic reactions in Caribbean-born patients', *Psychological Medicine*, 11: 303–18.

McAvoy, B. and Sayeed, A. (1990) 'Communication', in B. McAvoy and L. Donaldson (eds), *Health Care in Asians*. Oxford: Oxford Medical Publications.

Pearson, M. (1986) 'The politics of ethnic minority health studies', in T. Rathwell and D. Phillips (eds), *Health, Race and Ethnicity*. London: Croom Helm.

Pedersen, P. (1988) *A Handbook for Developing Multicultural Awareness*. Alexandria, VA: American Counseling Association.

Phillimore, P. (1989) 'Shortened lives: premature death in N. Tyneside', *Bristol Papers in Applied Social Studies*, No. 12.

Phizacklea, A. (1984) 'A sociology of race relations or "race relations" a view from Britain', *Current Sociology*, 32 (3): 199–218.

Pinsent, J. (1963) 'Morbidity in an immigrant population', *Lancet*, 1: 437–8.

President's Commission on Mental Health (1980). Report from the President's Commission on Mental Health. Washington, DC: Government Printing Office.

Qureshi, B. (1989) *Transcultural Medicine*. Dordrecht: Kluwer Academic.

Qureshi, B. (1990) in B. McAvoy and L. Donaldson (eds), *Health Care for Asians*. Oxford: Oxford Medical Publications. pp. 663–70.

Racy, J. (1980) 'Somatisation in Saudi women: a therapeutic challenge', *British Journal of Psychiatry*, 212–16.

Rawsley, K. and London, J.B. (1964) 'Epidemiology of mental disorder in a closed community', *British Journal of Psychiatry*, 110: 830–39.

Rex, J. (1982) 'West Indian and Asian youth', in E. Cashmore and B. Troyna (eds), *Black Youth in Crisis*. London: Allen and Unwin.

Roach, F. (1992) 'Community mental health services for black and ethnic minorities', *Counselling Psychology Quarterly*, 5 (3): 277–90.

Rwegellera, G. (1977) 'Mental illness among West Africans and West Indians living in London', *Psychological Medicine*, 7: 317–29.

Sanua, V.D. (1969) 'Immigrants, migration and mental illness: a review of the literature with special emphasis on schizophrenia', in E.B. Broby (ed.), *Behaviour in New Environments*. Beverly Hills, CA: Sage.

Sheldon, A. and Parker, H. (1992) 'The use of ethnicity and race in health research: a cautionary note', in W.I.U. Ahmad (ed.), *The Politics of Race and Health*. Bradford: University of Bradford.

Sivanandan, A. (1991) 'Black struggles against racism', in Northern Curriculum Development Group (eds), *Anti-Racist Social Work: 1, Setting the Context for Change*. London: CCETSW.

Skellington, R. and Morris, P. (1992) *Race in Britain Today*, London: Sage/Open University Press.

Smith, D.J. (1977) *Racial Disadvantage in Britain*. Harmondsworth: Penguin.

Smith, E.J. (1982) 'Counseling psychology in the market place: the status of ethnic minorities', *The Counseling Psychologist*, 10: 61–7.

Sue, D.W. (1990) 'Culture specific strategies in counselling: a conceptual framework', *Professional Psychology*, 24: 424–33.

Sue, D.W. and Sue, D. (1990) *Counseling the Culturally Different: Theory and Practice*. New York: Wiley.

Sue, D.W., Bernier, Y., Durran, A., Feinberg, L., Pedersen, P.G., Smith, E.J. and Vasquez-Nuttal, E. (1982) 'Position paper: cross-cultural counseling competencies', *The Counseling Psychologist*, 10: 45–52.

Sue, S., Akutsu, P.D. and Higashi, C. (1985) 'Training issues in conducting therapy with ethnic minority group clients', in P.B. Penderson (ed.), *Handbook of Cross-cultural Counseling and Therapy*. Westport, CT: Greenwood Press. pp. 275–80.

Swann Report, Department of Education and Science (1985) *Education for All*. London: HMSO.

Teja, J.S., Narang, F.L. and Aggarwal, A.K. (1971) 'Depression across cultures', *British Journal of Psychiatry*, 119: 253–60.

Teoh, J.-I. (1972) 'The changing psychopathology of Amok', *Psychiatry*, 35: 345–52.

Townsend, P. (1987) 'Deprivation', *Journal of Social Policy*, April: 122–45.

Zwi, A. (1991) *Racism in the Production and Reproduction of Knowledge in the Social and Biomedical Sciences* (mimeo). London School of Hygiene and Tropical Medicine.

4

MODELS OF COUNSELLING AND PSYCHOTHERAPY FOR A MULTIETHNIC SOCIETY

Waseem Alladin

This chapter begins by highlighting some conceptual differences between Western models of counselling and psychotherapy by focusing on the problems with the Western concept of the autonomous self. A brief case illustration shows how conceptual clashes in counselling and psychotherapy can be damaging. After a review of three models proposed for a multiethnic society, the focus will be on a nine-dimensional ethnomedical model which will be illustrated with a framework for counselling and psychotherapy and followed by detailed analysis of a case study. The question as to whether a transcultural model can be assimilated within mainstream Western models of counselling and psychotherapy is considered. It will be acknowledged that some concepts in indigenous counselling and psychotherapy may not be compatible for integration and may need to exist in parallel – a case of recognizing that the glass is not simply either half full or half empty, but more accurately both half full and half empty, at one and the same time.

In this chapter I will focus on one group of ethnic minority people who have made Britain their home – those from the Indian subcontinent – since I am more familiar with them, but hopefully my comments will have relevance for the counselling and psychotherapy of culturally different clients with diverse religious backgrounds. I will not consider the central issue of racism here, since this is specifically dealt with in Chapter 3 but suffice it to say that elsewhere I have addressed concerns about racism (Alladin, 1986, 1987, 1989, 1992) and the relevance of racial identity (Alladin, 1993a).

The glass is both half full and half empty

The influential roles played by shamans, witch-doctors and religious sages in helping their clients have been analysed by Kakar (1982) in his psychological inquiry into India and its healing traditions. Kakar describes nine different approaches ranging from tribal shamans, to Hindu and Muslim holy men and women, to Tantric and Ayurvedic practices. Similarly, there are numerous references in holy texts, for example the *Bhagavad Gita* and the Holy Qur'an, which can be used to compare and contrast models of counselling and psychotherapy. For example, Ajaya (1989), a clinical psychologist and a professional yogi, has attempted to integrate the psychotherapy of East and West in a unifying paradigm. More recently, Sheikh and Sheikh (1996) have brought together a range of topics spanning Hindu, Buddhist, Jewish, Christian and Islamic approaches and attempted to integrate these with those of psychology, modern physics and the neurosciences. These approaches, whilst relevant to counselling and psychotherapy, will not be considered here but readers are encouraged to consult these works.

Cognitive therapists hold that a glass is half full rather than half empty, and apparently this fits the perception of optimists as opposed to pessimists. Ironically, cognitive therapists on the one hand advise their clients not to engage in all-or-none categorical thinking, one of the thinking errors in cognitive therapy, yet they fail to see the error in their own thinking! However, to an Eastern way of thinking the glass is both half full and half empty simultaneously, and depending on the context, it may be more appropriate to focus on it being either one or the other.

It may seem harsh to suggest that Western counselling and psycho-therapy still peddles cultural imperialism. Cognitive behavioural therapy with its emphasis on a problem solving approach would seem to be immune from this charge. But is it? I have pointed out elsewhere that cognitive behavioural therapists may be guilty of imposing their world view on clients. People have no difficulty recognizing, for example, that a glass that is half full may be described as half empty, but some cognitive therapists dismiss this and assert that neither perspective is correct, claiming that it is 'only 6 fluid ounces in a 12 ounce glass'. Thus they are forcing psychometrics as *the* way of perceiving one's reality 'objectively' and dismissing 'subjective' perceptions and denying that moods colour our perceptions, which incidentally, is a central tenet of cognitive behavioural therapy. This does not mean that there is no merit in helping clients to adopt a detached viewpoint, but to present that as the proper and (implicitly) superior view is indefensible (Alladin, 1993b).

Pachuta (1996: 55–7) suggests that:

> the eastern way of healing is circular. Oneness with the universe is a given and one continually seeks balance and harmony within this oneness. Paradox is an illusion and can be mastered. Each individual is unique within the overall oneness. Sameness coexists with differences within and between all people. People are treated in the totality of bodymindspirit. . . . In contrast, the western healing systems are linear and emphasize differences. We have great difficulty in tolerating paradox. We stress the division of the person into body and mind, and the spirit is generally irrelevant to Western scientific medicine.

Pachuta (1996) uses the *Yin/Yang* concept in Chinese medicine to illustrate the duality within unity which he points out often poses problems for Western students of philosophy and medicine. He asserts that to the Western mind, things are black *and* white or black *or* white. But in the Eastern way, things are black/white. In the Judeo-Christian tradition all opposites are warring forces with the chief battle being good against evil. This is the 'cowboy versus Indians' world view of Hollywood. In the Eastern way, the inseparable *Yin* and *Yang* gently wrestle with each other. Nothing in the universe is one or the other. Everything contains *Yin/Yang*. They are part of the same reality. They are merely opposite polarities of the same magnet, and it is impossible to have one without the other. Westerners hold that light battles with darkness, life with death, good with evil, positive with negative. Watts (1975) has noted that thus the ideal to cultivate the former and be rid of the latter flourishes throughout much of the world. To the traditional way of Chinese thinking, this is as incomprehensible as electric currents without both positive and negative poles. The disappearance of one of them would be the disappearance of the entire system.

This has profound implications. For example, Western medicine in particular is overtly aggressive, someone with cancer for example is seen to be 'invaded by an evil that needs to be battled against' and in extremes leads to doctors playing God and finding ways to 'cheat' death. This is not to suggest that appropriate efforts to save life and extend lifespan are to be condemned, only that the contemporary Western tendency to see death as the end to our existence and 'save' a person at all costs is questionable and in Eastern terms even delusional! Dossey (1996) suggests that modern physics has abandoned the notion of linear time and that a revision of the view of time as allied to space would lead to sweeping changes in many commonly held views. For example, let us consider death. Beginnings, like endings, have no absolute status outside linear time. Dossey asserts that the goal of medicine, which is to extend life to the fullest extent possible, needs rethinking. With a new understanding and awareness there is something much less grim about the 'Grim Reaper' than Western science has heretofore imagined. He acknowledges that many traditions have long held the view that death is not final but what is new is that this belief can now be defended against the background of modern science.

Problems with the Western concept of the autonomous self

DeVos, Marsella and Hsu (1985) are at pains to stress that the Western cultural tradition is only one of a number of possible ways to conceptualize the person in society. They explain that the Western striving is towards the development of a solid well-functioning ego. The inner experience of self should be clearly delineated from the outside.

The Hindu striving goes in the opposite direction – to achieve union with the immutable self, which is ultimately indistinguishable from deity and the totality of the universe (see Bharati, 1985).

Does it really matter how the self is conceptualized by different peoples? This may sound academic, but Western cultural imperialism continues in counselling and psychotherapy encounters to damage clients and the counselling professions, as I hope to explain in this section.

To a Buddhist, the self is both an individual and collective delusion because there is no self. It is neither a thing nor a process and those who come to this realization are on their way to enlightenment. Ironically, Western discourse about the self implicitly recognizes this when reference is made to the self-concept which is nothing more than a *concept* of the self. In the terms of Gilbert Ryle, 'a category error' has been committed because a category has been elevated into a thing.

In Sufism, the Muslim mystical way to Universal Self, for example, the person's self is seen as an obstacle to development, as in the following anecdote involving the behaviour of a dog.

Shibli was asked: 'Who guided you in the Path?'
He said: 'A dog. One day I saw him, almost dead with thirst, standing by the water's edge.
Every time he looked at his reflection in the water, he was frightened, and withdrew, because he thought it was another dog.
Finally, such was his necessity, he cast away fear and leapt into the water, at which the "other dog" vanished.
The dog found that the obstacle, which was himself, the barrier between him and what he sought, melted away.
In this same way my own obstacle vanished, when I knew that it was what I took to be my own self. And my Way was first shown to me by the behaviour of a dog.' (Haschmi, 1973: 129, cited in Arasteh and Sheikh, 1996)

If we compare the Sufi example, we can tease out some interesting comparisons. We could say that the dog desensitized itself to its fear, helped by overwhelming thirst, or even that by taking the leap into the water the dog was practising flooding by facing its fear and thereby conquering it. The events were naturalistic and ecologically valid and needed no further experiments to validate the generalization of the finding. There was no need to do anything or apply noxious stimuli to the subject of the observation and no ethical principles were violated. On the other hand, Ivan Pavlov, in the Western tradition, conducted his conditioning experiments by observing the behaviours of salivating dogs, just as Martin Seligman put forward his learned helplessness theory after his fortuitous discovery in his experiments with dogs that were subjected to mild electric shocks.

Rose (1991) cautions that anthropologists and historians long ago recognized that the category of 'the self' was not universal, that different cultures and different historical periods specified human capacities differently and individualized humans in ways foreign to our own. He stresses that sociologists too have suggested that the free, rational, conscious, choosing, autonomous self is a creation of Western capitalist democracies. This is not to suggest that ethnic minorities are shackled, irrational, unconscious, incapable of making choices and refuse to accept responsibilities for their behaviours.

A telling example illustrates the unwitting clash of concepts in counselling and psychotherapy practice:

> 'I'll have to talk to my brother,' the female Pakistani graduate student told the female American counsellor. 'I can't decide what to do until I talk to him.' She was married and her husband was abusing her. He hit her, reviled her, and on at least one occasion burned her with his cigarette. Friends had encouraged her to see the counsellor. Her older brother was a post-doctoral researcher at an Ivy League institution. It was his guidance she said she needed.
>
> The counsellor saw the problem right away. Here was a woman unable to make up her own mind. She needed to assert herself. It was her life, not her brother's. The counsellor explained that the Pakistani woman needed to take responsibility for her own decisions. The Pakistani woman left the counselling session and never saw the counsellor again. (Thomas and Althen, 1989: 205)

I presented the above example at a postgraduate seminar/workshop and none of the participants could even understand why the counsellor's response was inappropriate! What was wrong with asking a grown woman to assert herself? Surely, an adult has to take responsibility for making her own decisions? The point is that:

1 It was premature to ask the Pakistani woman to assert herself, not that the assertion *per se* is inappropriate.
2 It also cannot be assumed that the Pakistani woman was incapable of asserting herself, for she may have assertive skills in her repertoire but has not yet decided to use them (see Alladin, 1988).
3 The notion that it was 'her life not her brother's' illustrates the problem that Laungani (1997a) has highlighted about imposing an individual or client centred approach on ethnic minorities.
4 The notion that anyone who is at least 18 years is an adult in law does not automatically mean that responsibility for making important decisions should be taken by the person alone. For the Pakistani woman, her elder brother is a person to be respected and consulted before a major decision is made.

Again, we have the clash between Individualism and Communalism, which Laungani (1997a) has highlighted, when an individual perspective is imposed on a family perspective, which I have considered elsewhere (Alladin, 1992) in criticizing the qualities that a person is required to have in a Western society to be judged psychologically well adjusted.

In Table 4.1, to a Western way of thinking the qualities in **bold** on the left are a 'good' thing to have, which are polarized with the 'undesirable'

Table 4.1 *Perspectives on concepts of normality and health*

Assertive	**Submissive**
(Arrogant)	(Humble)
Independent	**Dependent**
(Selfish)	(Caring)
Free expression of feelings	**Control of passions**
(Out-of-control)	(Dignified)
Individual	**Family**
(Egotistic)	(Communal)

Source: Alladin, 1992

qualities in **bold** on the left. However, from an Eastern or holistic perspective those 'desirable' qualities may be viewed differently, as shown in the terms in brackets on the left which may be perceived as undesirable behaviours whereas those on the right are 'desirable' behaviours to emulate. The mistake that Westernized counsellors often make is that the behaviours are abstracted from their context and judged as 'good' or 'bad', independent of the culture of the client.

Thomas and Althen (1989: 205) comment that the counsellor had made a mistake:

> She had (quite naturally) taken the individual-centred view that is the hallmark of most Western cultures. She had supposed that the Pakistani woman was immature and perhaps even a bit 'defective' in believing that she needed her brother's guidance. It had not occurred to the counsellor that this woman, in her own terms and those of all important to her, was behaving in a perfectly appropriate way. It was clear to the Pakistani woman that the counsellor simply did not understand.

The problem is that an Eastern woman was being judged from a Western frame of reference. In counselling and psychotherapy, there is an exhortation that we should not judge another's behaviour until we walk in their moccasins for a while. It could be argued that if a client has a more holistic conceptual system then the therapist who is indoctrinated or encapsulated in traditional Western thinking is not only liable to misunderstand the client but at risk of forcing the client into a way of thinking that becomes a strait-jacket for the client, and it is then hardly surprising that clients may drop out and never come back. It would be too easy then for a therapist to dismiss the client as lacking in motivation, psychological-mindedness or even as not being ready for therapy.

The concept of personality

Hsu (1985) asserts that the concept of personality is an expression of the Western ideal of individualism. Worse, it does not correspond even to the reality of how 'the Western Man lives in Western culture, far less any Man in any other culture'. He suggests that the main problem created by the concept of personality is that we tend to see it as a separate entity, distinct from society and culture. To put it more bluntly, the Western ideal of individualism (the egotistical preoccupation with 'me . . . me . . . and me' or 'looking after number 1') rejects the notion of interdependence, creates and perpetuates alienation and damages the ecology.

Modern physics has begun to converge on Eastern spiritual concepts to the point that Dossey (1996) has not only made a compelling case for the importance of modern physics to modern medicine but he understandably regrets the fact that the medical schools do not teach modern physics. Thus, for example, he states that one of the central features of classical physics is that nature can be 'atomized' – that is, it can be divided into units that are ultimately indivisible and separate. He asserts that this feature of separateness cannot be found in modern atomic physics since the idea of separately existing particles has been impossible to prove.

Hsu (1985) asserts that the meaning of being human is found in interpersonal relationships since no human being exists alone. Client centred counselling recognizes this when it is acknowledged that the relationship between client and counsellor is paramount, yet the practice of counselling and psychotherapy more often than not focuses on the individual at the expense of the relationship. Looked at in this context, Laungani's (1997b) critique of client centred counselling, which is widely but mistakenly regarded as 'neutral' or as the 'least culturally loaded', is not only courageous, since it goes against the received wisdom in the field, but also perceptive.

Ironically, client centred counselling recognizes that at the *heart* of the therapeutic enterprise is the *relationship* between counsellor and client. However, the counsellor or psychotherapist as expert unwittingly perpetuates a medical model yet most practitioners would be horrified to see their practice characterized in this manner. However, consider the constructivist approach underpinning Eastern healing systems such as the relationship between the *guru* (teacher) and disciple (pupil). De Berry (1991), a clinical psychologist and philosopher, has urged the adoption of constructivism which totally revises the notion of a psychotherapeutic 'cure', a concept that still underpins the biomedical and behavioural paradigms. The biobehavioural model speaks of diseases and maladaptive behaviours (or dysfunctional cognitions). An expert exists to fix, cure, change or in some fundamental way do something to and thus alter the client/patient. He stresses that in the constructivist model there are at least two people trying to understand how at least one of them constructs his (her) world. Thus this changes the role of psychotherapist from the medical position of one who cures to the more spiritual posture of one who guides or helps construct conditions for change. The fundamental point is that nothing exists independently. Everything is a matter of relation. De Berry (1991) stresses that this does not imply that behavioural or biological factors do not exist, only that they do not exist alone, that they are contextual, and as much a result as a cause.

Laungani (1997a) stresses that clients from the Indian subcontinent, for example, may expect their counsellor to be expert and may even be in awe of them. However, it is important not to confuse expertise with acting like an arrogant expert who knows it all. A counsellor or psychotherapist needs to speak authoritatively as it were, but this does not necessarily imply superior knowledge but that the therapy is a partnership where there is inevitably a power imbalance and the lead is taken by the therapist for the purpose of guiding the client. This is how I set about deconstructing the expert image in counselling and psychotherapy by communicating explicitly to my clients something along the lines of:

> I have expertise in psychotherapy, but you are the expert on yourself. Therefore, I would suggest that we view this relationship as a partnership in which you are encouraged to question, disagree and even challenge my interpretations. This would really help me help you. Unless you give me reason to believe otherwise (and I will tell you if this happens), I will accept your statements at face value. We are not seeking to establish the truth, I will attempt to offer you interpretations to reflect your concerns, much like holding up a mirror closer to you. However, I may not reflect your reality accurately and you can help me understand your concerns better by pointing out the distortions that may creep in and giving me feedback. How do you feel about this?

As I have pointed out elsewhere (Alladin, 1993b), my clients are delighted, if at first surprised, and report feeling that they can 'let their hair down and breathe more freely' since I am not going to analyse their every word and non-verbal behaviour and diagnose psychopathology in them. Besides, a partnership implies that we do not have to waste time playing games of one-upmanship.

A review of some models of counselling and psychotherapy

In this section, three models of counselling and psychotherapy are briefly reviewed. Laungani (1997a: 350) has criticized client centred counselling, asserting that it does not live up to its fundamental assumptions: 'Just because a therapy is seen as being attractive or is seen as being politically correct, or that it is in keeping with current social trends, does not in itself merit its usage unless one can establish its validity . . .'.

A culture centred model

Laungani argues that Western cultures in general and the English culture in particular can be distinguished from non-Western cultures in general and Indian culture in particular along four major factors. Western cultures emphasize Individualism, Cognitivism, Free Will and Materialism and Eastern cultures tend to emphasize Communalism, Emotionalism, Determinism and Spiritualism. He stresses that the concepts underlying each factor are not dichotomous but extend along a continuum so that the behaviour of groups of people may be described as more Individualism oriented and less Communalism oriented and over time may even move along the dimension from one end to the other. (For an extensive description of the theoretical basis for these dimensions see Laungani, 1992, 1993, 1994, 1995, 1996, 1997b). Laungani (1997a) states that hypotheses derived from the formulation have been subjected to rigorous empirical tests cross-culturally (Sachdev, 1992; Sookhoo, 1995).

Laungani (1997a) proposes that we move to a culture centred counselling, by outlining a framework more appropriate for ethnic minority clients which is detailed in his paper. Briefly, he argues that there is a lack of correspondence between the assumptions of counsellors and those of their client groups – even within their own culture. For ethnic minorities, particularly from the Indian subcontinent, there is a wide chasm. These clients do not understand or share the fundamental assumptions of their counsellors or, as I would put it, the counsellors do not understand or share their clients' fundamental beliefs.

Laungani (1997b) points out that unwittingly counsellors and indeed the majority of Westerners are misled by the perceived Westernization of their Indian clients. Should they meet with an Indian who speaks English fluently and colloquially, one who dresses in a Western manner, is involved in a professional occupation and for all appearances gives the impression of being a Westerner, they also assume the Indian to be a Westerner. The Indian is then imbued with a Western mind! He/she is then divested of most, if not all, of his/her cultural inheritance. However, Laungani cautions that beneath the easily acquired cosmetic Westernized persona is to be found a psyche whose roots can be traced back to one's own ancestral cultural upbringing, which exercises a profound influence on the individuals in terms of their evaluations of themselves, their identities and their own unique world views.

An integrative model

Jones (1985) proposed a model of psychological functioning in black Americans as a conceptual guide for use in psychotherapy. Four classes of variables are described:

1 reactions to racial oppression;
2 influence of the majority culture;
3 influence of traditional African-American culture;
4 individual and family experiences and endowments.

Jones stresses that in reality it is difficult to separate the influence of each of the classes of variables, since they overlap to a significant degree. He illustrates this point by using overlapping circles to show that each set of factors may be viewed as having both a separate influence on psychological functioning and an influence on the operation of the other factors. The specific content of each set of factors is derived from clinical assessment of the individual patient. Jones (1985) has been particularly interested in the development of clinical interventions that focus on the use of traditional African-American cultural experiences as a source of personal growth. He suggests that the general approach might well be useful for other ethnic minority clients as well.

The ethnomedical model

Alladin (1993c) proposed using the ethnomedical model of Ahmed and Fraser (1979) as a conceptual tool for transcultural counselling since it can be more universally applied without doing violence to other cultures, but this is a personally orientated paradigm which could facilitate therapeutic dialogue and increase transcultural sensitivity. Ahmed and Fraser (1979) locate individuals and their conception of sickness at the core of their ethnomedical model. They highlight the components that feed into an individual's conception of disease in any culture by a nine-dimensional model (labelled 1–9 below).

At the core is the individual's (1) sickness conception. Next, the most salient to the individual are the factors at the base of the cube: (2) body function beliefs, (3) wellbeing criteria, (4) causal/healing beliefs, (5) medical practice/efficacy beliefs. By using a three-dimensional cube surrounding the person they represent the different forces, concerns and components that affect the person's conception of 'being sick' and of health need. They use a bubble surrounding the individual to represent how the individual's cultural heritage permeates personal experience – the level that Laungani (1997a) stressed was often ignored by Westernized counsellors.

Counsellors need to consider the individual's beliefs about how effective and useful certain healing systems are, their personal beliefs about what causes healing and sickness, and beliefs about mind–body functioning. The final set of dimensions are (6) recognition of health need, (7) reliance on self-treatment and diagnosis, (8) cooperation with health advice, (9) acceptance of suggestions for health care.

The question is often asked whether it is possible to assimilate these multiethnic models of counselling and psychotherapy within the mainstream of Western models of counselling and psychotherapy. I do not think it would be advisable to 'assimilate' a more holistic transcultural model into Western intrapsychic models, even if this is possible. At worse they could run in parallel, at best the more holistic multiethnic models of counselling and psychotherapy should subsume the Western models of counselling and psychotherapy and not be assimilated. This is not a reverse of the cultural imperialism that currently prevails. The point is, a reductionist or atomistic model cannot subsume a more holistic model. That is why, for example, a culture centred counselling model or an ethnomedical model is not specifically for ethnic minorities but for all peoples everywhere.

In the case of Zohra, to be discussed below, the value of focusing on the dimensions of the ethnomedical model will become apparent.

The ethnomedical model has its roots in ethnomedicine and should not be confused with a medical model. The term 'ethnomedicine' suggests a personal paradigm within a cultural context but that biomedical factors are not ignored in considering wellbeing. Contrary to popular misconception, as Leslie (1976) has stressed, by commonly recognized criteria Chinese, Ayurvedic and Arabic medicine are scientific in substantial degrees. They involve the rational use of naturalistic theories to organize and interpret systematic empirical observations. These systems have explicit, orderly ways of recording and teaching this knowledge and they have some efficacious methods for promoting health and for curing illness.

Alladin and Ullah (1990) tested the validity of the ethnomedical model by devising an Ethnomedical Model Questionnaire and getting British subjects to rank the nine dimensions for personal importance. Sickness conception emerged as the most salient dimension, followed by wellbeing criteria and recognition of health need as the top three personally important dimensions. Not surprisingly, biological, psychological and environmental factors were given different weightings in causal links with disease and wellbeing.

Some suggestions are offered below for using the ethnomedical model as a conceptual tool in counselling and psychotherapy.

A Framework for Using the Ethnomedical Model in Counselling and Psychotherapy

Sickness conception

It is possible to feel sick without having biomedical pathology and have biomedical pathology without feeling sick. A religious client may believe that evil and sin are causes of sickness.

- Does the client adopt biomedical norms to conceptualize sickness?
- Has the client transgressed religious beliefs and sinned?
- Is the sickness punishment for transgression?
- Is the client or the family medicalizing interpersonal problems?

Causal/healing beliefs

Behaviours that are strange, unfamiliar and different from the prevailing norms should not be automatically assumed to signify psychological disturbance or medical pathology. Beliefs in the evil eye, ghosts, spirits and witchcraft are not uncommon and may even coexist with contemporary Western notions of disease.

- Are you clear what the implicit model of healing underpinning your approach to counselling and psychotherapy is and have you explained it to your client?
- Is your approach compatible to your client's beliefs?
- Have you familiarized yourself with your client's beliefs?
- Guard against the tendency to assume that all people from a particular culture necessarily share the same cultural beliefs.
- Middle class ethnic minority professions may be so Westernized or ashamed of their background that they may deny certain cultural beliefs which have currency only among the working class people of their culture or prematurely dismiss them as mere superstitions.

Wellbeing criteria

The tendency to regard health as the absence of sickness is an unfortunate medicalized viewpoint which separates the 'healthy' from the 'sick' by using statistical or biomedical norms. For more and more people, and especially ethnic minorities, a healthy person is someone in harmony with themselves and with nature. This implies the person functions adaptively and fulfils their social roles within their community.

- Does the client make a distinction between health, sickness and wellbeing and on what basis?
- If the client subscribes to folk beliefs, can you help the client to understand their problems within that context?
- Is the client so 'Westernized' they expect medication to solve interpersonal dysfunction or therapy to work miracles?
- Is the client so in awe of all things Western or ashamed of their own culture that there may be a significant problem with racism and racial identity? This would need to be addressed competently, otherwise there is a danger of collusion and perpetuation of the status quo.

Body function beliefs

According to Kleinman (1979), when the beliefs of individuals do not conflict with those of their practitioners, health care is optimized.

- A cultural perspective provides a more meaningful framework for diseases by using a social and not a biomedical or psychiatric yardstick.
- A biomedical or psychiatric yardstick still has a legitimate place but should not dominate the picture or impose an intrapsychic model on the client.
- What, if any, are the client's social and occupation impairments in daily living?

Health practice efficacy beliefs
Ethnic minority clients in particular may find it hard to believe that talking through their concerns is sufficient to produce therapeutic change. They expect practical suggestions which they can implement to resolve their concerns, that is why they have come to see a professional.

- Check out the client's expectations of therapy.
- Check out the client's expectations of you as their counsellor or psychotherapist.
- Can you help reconcile any mismatch between the above expectations?

In the case study presented below the value of focusing on the dimensions of the ethnomedical model will become apparent.

Case study: Zohra

Synopsis

Zohra is a 23-year-old Pakistani referred by her GP to a psychiatrist at the local community mental health centre as an outpatient. This case study (reproduced here with acknowledgement to the authors, [the late] Jafar Kareem and Roland Littlewood, with permission of Blackwell Scientific Publishers) contains only selective extracts taken from Kareem and Littlewood (1992).

For our present purpose, assume that Zohra is a new immigrant from Pakistan of a working class family. She lives with her husband, Khalid who is a second generation immigrant. However, Khalid manages his own factory and considers himself a middle class British Pakistani. His parents are from a working class background but came from Pakistan to the UK in 1960. The commentaries that follow are mine and they are only suggestive and by no means intended to be comprehensive or definitive.

Psychiatrist's notes

> Food given to her had been thrown out of the window. She has been observed coming down at night and making some food for herself. Patient again withdrawn and flat. When pressed she eventually said (through her husband) that her food was being poisoned and that was why she was ill. Husband thought that this was rubbish. He explained that 'she believes a lot in all that kind of superstitious stuff like "magic"'. He pointed to a leather amulet she was wearing round her neck – which she had got sent from Pakistan – and which she claimed was keeping her alive. He thought it was 'a lot of mumbo jumbo' and what she needed was admission and some 'real medicine'. (1992: 185)

Under each section is a commentary consisting of some key issues organized under the dimensions of the ethnomedical model together with several possible hypotheses to consider. After listing them, I will select what I consider are the most salient hypotheses and focus on these to convey a flavour of the issues that need pursing in Zohra's therapy.

Commentary

CAUSAL/HEALING BELIEFS Zohra's belief that her food was being poisoned can be interpreted in several ways.

1 If she had been prescribed medication and refused to take it, could it be that she was suspicious that care staff had laced her food with medication? We have no evidence to support this view.
2 It is interesting that her husband does not question on what basis she came to the conclusion that her food was being poisoned. Assuming that the majority of care staff were not from her culture, was she understandably suspicious that they were doing something to her through the food?
3 Zohra's conviction that her food is being poisoned is dismissed by her husband as superstitious mumbo jumbo. In the absence of evidence, it would be premature to diagnose her problem as one of paranoia.
4 The therapist can moderate the husband's 'Westernized' superior attitude. On what grounds is he so dismissive of his wife's beliefs which are probably shared by a significant proportion of people from Pakistan? Could it be that he is really ashamed of his own cultural beliefs?
5 Does only Western medicine qualify as 'real' medicine? If so, what kind of medicine does he think she needs, and why?

Western science, eastern superstition? It is not difficult to discern that even within ethnic minorities there may be an attitude which regards science as being 'Western' and therefore things Eastern as superstition.

Only recently, after the development of a pain theory that could help explain acupuncture to a 'Western' mind was acupuncture accepted as a legitimate treatment. Previously, it seemed a lot of 'mumbo jumbo' to expect sticking needles in a person to alleviate pain. After all, logically, needles inflict pain.

Spiritual beliefs Are spiritual beliefs any less 'real' than scientific beliefs? This is a difficult question to answer in a brief space. Avoiding controversy, a pragmatic approach would (1) stress that Zohra needs to eat to get nourishment and strength; (2) ask if she would eat the food if she observed it being prepared for her and if others in the family also ate from her plate. Thus, if she was being 'bewitched' they would not eat from the same plate as her. Hopefully, this could also put her mind at rest. The point is, this non-judgemental approach does not violate her beliefs, be they personal or cultural. A cognitive behavioural therapist would recognize the above intervention as setting up a situation in which the client would feel safe to experiment and test out her beliefs.

Zohra's account

Hasn't the doctor come today? Why have you [social worker] come instead of him? I'm ill, can't you see? How do I feel? I'm still very weak, and I've got a bad headache. Those tablets they gave me at the hospital were quite good, they gave me some relief, but most of the pain has come back now, it hurts here – and here – and here. It's so bad I can hardly move. I was really looking forward to coming to England . . . My husband's father is my [maternal uncle] so I thought I would really be treated well. I was at first, but it didn't last long . . . But then it got worse and worse, they [in-laws] were plotting together. My mother got very concerned. After I lost my baby she sent me this *tawiz* [talisman]. She got it from a very holy *pir* [religious leader and healer] who lives in the mountains behind our village. I have to wear it round my neck all the time to keep evil things away. It worked quite well for a while, but then I think they [in-laws] must have found something stronger. I began to grow weaker and weaker, and look at me now. I'm only young, and I'm growing old very fast. What can I do? Of course, I try to be very careful, especially about my food. That's how they make me ill. That's why I threw out that food the other day. I could see they had put something in it. But even if I make my own food, I'm not sure it will make me any better, they will find other ways. Just living in this house makes me ill. You've got to help me. But what can I do? I can't go back to Pakistan. There would be too much shame. But I can't survive like this either. What can I do? (1992: 186–7)

Commentary

SICKNESS CONCEPTION

1 Zohra is afraid that, one way or another, her in-laws will get her. Does she really believe they are trying to kill her? This needs further exploration.

2   A therapist knowledgeable about cultural beliefs would recognize this as 'countermagic to overcome the protection of her talisman'. If not, the therapist must consult with other knowledgeable professionals from Zohra's culture: swimming in deep waters on your own is not recommended!

3   The therapist could also ask other Pakistani people in Zohra's situation what they would normally do if they held her beliefs. Obviously, since there are bound to be individual differences within any one culture, it would be prudent to sample a range of views.

4   Irrespective of the therapist's personal beliefs, Zohra is expressing fear, helplessness and hopelessness and the therapist should recognize this explicitly and respond to her explicit request for help. Is there any practical help the therapist can offer? Does she or her family wish to consult a traditional healer as well?

5   Zohra could be asked to *test* her *belief* that even if she made her own food and ate it, it will not make her any better. The therapist could suggest that an undernourished person is less likely to fight off whatever she is facing and encourage her to eat adequately.

6   The statement 'living in this house makes me ill' implicates *family dynamics*. Is there a wish on her part to move out of the family home? Could it be that she has become ill to compel her husband to move out of the parental home? The inconsistent attribution of illness, first to the poisoning of her food and then to the parental home (the nuclear family that she is with) can be explored.

7   It is not unusual for religious people to believe that *evil and sin are causes of sickness*. What did she mean by having to 'keep evil things away'? Is there anybody else in the family who shares her beliefs? What are the antecedents to her belief that evil things are after her?

8   Does she believe that she is being punished for having done something wrong? Does she feel guilty? If so, what about? Is she clinically depressed? Is this primary or secondary to her life circumstances?

(Husband) Khalid's account

It's since we got to England that Zohra's health began to change. Perhaps the climate didn't suit her. She often got sick, so she even lost the child when she got pregnant. I don't know why that happened, but now she has got all sorts of silly ideas into her head about the way people are poisoning her. It's rubbish of course, she should have left all that kind of stuff behind her in Pakistan. But that's why she threw the food out of the window, you know, she thought it was poisoned. Everyone got right upset about that, especially my mum. I don't know why it is, but mum has really turned against her. I know Zohra sometimes says bad things but she doesn't really mean it. It's only because she's sick. That's why she doesn't do her work either. She's not lazy, she's sick. We must find a doctor to cure her, though I'm quite sure about this *hakim* [doctor of Unani medicine] my dad's got in mind. Perhaps she should have some more X-rays and a blood test. It's weakness in her bones, you know. Can you get her taken into hospital for treatment?

Unhappy? Why should she be unhappy? She always wanted to come to England. Lonely? No it can't be that. She has got lots of company here at home . . . Where do I go? All sorts of places . . . Sometimes I go down the club to play snooker. Night club? Oh, have you been listening to all that rubbish from Zohra? She thinks all clubs are like places you see in the movies, so she's got this idea that we have dancing girls all over the pool tables every night! . . . When she gets the big freeze, she won't even talk to me. She has only to think about pool halls and she freezes up just like an iceberg. It's stupid really, when it is all in her imagination.

But I don't see what all this has got to do with it really. Zohra is ill and weak, that's what the trouble really is. If she was stronger all these family problems would go away. So why are you asking me all these questions? It's finding out what's wrong with her and getting her some medicine that really matters. (1992: 88)

Commentary

BODY FUNCTION BELIEFS AND HEALTH NEED

1 Khalid obviously does not subscribe to the explanatory model proposed by the therapist but offers his own: medicine to make her stronger since she is ill and weak. He suggests that she has a weakness in her bones. This could be a folk category. Or perhaps he suspects rheumatism? Arthritis? Is Zohra's inadequate nourishment sufficient to explain her weakness?

2 It appears that there are family problems and these are being medicalized. The husband's simplistic view that if Zohra became stronger the problems would vanish is wishful thinking and needs confronting. It is, of course, possible that he was merely exaggerating in that he could be suggesting that she would cope better with family stresses if she were stronger.

3 Khalid's dad appears to share Zohra's explanatory model for her current condition but Khalid is unsure and appears to pin his faith in Western medicine. The reason for this could be revealing. It is worth noting that whilst he rubbishes his wife's view, he is not so dismissive of his father's view.

SICKNESS CONCEPTION

1 Zohra and her mother in Pakistan firmly believe that she has been 'bewitched'. Her husband, on the other hand, dismisses this as superstitious rubbish. He himself is at a loss as to the reasons for her miscarriage. Thus, he could be unwittingly feeding their belief. Did she have a satisfactory medical investigation or explanation for her miscarriage?

2   Is she suffering from post-natal depression?
3   Khalid confesses that he is at a loss as to why his mother has actually turned against his wife. Perhaps there needs to be more open communication between Khalid and his mother.
4   An explanation of how the 'evidence' of his mother's open hostility feeds the self-fulfilling prophecy (they are out to get me) via a vicious circle may prove illuminating and be an honourable (face-saving) way of improving the family situation.

General commentary

Throughout this discussion, I have attempted to consider alternative explanations for Zohra's illness behaviours. My purpose is to show that we need to consider alternative plausible explanations before a more robust 'differential diagnosis' can be arrived at. Sometimes folk beliefs can legitimately be re-framed into 'equivalent' Western concepts, but as I have cautioned (Alladin, 1993a), this needs to be done with extreme care and sensitivity, and the therapist must have knowledge and understanding of the client's culture. But re-framing may not be possible when the equivalence of illness categories are questionable.

The charge can be levelled that the spiritual explanation that she has indeed been 'bewitched' has not been taken seriously enough. Should, for example, a traditional healer be also consulted as Zohra's father wishes and be invited to join in her treatment? It is not unknown for ethnic minority and mainstream clients to sometimes use both traditional medicine and complementary therapy concurrently, but often for fear of ridicule this is done on the quiet. Hopefully this case study has illustrated that a more comprehensive and less prejudicial assessment of Zohra's problem can be reached by therapists who may not be very knowledgeable of the client's culture but who nevertheless systematically check out alternative explanations with the help of the client and her family.

In my suggestions towards an empowering psychotherapy (Alladin, 1993c) I expressed concern that too many therapists seem to adopt an artificial unconditional positive regard and felt that if they are doing the 'right' things (a dash of empathy here, a bit of warmth there) then they can't be doing any harm.

Now, there is nothing wrong in techniques *per se* but the tendency to use techniques in a mechanical manner still pervades much of Western counselling and psychotherapy. As Ajaya (1989: 240) stresses:

To the extent that the therapist is genuinely self-accepting (and not adopting an artificial unconditional positive regard), he [she] will provide an environment in which the client can discover self-acceptance. Techniques often camouflage and create diversions to hide the therapists' lack of self-acceptance. The self-accepting therapist is more likely to respond with spontaneity and innovation in his [her] encounter with a client, forging a unique intervention that is suited to the moment rather than rummaging through an old bag of tricks.

Perhaps in counselling and psychotherapy of the culturally different client, there is greater opportunity for the therapist to learn and grow. Alladin (1993c) stressed the need to establish a dialogue and a genuine learning relationship. Again, Ajaya (1989) is illuminating in this regard, for he suggests that the therapeutic relationship is far from one-sided and the therapist who is open to what the client is experiencing may learn as much if not more from the client. The client may also challenge the therapist's limiting assumptions and a client may present a way of experiencing that calls attention to the therapist's insensitivity or lack of awareness and points out an area in which the therapist can yet grow in compassion, fortitude and humility. A systemic therapy will recognize that instead of treating Zohra's problem as an intrapsychic problem to do with the mental state of one individual, the hypotheses have raised issues which imply a systemic view of the nature of Zohra's problem.

Conclusions

There are conceptual clashes between some key concepts of Western counselling and psychotherapy and Eastern healing traditions which I have tried to highlight in this chapter. The question as to whether a transcultural model can be assimilated within mainstream Western models of counselling and psychotherapy, in my view, cannot be answered with a simple 'yes' or 'no' response. It should be considered on a case by case basis. An excellent attempt to provide an integration is the volume entitled *Healing East and West*, edited by Sheikh and Sheikh (1996). Nevertheless, it is recognized that in general holistic models cannot be integrated or assimilated into an intrapsychic model without doing violence to the integrity of the former approach. In this case, it may be possible, some may say desirable, that both models exist in parallel and be drawn upon as necessary, again on a case by case basis.
  Systemic models of counselling and psychotherapy are more compatible with Eastern approaches. However, there is a danger and a tendency to become too relativistic in an effort to subscribe to the view that 'everyone has won and all must have prizes'. I have argued that a more holistic approach is necessarily more adaptive than an atomistic reductionist intrapsychic approach and therefore preferable and even superior in a functional sense. It is also important to stress that ethnic minorities should not be stereotyped as being of a particular kind of person any more than Westerners are, though the tendency to emerge as a modal person is strong world-wide. However, I feel it is justified to draw broad distinctions in speaking of the Western mind or the Eastern mind, but again it must be remembered that few people are wholly one

or the other and if we consider a continuum then we are less likely to stereotype our clients. Then there are people who are in between, more of one and less of the other. At the end of the day, we are all concerned about the ultimate existential issue: Who are we? Why are we here? Where are we going? There is more than one way to live one's life and cope with the problems of living. Different ways of being need to be respected and not just paid lip service in therapy.

Key points

- Ignorance of conceptual differences between Eastern and Western models of counselling and psychotherapy can be damaging.
- The nine-dimensional ethnomedical model can be used as a framework for counselling and psychotherapy.
- Eastern concepts in counselling and psychotherapy may not be compatible for integration and may need to exist in parallel – the glass is half full and half empty.
- A reductionist or atomistic model cannot subsume a more holistic model.
- Western healing systems are linear and emphasize differences. In Eastern healing, sameness coexists with differences within and between all people who should be treated in the totality of bodymindspirit.
- Issues of racism, racial identity and cultural imperialism need addressing.
- Western counselling and psychotherapy, including cognitive behavioural therapy, still peddle cultural imperialism.
- The contemporary Western tendency to see death as the end to our existence is questionable in modern physics and in Eastern terms even delusional.
- It is a mistake for behaviours to be abstracted from their context and judged as 'good' or 'bad', independent of the culture of the client.
- The Western ideal of individualism undermines interdependence, creates and perpetuates alienation and damages the ecology.
- Client centred counselling recognizes that at the heart of the therapeutic enterprise is the relationship between counsellor and client but unwittingly perpetuates a medical model.
- The expert image in counselling and psychotherapy needs deconstructing.
- The constructivist approach underpinning Eastern healing systems such as the relationship between the *guru* (teacher) and disciple (pupil) changes the role of psychotherapists to the more spiritual posture of one who guides or helps construct conditions for change.
- Laungani's culture centred model, Jones's integrative model and Alladin's adaptation of the ethnomedical model can all facilitate therapeutic dialogue and increase transcultural sensitivity.

- A culture centred counselling model or an ethnomedical model is not specifically for ethnic minorities but for all peoples everywhere.

DISCUSSION ISSUES

Can a transcultural model of counselling be successfully assimilated within Western models?

Western counselling and psychotherapy still peddles cultural imperialism. Discuss.

What are the problems with the Western concept of the autonomous self when applied cross-culturally?

What is your understanding of the ethnomedical model?

References

Ahmed, P.I. and Fraser, R.W. (1979) 'International health planning: psychosocial issues and implications for development assistance', in P.I. Ahmed and G.V. Coelho (eds), *Towards a New Definition of Health: Psychosocial Dimensions*. New York: Plenum.

Ajaya, S. (1989) *Psychotherapy East & West: a Unifying Paradigm*. Pennsylvania: Himalayan Publishers.

Alladin, W.J. (1986) 'Ethnic minorities and clinical psychology: an inside view', *Clinical Psychology Forum*, 5: 28–32.

Alladin, W.J. (1987) 'Ethnic minorities and clinical psychology: beyond a culturalist approach', *Clinical Psychology Forum*, 10: 42–3.

Alladin, W.J. (1988) 'Cognitive-behavioural group therapy', in M. Aveline and W. Dryden (eds), *Group Therapy in Britain*. Milton Keynes: Open University Press.

Alladin, W.J. (1989) 'Counselling women and ethnic minorities: problems and prospects', in Special Issue: Counselling Women and Ethnic Minorities. *Counselling Psychology Quarterly*, 2 (2): 101–4.

Alladin, W.J. (1992) 'Clinical psychology provision: models, policies and prospects', in W.I.U. Ahmad (ed.), *Race and Politics in Health*, Bradford: University of Bradford Press.

Alladin, W.J. (1993a) 'Ethnic matching in counselling', in W. Dryden (ed.), *Questions and Answers on Counselling in Action*. London: Sage.

Alladin, W.J. (1993b) 'The ethnomedical model as a conceptual tool for counselling in health-care decision-making', *British Journal of Guidance and Counselling*, 21 (1): 8–19.

Alladin, W.J. (1993c) 'More reflections on Masson and psychotherapy', *Clinical Psychology Forum*, 43: 23–5.

Alladin, W.J. and Ullah, R. (1990) An Empirical Test of the Ethnomedical Model.

Poster prepared for the International Conference in Health Psychology, Edinburgh, 1990.

Arasteh, A.R. and Sheikh, A.A. (1996) 'Sufism: the way to Universal Self', in A.A. Sheikh and K.S. Sheikh (eds), *Healing East and West: Ancient Wisdom and Modern Psychology*. New York and Chichester: Wiley (previously published as *Eastern and Western Approaches in Healing*).

Bharati, A. (1985) 'The self in Hindu thought and action', in A.J. Marsella, G. DeVos and F.L.K. Hsu (eds), *Culture and Self: Asian and Western Perspectives*. New York and London: Tavistock Publications.

De Berry, S.T. (1991) *The Externalization of Consciousness and the Psychopathology of Everyday Life*. London: Greenwood Press.

DeVos, G., Marsella, A.J. and Hsu, F.L.K. (1985) 'Introduction: approaches to culture and self', in A.J. Marsella, G. DeVos and F.L.K. Hsu (eds), *Culture and Self: Asian and Western Perspectives*. New York and London: Tavistock Publications.

Dossey, L. (1996) 'The importance of modern physics for modern medicine', in A.A. Sheikh and K.S. Sheikh (eds), *Healing East and West: Ancient Wisdom and Modern Psychology*. New York & Chichester: Wiley (previously published as *Eastern and Western Approaches in Healing*).

Haschmi, M.Y. (1973) 'Spirituality: science and psychology in the Sufi way', in L.F.R. Williams (ed.), *Sufi Studies: East and West*. New York: Dutton.

Hsu, F.L.K. (1985) 'The self in cross-cultural perspective', in A.J. Marsella, G. DeVos and F.L.K. Hsu (eds), *Culture and Self: Asian and Western Perspectives*. New York and London: Tavistock Publications.

Jones, A.C. (1985) 'Psychological functioning in Black Americans: a conceptual guide for use in psychotherapy', *Psychotherapy*, 22 (2): 363–9. (In G.R. Dudley and M.L. Rawlins [guest eds], Special Issue: Psychotherapy with Ethnic Minorities.)

Kakar, S. (1982) *Shamans, Mystics and Doctors: a Psychological Inquiry into India and Its Healing Tradition*. London: Mandala Books.

Kareem, J. and Littlewood, R. (eds) (1992) *Intercultural Therapy: Themes, Interpretations and Practice*. Oxford: Blackwell Scientific Publications.

Kleinman, A. (1979) 'Sickness as cultural semantics: issues for an anthropological medicine and psychiatry', in P.I. Ahmed and G.V. Coelho (eds), *Toward a New Definition of Health: Psychosocial Dimensions*. New York: Plenum.

Laungani, P. (1992) *It Shouldn't Happen to a Patient: a Survivor's Guide to Fighting Life-Threatening Illness*. London: Whiting & Birch.

Laungani, P. (1993) 'Cultural differences in stress and its management', *Stress Medicine*, 9: 37–43.

Laungani, P. (1994) 'Cultural differences in stress: India and England', *Counselling Psychology Review*, 9: 25–37.

Laungani, P. (1995) 'Stress in eastern and western cultures', in J. Brebner, E. Greenglass, P. Laungani and A. O'Roark (eds) (series editors C.D. Spielberger and I.G. Sarason), *Stress and Emotion*, vol. 15. Washington, DC: Taylor & Francis. pp. 265–80.

Laungani, P. (1996) 'Death in a Hindu family', in C.M. Parkes, P. Laungani and W. Young (eds), *Death and Bereavement Across Cultures*. London: Routledge. pp. 52–72.

Laungani, P. (1997a) 'Mental illness in India and Britain: theory and practice', *Medicine and Law*, 16: 509–40.

Laungani, P. (1997b) 'Replacing client-centred counselling with culture-centred counselling', *Counselling Psychology Quarterly*, 10 (4): 343–52.

Leslie, C. (1976) *Asian Medical Systems*. Berkeley, CA: University of California Press.

Pachuta, D.M. (1996) 'Chinese medicine: the law of five elements', in A.A. Sheikh and K.S. Sheikh (eds), *Healing East & West: Ancient Wisdom and Modern Psychology*. New York and Chichester: Wiley (previously published as *Eastern and Western Approaches in Healing*).

Rose, N. (1991) *Governing the Soul: the Shaping of the Private Self*. London and New York: Routledge.

Sachdev, D. (1992) 'Effects of psychocultural factors on the socialisation of British born Indian children and indigenous British children living in England'. Unpublished doctoral dissertation, South Bank University, London.

Sheikh, A.A. and Sheikh, K.S. (eds) (1996) *Healing East and West: Ancient Wisdom and Modern Psychology*. New York and Chichester: Wiley (previously published as *Eastern and Western Approaches in Healing*).

Sookhoo, D. (1995) 'A comparative study of the health beliefs and health practices of British whites and Asian adults with and without myocardial infarction', Paper read at the 53rd Annual Convention of the International Council of Psychologists, Taipei, Taiwan.

Thomas, K. and Althen, G. (1989) 'Counseling foreign students', in P.B. Pedersen, J.G., Draguns, W.J. Lonner and J.E. Trimble (eds), *Counseling Across Cultures*, rev. edn. Honolulu: University of Hawaii Press.

Watts, A. (1975) *Tao, the Watercourse Way*. New York: Pantheon Books.

5

ASSESSING THE COUNSELLING NEEDS OF THE ETHNIC MINORITIES IN BRITAIN

Zack Eleftheriadou

This chapter outlines the specific counselling needs of those who come from different racial or cultural backgrounds. The focus of this chapter is how a counsellor can take into account the client's cultural context. This is a delicate task as it can result in generalizations that all Asians or all West Indians are the same and therefore have the same needs. Inevitably, there are shared group values and as a result different groups have different needs, but quite often they are responded to in a rather stereotypical way which does not take into account their individual preferences and cultural influences. Hence the task at hand is to consider the impact of their sociocultural context, including socialization patterns, religion and other possible social influences on their psychological development, without stereotyping on the one hand and ignoring the person's racial and cultural roots on the other.

An overview of the multicultural population of Britain

Currently, the predominant minority ethnic groups in the United Kingdom come from India, Pakistan, the West Indies, Africa, Cyprus and Turkey. These populations share commonalities in that they are often seen to be 'different', 'foreign' and they are even labelled as being 'alien'. Although they are perceived to be rather different from the majority population they have just as many differences between and within them as they do when compared with the majority population, namely in terms of languages and religions. The common issues presented by the different racial and cultural groups will be examined and the acculturation process. In order to examine specific issues which arise within the groups, the different groups will be divided into first generation immigrants, second generation immigrants, international students and guest workers, refugees, exiles and victims of torture, and people with biracial or bicultural identity from birth.

Visible and invisible minorities

It is important to understand how in Britain minority groups tend to be divided, and in fact at time divide themselves, into several groupings. The 'internal immigrants', for example, are those who originally come from Scotland, Wales and Ireland. 'White ethnics' include immigrants from North America and European countries. (Some European Jewish groups were also minority groups before they came to settle in Britain.) The grouping 'ethnic minorities' includes immigrants who come from previous Commonwealth countries, such as the West Indies and Cyprus, and the term is usually applied to those of 'colour'.

In British society the different ethnic groups tend to be divided purely on racial characteristics, despite the fact that race itself is no longer viewed to be a scientifically valid concept (Fernando, 1991). There is evidence to indicate that those who are from 'visible' minority backgrounds have a more difficult time settling in the new environment than religious and other white ethnic minorities as the latter tend to remain more 'invisible', for example those of Jewish origin, especially if they have taken on the culture's behaviours, language and mannerisms. When there are noticeable differences ethnic minorities often prefer to keep them secret in order not to intensify racism or to avoid being labelled as 'defective'. For example, Greeks and Greek Cypriots, Turks, Chinese, Bangladeshi, West Indians amongst others do not openly talk about the hereditary sickle cell anaemia or thalassaemia trait. As a result, it has been rather difficult to provide formal counselling support, although this is not to say that these ethnic groups would not use a counselling service.

The social reality for ethnic minorities

Many ethnic minority groups experience deprivation in terms of housing, education, employment and health care. Littlewood and Lipsedge (1989) and Fernando (1995) have demonstrated in great depth how ethnic minorities, especially those of black origin, are overrepresented in the psychiatric services due to racism, oppression and a genuine lack of understanding of their cultural and individual needs.

By examining a person's sociocultural context one allows the person to discover the meaningful elements from their social environment. This is something which emerges from the first counselling meeting. Some important questions that arise are: What sort of community structure did they have in the home country and what do they maintain in the new environment? What significant historical factors have shaped their beliefs and values? What is their cultural group experience in Britain? How do they define themselves, ethnically? For example, it is a common experience that if there is an upheaval in terms of sociopolitical events in their home country this will preoccupy them during counselling sessions, especially when there is a significant event such as a political election or the occurrence of a natural disaster.

Common psychological issues

Sense of self before moving and reasons for moving to another culture

People are now moving more extensively around the world and it is becoming more and more common as communications become easier. We are witnessing whole families moving, and it has become such a common event that it is important we do not underestimate its unique stresses and pressures. There are obvious differences when one chooses to move than when there is forced separation from one's home due to political, ideological reasons or natural disasters. Migrants have different reasons for moving to another country. It is important to bear in mind that some of these reasons do not unfold until they have moved to the new environment.

For example, some people feel that they have always been the 'odd one out' of their family, or have had to deal with so many internal problems which seem overwhelming that the person places importance on a change of environment in order to overcome these problems. Therefore the person has left in order to seek something better, to learn more or in order to escape from something which feels persecutory. They equate moving with a 'new start' and a hope that all will change. The new country is looked upon as full of potential and hope. Of course, both the wish to find something better and to escape something can be seen to have positive and negative qualities depending on how a person has made sense of them. Broadly speaking, there are those people who seek adventure and (sometimes) risk-taking, wanting to visit new places, and those who need many familiar people around them.

Primary stress and dislocation

There are numerous myths that have tried to explore the themes of people moving, such as the 'Tower of Babel' myth where there is desire to 'reach heaven' or the ideal, Jules Verne's writings, or the book *A Thousand and One Nights*, which is a voyage of curiosity, and discovery of things that are almost forbidden. The feelings of those who wish to move on are a mixture of sadness, anxiety and nostalgia, which is sometimes exaggerated, but also there are expectations and hopes to know more and to have new experiences. The confusion can sometimes be experienced as a punishment for wanting to know more, as those who leave can often experience guilt for wanting more than the 'mother culture' can offer.

'Cultural inheritance' (Winnicott, 1971) is necessary to ensure continuity of existence. Cultural inheritance is the 'potential space' between the individual and the environment. The person makes sense of this space according to the notion of 'me' and 'not-me', being within the group of origin and an outside group. Migrants need to develop 'potential space' between the lost mother country and the new one in a similar way to a child needing to play, creating a link between the self and the environment. For an immigrant it is also a process of gaining new self skills and exploration and developing a new internal and external relationship with the new culture. If this becomes difficult the person may end up experiencing distress and isolation./The separation from one's culture can be compared to the loss of the 'containing object' (Bion, 1970) or the space to feel one is safe and understood, which can make people feel that there will never be a sense of 'wholeness' again. There may be strivings to create a new family and ancestors in the new environment. *N*

The acculturation process

Acculturation refers to 'the changes that an individual experiences as a result of being in contact with other cultures and as a result of participating in the process of acculturation that his cultural or ethnic group is undergoing' (Berry et al., 1992: 271–2). It is the experience of cognitive (how others think or conceptualize), behavioural (how others behave and the reasons for particular gestures, rituals etc.) and emotional (how, when, to what degree and with whom is it appropriate to express emotionality) adjustment into a new culture. It requires the learning of new skills.

When a new culture is encountered there is often what has been termed 'culture shock'. This is the encounter of a completely different set of ideas, values and beliefs which is a challenge to the person's own. The deviation from cultural norms gives rise to prejudices and stereotypes of people from a different race, culture etc. Littlewood and Lipsedge (1989) are amongst some of the researchers who have discussed the problems encountered by those who migrate. The term 'culture shock' was used to describe the experience of confusion, rejection, a sense of loss, anxiety, surprise, amongst many complex feelings, when encountering a new culture. One has to reinterpret the familiar notion of acceptable behaviour and emotional expression and seek to understand new cues and experiences.

Many protect themselves in the new culture and continue behaving as if they are still living at home. There comes a time though when contact with people, places and practices which are different and often challenging can no longer be avoided. There is great individual and group variation in what value is placed on separating or integrating into the new culture.

The new culture may be rejected completely and perceived as inaccurate, or the newcomers may reject their own culture and view the new culture as the ideal place which will offer them good things. Alternatively, there may be a struggle to integrate different elements from both cultures and live biculturally, or another way of coping may be the complete rejection of both cultures. In the former two patterns, dissociative mechanisms are often utilized, such as idealizing the new culture and regarding what has been left behind as 'not-good-enough'. Through this process mourning is avoided, which is intensified if the migration has been a voluntary one. The process of splitting denies the losses and grief, the anxiety and the guilt which goes with migration. According to Grinberg and Grinberg (1989: 9):

> It becomes essential for the emigrant to maintain the dissociation: good on one side, bad on the other, irrespective of which country represents either characteristics, because if the dissociation breaks down, the inevitable result is confusion and anxiety, with all its feared consequences: one no longer knows who is a friend and who is an enemy, where one can succeed and where one must fail, how to distinguish between the useful and the harmful, how to discriminate between love and hate, life and death.

Paul Pedersen, one of the most prominent researchers and theoreticians in the cross-cultural field, has challenged the notion that immigrants go through a linear process in adjusting to a new culture. Through extensive research he reviews the different responses people have to the new culture. He demonstrates how the adjustment process is different for every individual and depends on different factors. For some people it may be experienced as very difficult at first, but it may enable them to 'adjust' in the long term. Contrary to the belief that culture shock is a negative experience, sometimes those who have had the experience of culture shock seem able to adjust more successfully in the long term. There are different models illustrating the adjustment process. For some people it may be experienced as a 'subtractive process'. This is because they may feel that they are subtracting or losing something of their background through the learning of new ideas, experiencing new ways of thinking and behaving. For others it may be seen as an 'additive process' where learning from other cultures is a positive process because the learning from the new culture either complements their own cultural upbringing (and they may even wish to replace some cultural patterns), or is perhaps included alongside some more traditional patterns they practise. It appears that when (cultural) groups come together under favourable circumstances the outcome is positive (Pedersen, 1996).

Adjustment also may mean having to go through a mourning process before one can begin to take on board the new people, places etc. Each person of course deals with the experience according to his or her personal psychological resources, that is, the resources the person has internalized from the way they were brought up in their family from childhood. Another significant factor is whether there has been support at the time from relations and friends. It is common to have a period of 'relapse' as many cross-cultural issues and conflicts are on-going.

External aspects which contribute to the adjustment process

HOME BELONGINGS   To feel like oneself one needs to hold on to the significant elements from the home culture (such as music, objects, myths, landscape). Decorating with objects from home demonstrates a link with the past, links with one's roots, history and past generations. It becomes extremely important for people to have furniture and belongings around them (Espin, 1992). Those that try to take everything with them try to fill up with the good and familiar things. It is common for people to feel 'better' and report feeling 'back to normal' when their belongings have arrived. For some cultural groups, like Greek Cypriots, roots are very important and ownership of a home and land which is then passed on to one's children is very important. As one refugee stated, 'I miss my country and my familiar earth' (see personal account of Parvanta, 1992).

RESPONSE OF THE NEW CULTURE   Adjustment is also dependent on how the new cultural group behaves, psychologically, physically and economically. The feelings of being an outsider are also reinforced by the majority culture which may experience the newcomers as 'foreign bodies', 'aliens' who are threatening, and it becomes safer to keep them at bay. It can alienate different cultural groups further. The immigrant may be viewed as 'sensitive' and 'needy', and indeed this is often the case, as they need more guidance. They will be treated differently if the host community has participated in the arrival of newcomers, for example, by 'invitation'. However, there is often a feeling of intrusion and it is common that paranoid anxieties of the group increase, with thoughts such as that all the newcomers will take over their jobs. There may be overt or covert hostility, for example, finding it difficult to understand their language whatever their fluency is like, making divides harder to cross by references to historical, political events that they may not be familiar with. Of course this will also depend on what the newcomers project on to the new environment. Even when there is formal help it may be difficult for the newcomer to accept it because they feel it is humiliating or that they are being infantilized (that is, treated as if they are not mature enough emotionally or cognitively) or dehumanized.

Racism

Many ethnic minority groups experience social deprivation in many spheres of their lives, including housing, education, employment and health care. Many counsellors state that they are not racist because it is associated as being an external or sociopolitical issue. However, when one begins to take the issues on board the political filters into the psychological. Racism is everyone's concern because it is linked with human deprivation, a hierarchical system, lack of human freedom and dignity. Racism creates feelings of envy, anger, jealousy, aggression, greed, deprivation, mistrust, fear and powerlessness and it is vital that it is worked with on an interpsychic and intrapsychic level. (For a more comprehensive discussion of racism, see Chapter 3.)

Links with the home country

Settling into the culture will depend on the links with those left behind, and in turn the feelings of those left behind towards the emigrant. The reactions about someone leaving may be supportive, critical and anxious or even envious. The person may be seen as a scapegoat taking all the bad away from them so they can carry on living, or there may be pleasure that someone has been able to leave or escape, unlike them. Those left behind react using defence mechanisms sometimes to the same degree as the person who is leaving. The reactions will be different when there has been a close relationship than when there has been an ambivalent relationship. Those left behind may experience hypochondriacal symptoms or real symptoms soon after a loved one's departure. The person leaving may contribute to their reactions by a need to exaggerate what they are leaving behind and what the new place represents. The person may oscillate between a feeling of loss and that of excitement and relief.

Permanent or temporary stay?

A theme that is very poignant for many ethnic minorities is the hoped for return 'back home'. It is common to hear people say that one day they will return 'home' but years later they have not returned and many never do. This is an issue for both second or third generation immigrants as well as for their parents. The children build up ties in the new environment, which include their parents. If the parents decide to return to the homeland many of the children go through tremendous feelings of loss, and even guilt that they are not 'good enough' to make the parents remain in the new 'homeland'. For the parents the return is equally difficult, as the homeland is now different and brings a new emotional upheaval.

Neither those who left nor those who stayed at home are the same: everyone has felt the impact of the separation, and beneath the surface, each reproaches the other for having abandoned him. Nearly everything must be rebuilt, like a house after a tempest: fallen trees cleared away, cracked roofs repaired, rubble swept away. And as for the structure itself surely a different house is needed, for the returning person inhabits a different reality. The one thing certain is they will feel a new kind of homesickness, a new kind of grief. (Grinberg and Grinberg, 1989: 188)

Identity development in relation to the sociocultural environment: an examination of different populations

First generation immigrants

Clients may be perceived as belonging to one national category and they may in fact adhere to another. For example, they may define themselves as 'black British' or 'Afro-British', whilst they may be labelled by society as 'black' or they may define themselves as 'Muslim' or 'Hindu' whilst they are labelled by others under the vast and rather anonymous umbrella 'Asian', which in fact consists of more than one hundred subgroups, languages and traditions.

Immigrants, refugees and exiles can sometimes view the new country as the cause of their problems rather than the country they fled from. However, it is easier for them to see it in this light rather than to have angry feelings for their own country. This process is similar with those who have been adopted; somehow they have to make the new parents suffer because, paradoxically, they now feel safer than they felt in the fleeing process. There may be a feeling that they are imprisoned because they have had to leave and they cannot go back.

Many immigrants speak of the importance of bringing up children according to their own culture in a way that surprises them. One South American woman in her mid-twenties said to me that she did not realize how important her roots were to her until she had children. Having children means different things for different people, but it is often a way of continuing the family and the culture. For those who chose to emigrate because of financial factors, there is a wish for the children not to have to suffer as the parents did. This can put a great deal of pressure on the children to do well at school and to excel in their future jobs. For Cypriot children there is often the pressure of attending an English school during the week and Greek school on Saturdays, which is where the active cultural transmission takes place. Children learn to speak Greek, they learn about the culture and customs, including Greek dances and cooking.

It is a particularly significant experience for women who have been separated from their husbands for the first time or who have to go out to work. It may mean that they are the breadwinners for the first time. The home sphere is the only area of control for some women, who have never worked outside the home. The men were the mediators between the outside world and the home. All of a sudden these women find themselves having to communicate and interact with others in a completely different sphere. 'Identification within any culture is essentially independent of identification with any culture. In other words, identifying with one culture in no way diminishes the ability of an individual to identify with any other culture' (Casas and Pytluk, 1995: 173). An individual who is brought up within two cultural systems may exercise a choice in what they practise. In the same way, it is common that individuals who are seen as 'acculturated' are not given the opportunity to talk about their own cultural heritage and experiences.

Second and third generation immigrants

Second or third generation immigrants have their own unique issues, namely that it is not clear when they stop being called 'minorities' or being seen as different. In many contexts they are no longer migrant as it is assumed they are growing up in one environment and not moving into other cultures. But I would argue that they are also 'immigrants' in some way because they have to negotiate different types of cultures on a different scale, every day. The home can represent one reality and the majority culture another reality which holds distinct values. There may be conflict in terms of religious ideology between the two, different behaviours are permitted/discouraged and exhibited or remain hidden, different ways of thinking and language are used, among many other differences. Often second generation immigrants can become the mediators between the new culture and their mother culture, literally by being the ones who communicate and arrange matters outside the home and even psychologically by almost buffering the other members of the family, usually older members, from the new practices.

The younger members of the ethnic minority communities, in particular, can start behaving like chameleons. This is in order to cope with the contradictions found when they try to incorporate more than one set of cultural beliefs. They may be more flexible and find creative ways to adjust more easily than the older immigrants, but there is a danger that this may be at a cost. Thomas (1995) talks about the 'proxy self' that may develop, where the chameleon state is taken to such an extreme that the child strongly wants to believe they belong to another culture or race and resents their own. Although people (irrespective of their age) may wish to be associated with only one cultural or racial group and become rather resentful about being seen as 'foreign', this may change later. Parents may also feel they are the only ones who are trying hard to maintain the cultural values. It may result in attempts to encourage the children to mix more with the same cultural group peers, and in not only regulating but in some cases prohibiting meetings with majority culture peers outside school hours. For example, Greek children who are sent to Greek school on Saturdays may view it as time away from friends and play since it is an extracurricular activity. As a consequence they may resist attending or become unruly and disruptive at the school (Constantinides, 1991). Children may find it easier if they have been brought up with 'acculturated' parents who convey one model of functioning and the divide between school and home life is less marked.

However, even if there has not been any discussion of their roots it is common that around adolescence children seek to know more about their cultural and racial ancestry. Even if their heritage has not been made explicit much has been transmitted. A good example of how racial and cultural material is transmitted through the generations is children and grandchildren of parents who were Jewish holocaust survivors. The guilt of survivors is something that still remains a rather secretive issue, and yet it can preoccupy the younger generations even though they may have witnessed very little to none of the horrors that their parents or grandparents witnessed. One of my clients, John, told me right from the beginning of the counselling relationship that the events of the holocaust were something that he had grown up with. He could not remember when he had first heard about it; it was something that he had always had with him. He said that his father reminded the children of the holocaust, and it felt almost like they had a memorial in the house and you could never get too carried away with laughter as you would be reminded of what the living family generations symbolized.

CASE EXAMPLE: GITA   Another example of the influence of culture on the identity of second generation children can be seen in this case of an Indian woman who came for counselling for what appeared to be reasons unrelated to her culture.

Gita came to see me for problems in her relationship. She was second generation Indian and was involved with an Indian man. In the beginning she appeared very 'Westernized'. During the initial counselling sessions she spoke in a highly academic manner and did not refer to her feelings or make any reference to her ethnic background, despite my attempt to find out more about her upbringing influences. About a month into the counselling, her father fell ill and shortly after was diagnosed as suffering from leukaemia. Gita was devastated by this news and feared the worst. He was hospitalized soon after his diagnosis and Gita spent most evenings by his bedside at the hospital. Those few weeks after her father's diagnosis seemed to trigger off a great deal of cultural material in our sessions that she had not referred to before. For example, she had never visited India as her parents had always wished for her to become 'fully integrated in British society'. Even her partner had urged them to make a joint visit, but she had always underestimated its importance.

After her father died, she carried on coming to see me for a few months where she mourned her father. What she had not anticipated is that she was also mourning for the cultural heritage she had not really allowed herself to experience as it was easier to cope with one set of values. Her partner had been the link with the new culture and her father was the link with the Indian culture, religion and language. She saw her mother as the emotional support and her father as helping her to become socially and politically aware. She felt quite 'special' as the only one who engaged in these sociopolitical discussions unlike her siblings. However, this was almost something private between her and her father and when he became ill she felt very alone.

She wrote to me after we had ended counselling to tell me how she had decided it was time to visit India, to see her parents' birthplace and meet some of her relations. She planned to stay there for a few months. On her return she was in touch with me (as we had planned) and came back to see me for a few final sessions. The change in her was striking. She had grown her hair in the time that we had not met and wore a sari. I was struck at how relaxed she seemed in it. She talked of how India had opened up a whole new way of life for her and she was able to make links with her parental culture. When I commented on how different she seemed and that the visit to India seemed to have had a profound effect on her, she cried. Her tears were of enormous relief, being in touch with the potential loss had she not reconnected with the richness of her parental culture. She realized how much had not been considered in the past, and yet her childhood cultural influences had had a significant impact on her identity. There was a recognition that there was still a long path ahead. She felt she could proceed to take on board her different cultural worlds with the (new found) support of peers of the same 'mixture' of cultures as herself. Through the therapeutic process she felt she gained the resources to deal with her conflicts. Moreover, she had the insight that the new cultural richness might bring other conflicts in the future, but for now, everything felt more manageable.

International students and guest workers

For those who choose to move because of economic factors or educational factors, the experience may be quite different in that they often see the new culture as their host culture for a few years, with specific goals to fulfil. They wish to gain the culture's good aspects and not have any involvement in other areas. Students often come to the countries which originally colonized their countries of origin with the view of gaining a 'good education'. Similarly, for those who seek work abroad it may be seen as a temporary sacrifice to gain experience or improve their financial situation before returning to the home country. The impact may be greater for their partners, the many women who come abroad and lose their own jobs and status, and it may take a long time before they are able to find employment, if this is possible, in the new country. Those that travel because of their jobs face quite different issues because, although much may be lost, there may be gain in their new career opportunities.

Refugees

There are over 15 million refugees in the world today (US Committee for Refugees, 1990) and there is currently an emotive debate on who is 'eligible' to be in which host country. In recent years Britain has seen an influx of refugees from around the world. For example, many Greek Cypriots came to Britain after the Turkish invasion of Cyprus in 1974, and more recently refugees have come from the former Yugoslavia, Bangladesh and Somalia.

The abrupt nature of events often means that the person does not experience the shock until a later stage. Generally, there is a latency period between the traumatic event(s) and the after effects (Grinberg and Grinberg, 1989). How and when the trauma manifests depends on the personality structures and other important factors such as the duration and severity of the trauma. The impact can be almost like post-traumatic stress disorder (PTSD) where flashbacks or dreams return much later (Espin, 1992). For many the primary reason for evacuation from their homes was physical safety, therefore one has to think quickly and economically. Often there has not been time to say a proper goodbye to the mother country, and there may be a strong attachment to it for a long time. One has to grieve for the impossible return, the loss of identity.

Attachment to the new country can be experienced as temporary since the attachment with the home country is still very strong. Those who escaped war situations may feel too guilty, what has become known as the 'survivor syndrome', to gain from the new environment that has no violence. Sometimes refugees or exiles may be treated as heroes, which may make it hard for them to cope with the loss because 'they should be grateful' or seen as strong. But this is not the view they have of themselves. Often people feel relieved that they are in a safe land and are free. However, the cost of being free may result in feelings of guilt that they survived whilst others were left behind. There is anxiety about what has happened to them, whether they have survived and the fear of what it would have been like to have remained in the homeland under occupation.

Most refugees have experienced a feeling of having to escape abruptly from situations where their personal safety was threatened, usually by a group of others. It is widely known that female refugees around the world experience a great deal of persecution, such as rape, abduction, physical punishment, as well as mental torture during war situations. For some, flight becomes a necessary risk to take in order to obtain freedom and safety. In such an abrupt ending, people are deprived of the right to go through the ritual of saying goodbyes. There is no time to plan and to know when you will leave, how safe you will be and whether there will be a return. There is a feeling of permanent loss, anger, resentment, bitterness and frustration and a feeling that life will never really be the same again, which is very different from the immigrant who will return to the same people and places. The refugee has to deal with many concerns about those who may be left behind, and the fear that 'we shall never meet again'. Furthermore, the wish to be buried at home becomes impossible, which may further intensify feelings around death and loss. Overall, refugees feel they have no choice, control over or mastery of their situation.

Exiles and victims of torture

This group present their own unique issues. It is important they should be seen for therapy as soon as possible when they enter the country, although due to their experiences they usually find it difficult to trust others. Like refugees, they may experience post-traumatic stress symptoms such as intrusive thoughts and flashbacks, depression, physical symptoms such as sexual problems, anxiety, problems with memory and concentration, chronic hyperventilation syndrome, much later after the event has occurred. They have often experienced psychological and physical abuse and humiliation, and have often been teased by their captors regarding their release. People may try to adapt through internal numbing; for example, repression, pushing any powerful thoughts aside or externally avoiding certain places. For these people, like refugees, loss began in their own country and continued in the new one with additional losses. Their nightmares usually reveal frightening hidden secrets which may be shocking to the person to verbalize or relive. They have a strong sense of hopelessness and helplessness, sense of paralysis and impotence. The counsellor must be very careful not to create secondary victimization, that is, to inflict further aggression.

In hearing the stories it is important to restore a sense of dignity to the person and self-respect; to help them turn the perverse experience of torture into a healing relationship. The counsellor can encourage the person to reclaim a sense of space, self, body and mind, as often they feel they have been intruded upon by the persecutor and fear they will never be rid of them. At the same time there may be ambiguous feelings towards the torturer which have to be explored. It is important to keep within the individual's level of tolerance. Sometimes, the person may need psychological debriefing which might take a few hours rather than the conventional session time. Eventually the person may be helped to take their case to the authorities if they wish to do so.

People with biracial or bicultural identity from birth

Demographic trends indicate that numbers of mixed race children are increasing as more people intermarry. According to Smolowe (1993), in the US the birth rate of babies who are of multiracial parentage is 26 times higher compared to any other group. This increase suggests it is time that the issues were examined more closely.

People of mixed parentage have to integrate two or more racial and cultural backgrounds from birth. This means that their gender and ethnic identification process is rather more complicated than children who are brought up in monoracial or monocultural families. Mixed race children often experience the same degree of discrimination as ethnic minority groups. They tend to experience different levels of discrimination depending on their racial composition. Nevertheless, often whatever colour of skin they have they are perceived to be black. There is a myth that they must identify with only one group (Kerwin and Ponterotto, 1995), which of course is to deny the heritage of one parent. There is very little research and literature on individuals of mixed racial or cultural parentage and the implications of their identity formation. The available research has tended to view them as 'marginal', as they are neither 'black' nor 'white', and to suggest that mixed parentage has negative implications on their identity. However, recent work by Tizard and Phoenix (1989) has introduced a different picture. In one study they saw 58 young people aged 15–16 years who all had one parent who was white and one who was either black African or African-Caribbean. Just under half of the group perceived themselves as 'black', the rest saw themselves as 'coloured', 'brown' or 'half and half'. Interestingly none of them described themselves as 'white', although they were aware of having a white part. About two-thirds of them were very positive about their mixed race, but they seemed to have had a more negative perception when younger. Another interesting point is that half of them had wanted to be white when they were much younger. They seemed to have experienced more problems than either white or black groups. Factors such as parental attitudes to their mixed race, relationships with their parents, social class background and schooling environment, and inevitably societal perceptions and racism, contributed to their identity development. Study of the psychology and social position of mixed race individuals has had an impact on understanding their needs and on a social policy level has helped to inform adoption, fostering and psychotherapy practice. Mixed race identity formation in the context of different racial/cultural contexts is demonstrated in the case study of Jackie (presented as an Appendix to the chapter), who was brought up with only one white parent, and in the example of Michael (below), who was brought up in different environments.

CASE EXAMPLE: MICHAEL One of my young clients, Michael, an adolescent of mixed race, was sent to therapy after many changes in his foster home placements. After about the fourth session we began to talk about his upbringing and how many different families he had had to get used to. I asked about the racial background of the families and he said they had all been black, but his current foster mother was white. He went on to say that there was no one who was mixed race like himself and I asked him what that felt like. At first he said it did not matter, but later told me that they always saw him as black. I then wondered how he saw himself. He said, 'I am mixed race of course!' He then asked me whether I was mixed race? Before I even had a chance to gather my thoughts, he said 'But of course you are mixed race *and* Greek'. We discussed what this meant and it is interesting how in one way he viewed us as having similar experiences, but I was also different. Michael had a West Indian father and a white English mother and he never really saw how the two of them were together. He would often enquire whether I got on with my black colleagues and one day he broached the subject of race with a curiosity about the 'black man he had seen in the waiting room at Nafsiyat [Therapy Centre]'.

When should a referral be made to a counsellor/centre of the same ethnic background?

There may be times when it is appropriate that clients are referred to centres where they can work with someone who shares their racial or cultural background or their language or people who have had specific life experiences and training in the cross-cultural field. It is important that this decision is made carefully with much discussion with the client so as not to make the presenting problem in counselling into a race or cultural issue, or to suggest that the client's distress can only be handled by someone from their own cultural or racial background, as this may not be the case.

Conclusion

This chapter focuses on the needs of specific minority groups in Britain. It is not intended to create or reinforce stereotypes about particular groups, but rather to educate the counsellor on the reality and difference of the client's external world. The aim is to highlight the common as well as quite specific issues presented by different types of immigrants; for example, those who are first generation immigrants who had a choice in leaving their culture will have different psychological needs from those who left abruptly due to involuntary circumstances like a natural disaster or who escaped a war situation.

Both through theory and clinical vignettes this chapter has illustrated that people react differently to cultural moves. The different patterns are paths that individuals choose, but the views of any one individual may alternate at different times, taking a different amount of time to 'adjust'. In fact, most people change their views according to the environment they are in. This is a way of dealing with conflicting values/ideas and traditions that had never been questioned before. Hence, the process of acculturation can occur on different levels for different areas (for example, one can be acculturated in terms of friendships, but not in terms of ethnic choice of partner) and it is by no means directional, with a common outcome. Whatever form it takes, people need time when they are going through the adjustment process, sometimes a rather prolonged period.

In counselling it is important to explore to what extent the person feels able to reconstruct or recreate part of their environment in the new country. Also, of course, how much the new country is facilitating this process.

In conclusion, it becomes essential that the counsellor becomes familiar with the sociopolitical reality of the clients they are going to be working with, in order to understand the impact on their psycho-racial/cultural identity. Through counselling the counsellor can facilitate the client's psychological exploration of their cultural or ancestral heritage and how it can be kept alive and integrated into the new experiences.

DISCUSSION ISSUES

In what ways is acculturation a cognitive, behavioural and emotional process?

The experience of culture shock is not a linear process. Discuss.

Why may refugees or exiles find the adjustment more difficult?

Mixed race/culture individuals have to deal with being part of two worlds from the beginning. Discuss.

References and further reading

Adamopoulou, A., Garyfallos, G., Bouras, N. and Kouloumas, G. (1990) 'Mental health and primary care in ethnic groups', *International Journal of Social Psychiatry*, 36: 244–51.

Atkinson, D.R., Morten, G. and Sue, D.W. (1989) 'A minority identity development model', in D.R. Atkinson, G. Morten and D.W. Sue (eds), *Counseling American Minorities*. Dubuque, IA: W.C. Brown. pp. 35–52.

Berry, J.W., Poortinga, Y.H., Segall, M.H. and Dasen, P.R. (1992) *Cross-cultural Psychology*. New York: Cambridge University Press.

Bion, W. (1970) *Attention and Interpretation*. London: Heinemann.

Casas, J.M. and Pytluk, S.D. (1995) 'Greek Cypriots in London: a preliminary investigation', in J.G. Ponterotto, J.M. Casas, L.A. Suzuki and C.M. Alexander (eds), *Handbook of Multicultural Counseling*. London: Sage.

Constantinides, P. (1991) 'The Greek Cypriots: factors in the maintenance of ethnic identity', in J.L. Watson (ed.), *Between Two Cultures: Migrants and Minorities in Britain*. Oxford: Basil Blackwell.

Eleftheriadou, Z. (1992) 'Multi-cultural counselling and psychotherapy: a philosophical framework', *Psychologos: an international Review of Psychology*, 3: 21–9.

Eleftheriadou, Z. (1993) 'Application of a philosophical framework to transcultural counselling', *Journal of the Society for Existential Analysis*, 4: 116–23.

Eleftheriadou, Z. (1994) *Transcultural Counselling*. London: Central Publishing House.

Eleftheriadou, Z. (1995) 'Psycho-social aspects of thalassaemia: a psychodynamic understanding', *Psychodynamic Counselling*, 2: 283–6.

Eleftheriadou, Z. (1996a) 'Skills for communicating with patients from different cultural backgrounds', in R. Bor and M. Lloyd (eds), *Communication Skills for Medicine*. Edinburgh: Churchill Livingstone.

Eleftheriadou, Z. (1996b) 'Notions of culture', in S. Sharples (ed.) *Changing Cultures: Developments in Cross-Cultural Theory and Practice*. London: UKCOSA.

Eleftheriadou, Z. (1997) 'The need to understand and accept cultural differences', in I. Horton and V. Varma (eds), *The Needs of Counsellors and Psychotherapists*. London: Sage.

Espin, O.M. (1992) 'The roots uprooted: the psychological impact of historical/political dislocation', in E. Cole, O.M. Espin and E.D. Rothblum (eds), *Refugee Women and Their Mental Health: Shattered Societies, Shattered Lives*. London: Harrington Park Press.

Fernando, S. (1991) *Mental Health, Race and Culture*. London: Macmillan/MIND.

Fernando, S. (ed.) (1995) *Mental Health in a Multi-Ethnic Society*. London: Routledge.

Furnham, A. and Bochner, S. (1986) *Culture Shock: Psychological Reactions to Unfamiliar Environments*. London: Methuen.

Garyfallos, G., Adamopoulou, A. and Bouras, N. (1991) 'Psychological problems in primary care: a comparison of Greeks to Greek Cypriots and English', *Neurological Psychiatry*, 12: 71–7.

Grinberg, L. and Grinberg, R. (1989) *Psychoanalytic Perspectives on Migration and Exile*. London: Yale.

Kerwin, C. and Ponterotto, J.G. (1995) 'Biracial identity development', in J.G. Ponterotto, J.M. Casas, L.A. Suzuki and C.M. Alexander (eds), *Handbook of Multicultural Counseling*. London: Sage.

Levine, R. and Campbell, D.T. (1972) *Ethnocentrism: Theories of Conflict, Ethnic Attitudes and Group Behaviour*. New York: Wiley.

Littlewood, R. and Lipsedge, M. (1989) *Aliens and Alienists*. London: Unwin Hyman.

Parvanta, S. (1992) 'The balancing act: plight of Afghan women refugees', in E. Cole, O.M. Espin and E.D. Rothblum (eds), *Refugee Women and Their Mental Health: Shattered Societies, Shattered Lives*. London: Harrington Park Press.

Pedersen, P. (ed.) (1987) *Handbook of Cross-Cultural Counselling and Therapy*. London: Praeger.

Pedersen, P. (1996) 'Recent trends in cross-cultural theories', in S. Sharples (ed.), *Changing Cultures: Developments in Cross-Cultural Theory and Practice*. UKCOSA.

Pedersen, P.B., Draguns, J.G., Lonner, W.J. and Trimble, J.E. (eds) (1989) *Counseling Across Cultures*, 3rd edn. Honolulu: University of Hawaii Press.

Shweder, R.A. (1991) *Thinking Through Cultures: Expeditions in Cultural Psychology*. London: Harvard.

Smolowe, J. (1993) 'Intermarried . . . with children', *Time*, 142 (21): 64–5.

Thomas, L. (1995) 'Psychotherapy in the context of race and culture: an intercultural therapeutic approach', in S. Fernando (ed.), *Mental Health in a Multi-Ethnic Society*. London: Routledge.

Tizard, B. and Phoenix, A. (1989) 'Black identity and transracial adoption', *New Community*, 15: 427–37.

US Committee for Refugees (1990) *World Refugee Survey: 1989 in Review*. Washington, DC: US Committee for Refugees.

Winnicott, D. (1971) *Playing and Reality*. London: Routledge.

Appendix to Chapter 5
A Case Study Demonstrating the Complexity of Identity Formation: Jackie

Jackie, a woman of mixed race in her early twenties, came to see me after a decision to leave home. She had grown up with her then teenage white mother and her mother's white boyfriend until she was about 6 years old and then she went to live with her aunt. It was thought that her aunt could take better care of her since she was older than Jackie's mother. Her aunt was also used to children since she had two of her own. Jackie had regular, but rather infrequent contact with her mother which began to upset her a great deal. Many of the feelings about her mother had been triggered by her own pregnancy and subsequent miscarriage. She had had ambivalent feelings about her own pregnancy: a part of her desperately wanted a child and another part felt that she was not ready. She was not in a position to support a child financially or psychologically. She felt far too insecure in her relationship to expect support from her partner. Initially, her partner made it clear that he did not want her to go ahead with the pregnancy, but at the end had left it up to her to decide. She had almost made the decision to have a termination of the pregnancy when she had a miscarriage. She felt guilty after the miscarriage, although she was also so aware that if she had had the baby she would have repeated a rather similar path to her mother.

In one session she talked with great distress of an event she had attended with her mother. She was devastated that many people did not know who she was, and when she explained people were surprised and she felt she had to go through explanations of the living arrangements. She desperately wanted to be part of a family and to be included in her mother's family. She always said how much she loved her aunt dearly and she was very grateful to her for all that she had done, but she wished her relationship with her own parents was closer. Everyone from her mother's family, especially her aunt, saw her as white and gave her 'white food' and spoke 'white language'. She was viewed as 'black' by other white people, however, and people showed the inevitable surprise about her being a different colour from her mother. She herself could not feel she was either one or the other. Recently, she would frequently get rather upset that she was not 'black enough' and that somehow she would be 'found out'. When we explored this further she was anxious that they might ask her questions about sociopolitical events and practices in the West Indies that she might not be able to answer accurately or with much detail.

Towards the end of her therapy Jackie felt that she had a clearer identity, although she acknowledged that since she was a combination of two racial heritages, however much she could integrate the two she would always be a 'mixture' to others, although she could appreciate the complexity of it herself. All the issues relating to her racial identity were linked to a time when she was thinking of leaving home and this brought into question where she belonged and how she wanted to live. Many other issues emerged about being brought up by a very young mother who could not really fulfil all her needs and facilitate her psychological and social-racial identity development. In fact, she had always picked up her mother's strong negative feelings about her father and found it difficult to separate the 'father' part she had inherited from her father from her mother's perception. She was also a similar age to when her parents had met and became involved. When she was younger she had wanted to be white, but as she grew older she felt less and less need to be different. Everything she knew about her identity she had found out on her own by having black and mixed race female friends. She was able to explore a different social sphere from that of her aunt's family because she could use her aunt as a safe psychological base to return to.

During the sessions she made contact with her father and told him much of what she had felt. They had not met for a few years following a big argument where Jackie had been furious with him. To her surprise, he became distressed by her telephone call and asked to meet with her soon after. When they met Jackie felt something had lifted from her. She did not get the explanations she would have wanted, but she was able to understand more about him and his relationship with her mother. She felt she had much to learn about her cultural heritage from her father's side and enquired about other family members whom she had never met. She knew that she would never relive all the years she had missed with her father, but that they could try to maintain more contact and get to know each other more now.

She found it useful to work with me because she did not see me as one or the other, black or white, although she did perceive me as being different from her. I experienced this as providing an appropriate distance where she could reflect and at the same time she could feel intimate with me, and that I would have an understanding of what it was to be 'mixed'.

Towards the end of the counselling she felt she was more integrated in terms of all the different components; the white part and her mother and the black part and her father. Jackie had experienced many losses in her life; she had grown up with little experience of mothering and even less of fathering and had very little information about her black heritage. Through counselling she was able to experience a certain level of, symbolically speaking, 'mothering' from me and at the same time a vital exploration into her fragmented racial and cultural identity.

6

CLIENT CENTRED OR CULTURE CENTRED COUNSELLING?

Pittu Laungani

To answer the question which forms the title of this chapter, we shall first examine the nature and process of client centred counselling. We shall then turn to culture centred counselling. In so doing we shall be able to distinguish between the two approaches. We will then, hopefully, be in a position to offer tentative answers to a question that is of serious concern to counsellors – and indeed to the client groups of different ethnic origins who live in the UK and in other Western countries. The question when phrased carefully is this: in offering counselling and/or therapeutic services to members of ethnic minorities (for example, persons of Indian ancestry), which of the two counselling approaches is likely to be more effective with such client groups?

The question assumes that one of the two approaches is likely to be more effective than the other. After a close examination it may transpire that *neither* of the approaches has a proven success rate; or that both approaches – each in its own idiosyncratic way – meet with a limited degree of success. Moreover, in the absence of carefully conducted studies which would provide clear, operational definitions as to what one means by 'effect', and the criteria used to measure effectiveness, it may prove difficult in any event to determine the superiority of one over the other. Although one may not be able to settle the argument satisfactorily and unequivocally – such arguments seldom are – the very process of discourse and disputation will help us to throw light on this extremely vital problem.

In a consumer-driven society where consumer is king or queen, it is necessary that the consumer is offered all the 'wares' of counselling that are readily available, so that the consumer is able to make informed choices (Laungani, 1995a). It does not make good therapeutic (and economic) sense to offer one particular 'brand' of counselling on no other grounds than that counsellors are familiar and well-versed with that particular brand of counselling – *regardless of whether it turns out to be appropriate or inappropriate for the particular client group!* To present a client with such a *fait accompli* raises very serious moral problems. For instance, are the counsellors justified in promoting a particular brand of therapy to the exclusion of others? Are the clients made aware of other options which are open to them? Do the counsellors have any firm evidence of the efficacy of their brand of counselling on client groups from ethnic minorities? To offer a particular brand of counselling because the counsellor is convinced that it works is a mistaken argument. All convictions form part of the structure of all our psychological belief systems. The firm convictions of counsellors concerning the efficacy (or otherwise) of their brand of counselling need to be seen as nothing more and nothing less than such patterns of belief systems. Beliefs and convictions, however strong and unshakeable, are independent of and unrelated to the efficacy (validity) or otherwise of a given form of counselling and/or therapy (Popper, 1972).

It is important therefore that counsellors adopt a more reflective approach, stand back and look inward so to speak, and consider the very serious moral implications of their approach to counselling both indigenous and multicultural client groups.

Origins of client centred counselling

Carl Rogers 'founded' client centred or person centred counselling (Rogers, 1961, 1970, 1972). A growing disenchantment with behaviourist psychology and with Freudian psychology, both of which the disaffected group of psychologists felt did not address the issues which were of vital concern to human beings in general, led to the founding of what has come to be referred to as a third 'force' in psychology. The problems which were of serious concern to Rogers, Maslow, Rollo May and several other existentialists and psychotherapists, at a general level, were not dissimilar to those that were first voiced by Socrates in the 4th century BC when he asked the question: What constitutes the good life? What are the ingredients which need to blend in order to enable individuals to realize their innate potential, which would assert the uniqueness of their being and make it possible for them to live in peace and harmony within themselves and with their fellow human beings? No satisfactory answer, it would appear, has ever been proposed to the above question.

Although Rogers did not ignore the Socratic question, his main concern was with contemporary deep-seated existential problems. In this he was not alone. The origins of existential philosophy can be traced to the writings of the Danish philosopher Kierkegaard, but the movement came into bloom following the Second World War with the writings of Sartre, Camus and several others, including Heidegger, Husserl, Tillich and May.

Rogers, by all accounts, was a good man. Reputedly, he was a kind man: warm, approachable and caring. He had a natural tendency to hold people in high positive regard and by his unique methods of acceptance and trust, he attempted to make all his clients feel the same way about themselves. Being with Rogers had a 'feel-good' factor for all those who came in contact with him. He believed that people were innately good, and given the appropriate conditions would display such goodness.

It is here that we are faced with an interesting dilemma. There is a tendency or an optimistic expectation in most people that good flows from good and evil from evil. Carrying these early Christian expectations a step further, one might venture to suggest that 'good' theories are also produced by 'good' persons. Such an expectation, regrettably, is naïve, unfounded and potentially dangerous. Even the kindest souls (Einstein, for example) may produce a theory whose applications may lead to terrible and devastating consequences for humanity, as was evidenced by the dropping of two atomic bombs at the end of the Second World War. In so far as Rogers is concerned, there is among his adherents a strong belief that his non-directive therapeutic approach, or his subsequent, person centred therapeutic model, helps his clients to reappraise their life situations and eventually make the kind of positive choices which lead to a fuller realization of their innate potential.

It should be emphasized here that the popularity of a theory or therapy should not be considered as a measure of its efficacy. A theory or therapy may be popular, it may even have a universal following, without being effective. Conversely, a theory or therapy may be unpopular, may be severely criticized and even ridiculed, and yet may turn out to be extremely effective. The popularity or unpopularity, the acceptance or rejection, the approbation or misapprobation of a theory, it needs to be stressed, is *independent of a theory's validity*.

A theory, as Lakatos (1970) states, may be valid even if no one believes in it and may be invalid even if the whole world believes in it – as was the case with the universal belief in Ptolemy's *geocentric model* of the universe. This mistaken belief lasted for almost fifteen hundred years, before it was replaced by the *Copernican heliocentric* model. Beliefs and disbeliefs, as has already been pointed out earlier, need to be understood within the context of cultural and social psychological factors. The methods by which beliefs are acquired fall within the realm of social psychological processes. They have little to do with the validity of a theory. Popper, in his classic book *Objective Knowledge* (1972), points out that even the testing of a theory is independent of the beliefs concerning a given theory.

Thus, whether counsellors generally believe in the efficacy of Rogerian counselling or not should not in any way influence us into accepting (or rejecting) its efficacy.

Nature of client centred counselling

Three stages of development which occurred in Rogers's thinking concern the nature and process of counselling. These stages, which reflect Rogers's own development, have been summarized by Ivey, Ivey and Simek-Morgan (1993) as follows:

1 *Stage I: Non-directive (1940–50)*
   Acceptance of the client, trust in the client's wisdom, and permissiveness, clarification of the client's world as the main technique.
2 *Stage II: Client centred (1950–61)*
   Reflecting the feeling of the client, resolving incongruities between the ideal and the real self, using reflection as the main technique.
3 *Stage III: Person centred (1961–87)*
   Increased personal involvement, stress on relational issues, in the here and now; more active, self-disclosing role for the counsellor.

To avoid any chance of confusion, it should be pointed out that our use of the term 'client centred counselling' reflects all three stages outlined above.

Mechanics of client centred counselling

Client centred counselling, which is also referred to as non-directive counselling and person centred counselling, involves a subtle, close and complex encounter of two minds: the mind of the client and the mind of the counsellor. For the encounter to be meaningful, in other words, for both the client and the counsellor to be able to pursue a meaningful and productive dialogue over time, it is necessary that both of them are aware or become aware of the rules which guide and foster their dialogues. In so far as the two actors in the encounter are fully cognizant of the rules, communication is likely to proceed smoothly. But for either party to misunderstand the rules, or to flaunt the rules, or to arbitrarily change the rules during the course of the encounters, is likely to lead to an impasse – which of course has serious repercussions on the outcomes of these encounters. The rules which guide these encounters are generally unwritten. They are seldom articulated, nor are they ever specified. They exist within the social, existential and cultural milieu of the client and the counsellor. They are part of the cultural legacy inherited by the two dramatis personae.

This needs some elaboration. For effective communication between the counsellor and the client it is essential that the following three conditions are met:

1   that the persons concerned share a common set of assumptions;
2   that the persons concerned share, to a large extent, a common cultural ideology;
3   that the counsellor and the client share, to a large extent, the theoretical assumptions underlying the process of client centred counselling.

Let us examine the three conditions briefly.

1 SHARING COMMON SETS OF ASSUMPTIONS   Each culture, or a subgroup within a given culture, comes to acquire over time a set of shared assumptions. It is not easy to define what shared assumptions are, nor is it particularly easy to articulate them with any degree of precision. However, it is reasonable to suggest that most of us have an intuitive understanding of what the concept subsumes.

Assumptions refer to commonly held beliefs, attitudes and values shared by people in a given culture. Each culture, over time, comes to acquire its own notions concerning right and wrong, good and bad, proper and improper, healthy and unhealthy, normal and abnormal. When pressed why we hold *such* beliefs dearly and not others, why *this* is important and *that* less so, we may be unable to offer plausible explanations. None the less, our beliefs and values whose origins are often lost in antiquity, pervade our cultural atmosphere. Like air, we imbibe them, often without a conscious awareness of their origins. What is not always fully appreciated is the extent to which one is a prisoner of one's culture, handcuffed to it, as it were, by past history.

The mechanics by which such beliefs are culturally transmitted and internalized are of course open to conjecture. However, it is the sharing or not sharing of such beliefs which, in a sense, brings cultures close to one another, or moves them apart. Clearly, some cultures are 'closer' to one another, and others 'apart'. Although geographical location may play a vital role in the closeness or otherwise of cultures, it need not, as is evidenced by the similarities between Britain and Australia, always be the case. And although cultures may be enjoined by a common course of history, they may yet remain apart, as is evidenced by the differences between Britain and India. If the underlying assumptions commonly shared by members of one culture are *not* shared by members of another culture, nor is any serious attempt made to understand them, effective communication is likely to be imperilled, and may, under some circumstances, break down altogether.

An example or two may clarify our meaning further. A woman living in India may accept a firmly established system of folk 'theories' as to what constitutes illness and its causes. The belief system which she takes for granted is the one which is culturally accepted in her country. To her, the dysentery in her child might seem to be the definite influence of the 'evil eye', and although it may be diagnosed as due to bacteria by an Indian doctor trained in Western medicine, her view would be unlikely to be subjected to ridicule. The two views – the natural and the supernatural – would reside side by side; pills, potions and amulets, mixing freely with antibiotics. Over time, the woman in question may come round to believing that her child's illness was caused by armies of unknown, unseen 'germs'. Thus the bacteriological view might ultimately come to prevail. But whether she does or does not come round to accepting the bacteriological view, her own views concerning the causes of her child's illness are the ones which find ready acceptance among her own people and within her own community.

In England, however, the same Asian woman would find herself out of step, and out of sympathy – with the added danger of finding her own sanity being questioned were she to persist in supernatural explanations of her child's illness.

Thus, the assumptions shared by two persons or a group of people may be **linguistic** (e.g. sharing a common language), **semantic** (e.g. an ability to interpret and understand the subtle nuances of the shared language), **non-linguistic** (e.g. an understanding of the non-verbal means of communication, which would include the expression of feelings, emotions and empathy conveyed through gestures, eye contact, facial expressions, bodily postures etc.), **ethical** (e.g. an appreciation of the normative moral rules which prescribe one's private and social behaviours), or **political** (e.g. an internalization of the values underlying an elected constitutional government, notions of 'natural justice' etc.).

Without shared assumptions, effective communication between two or more persons is likely to be seriously impeded. Such impediments can and do occur even between indigenous groups of people sharing a common language and, to a large extent, the fundamental values of their own culture. This can be evidenced in England where members of different social classes often experience serious difficulties in communicating with one another – and more poignantly, between medical doctors and their patients (Laungani, 1992).

Let me illustrate the above points with an example. The example, trivial in itself, none the less demonstrates how even the most ordinary and mundane encounters between two persons of the same culture, speaking the same language, may lead to misunderstandings.

About two years ago, when I was in India, I ran into one of my old teachers (now retired) who taught psychology at the University of Bombay. In keeping with the ancient Indian custom of displaying reverence, respect and deference to one's elders, particularly one's teachers, I bowed down before him, touched his feet, and he, in turn, blessed me and wished me a long and happy life. The next day, on an off-chance, he came to visit me around four in the afternoon. Since it was time for tea, I asked him if he would like some tea. He shook his head. I repeated my request. He shook his head for the second time, and said no. I went into the kitchen and requested cook to get me my tea. When tea arrived, there was on the tray next to a plate of biscuits, only one cup, which I poured for myself. As I started to drink my cup of tea, he turned to me, genuinely puzzled.

'Where's *my* tea?' he asked in a hurtful tone.

I was bewildered and mortified by his question.

'But, Sir, I thought you didn't want any tea. I asked you twice. The first time you shook your head, the second time, you shook your head and said no. I thought you didn't want any.'

'You're wrong,' he replied smiling at my discomfiture.

How did this very simple but yet very embarrassing misunderstanding occur?

First, in India there are seldom any clear distinctions between shaking or nodding one's head, as there are in the West, where nodding implies affirming, and shaking, negating. It is not uncommon in India for people to nod or shake or nod *and* shake their heads to mean yes or no. One has to glean the meaning from the context of the social encounter. It was obvious that having lived in the West for over 25 years I had forgotten this elementary lesson in non-verbal communication.

Secondly, although he had said no to tea, when I asked him the second time, I had once again forgotten that in India it is not uncommon for people to make an overt show of refusal of hospitality. The refusal is ritualized and is culturally sanctioned. One goes through the refusal process a few times, before one reluctantly, as it were, accepts the kind hospitality of one's host.

Thirdly, I had clearly committed a gross social blunder by taking him at his word, and not seeing through the verbal and non-verbal rituals. I ought to have repeated my offer of tea a few more times. Had I done so, he would eventually have said yes.

His final comment delivered in a velvet glove, was: 'Oh, you have become an Englishman!'

I doubt he has met more than a handful of Englishmen in his entire life, but that did not prevent him from using a convenient stereotype as an explanatory device for my social lapses. It was evident from what he said that I had forgotten, if not forsaken, my own cultural roots.

2 SHARING A COMMON CULTURAL IDEOLOGY It is not being suggested that meaningful intercultural communications are never possible unless the persons concerned share a common cultural ideology. Such an argument would involve the acceptance of an extreme relativistic position. Relativistic doctrines, despite their seeming attractions and their recent upsurge with certain academic circles, have very little merit

in them (Laungani, 1997). The value of relativism as a valid explanatory concept has come to be seriously questioned by several writers (Bloom, 1987; Doyal and Harris, 1986; Gellner, 1985; Laungani, 1997; Musgrove, 1982; Williams, 1985). The acceptance of an extreme relativistic position is to present an argument which ends all arguments – for there is nothing left to say. It leads to what Popper refers to as an epistemological *cul-de-sac* (Popper, 1972). Such a position does not permit any meaningful comparisons within and between groups of people on factors of significant importance. From a practical point of view, the acceptance of a relativistic position is likely to lead to arbitrary, pejorative and even dangerous divisions within any society.

It is asserted that meaningful intercultural communications are possible. However, such processes are not without their own unique hazards. The potential hazards of intercultural communication – in our case intercultural counselling and therapy – and the means by which they may be overcome will be examined later.

What distinguishes one culture from another is the fact that cultures vary with respect to their value systems, which have a significant bearing on the religious beliefs, kinship patterns, social arrangements, communication networks, including regulatory norms of personal, familial and social conduct (Laungani, 1995a; Parkes et al., 1996). Values are best defined as the currently held normative expectations that underlie individual and social conduct (Laungani, 1995a). Salient beliefs concerning right and wrong, good and bad, normal and abnormal, appropriate and inappropriate, proper and improper, and the like, are, to a large extent, influenced by the values operative in the culture. Because certain values are culture-specific, it follows that many assumptions and expectations underlying the appropriateness or otherwise of certain behaviours are also culture-specific. This factor evidently has extremely serious implications for counselling persons from different cultures. It is argued that Western cultures in general and English culture in particular can be distinguished from non-Western cultures in general and Indian culture in particular along four major factors, which are:

- **Individualism . . . Communalism (Collectivism)**
- **Cognitivism . . . Emotionalism**
- **Free Will . . . Determinism**
- **Materialism . . . Spiritualism**

Since the theoretical model, purporting to distinguish Western cultures from non-Western cultures, or more specifically, English culture from Indian culture, has been described at length elsewhere (Chapter 2), it need not be repeated here. Suffice it to say that several hypotheses deduced from the above formulation have been subjected to rigorous empirical tests in India and in England (Sachdev, 1992; Sookhoo, 1995), thus providing empirical validity to the above formulations. Although no attempt will be made to discuss the above model in detail, references will be made to those features which have a direct bearing on the problems related to the nature, the process and the outcome of the client centred counselling.

3 THEORETICAL ASSUMPTIONS IN CLIENT CENTRED COUNSELLING   All therapies – and client centred therapy is no exception – have their own theoretical assumptions. In some instances, the assumptions are clearly stipulated (for example, in Freudian psychotherapy, and in behaviour therapy) and in others they may not be clearly articulated and may need to be inferred from the nature of the relationship between the therapist and the client, the process of counselling and the types of interpretations offered by the counsellor or therapist. *No form of counselling is atheoretical.*

It should also be recognized that theories are not constructed in a social vacuum. All theories are social constructions (Popper, 1972; Ziman, 1978). They are rooted in social reality. As has been argued elsewhere:

> a theory also needs to take into account its historical antecedents, its prevalent social, religious, economic (and other) conditions, including the objective and subjective states of knowledge which exist in a given society at a specific point in time. All these factors collectively influence the manner in which theories are conceptualised, formulated, and tested. Failure to take account of these factors may impose severe constraints on rationalist theories and may even render them meaningless. (Laungani, 1997: 510–11)

The theoretical assumptions underlying Rogerian counselling are too well known to merit a detailed discussion. However, the major features which have a pertinent bearing on our subsequent discussion of culture centred counselling are shown in Table 6.1.

The theoretical assumptions which underlie client centred counselling are seldom or never presented to the client as one might present a menu, a price list or a catalogue. Although the counsellor may offer some initial insights into the nature of the counselling process, it is, however, the client who, over a series of encounters, is expected to infer the theoretical basis of the counselling process. Right from the beginning, the client is (unwittingly) involved in a guessing game in terms of what to expect from the counsellor and what is expected of him/her by the counsellor. This places the client at a disadvantage and the counsellor at a distinct advantage, first because the counsellor knows and the client doesn't know the unwritten rules of the encounter. Such a practice compromises the fundamental assumption of non-hierarchical relationships. Like most relationships in psychotherapies of one kind or another, this one too turns into an *asymmetrical* relationship

Table 6.1 *Major features underlying client centred counselling*

1 Secular
2 Holistic
3 Rooted in the neo-Kantian humanist tradition
4 Importance of non-hierarchical relationship between client and counsellor
5 Total acceptance of client's beliefs, attitudes and values
6 Cognitive factors important in the counselling process
7 Non-directive
8 Counsellor as facilitator
9 Relationship between client and counsellor 'contractual'
10 Individuality of client (and counsellor) recognized and respected

in which the counsellor is in a position which is superior to that of the client. All the other factors too 'conspire' to perpetuate the non-hierarchical nature of the relationship. It is the client who is expected to keep his/her appointments with the counsellor. It is the client who is kept waiting should the counsellor, for one reason or another, be busy. On the other hand, it is not the client but the counsellor who initiates the session, and who, after the agreed hour or fifty minutes, terminates the session. It is the counsellor who is construed as the 'expert' who has within his or her means the power to unravel the complexities and conundrums of the client's existential dilemmas, and 'guide' him or her along a path which will lead to a successful resolution of the client's psychological conflicts. Whether such constructions of expertise of the counsellor are justified or not is not the point. Whether the counsellor is imbued with the powers to understand the client's conflicts is also not the point. It is sufficient that such constructions form part of the world view of the client and that the counsellor is seen as *the expert*. Without such a construction it is hard to envisage how the very process of counselling can be initiated.

It would seem therefore that at an *overt* level there is a semblance of a non-hierarchical relationship, but at a *covert* level, the relationship between the counsellor and the client is one based on a hierarchical structure, in which the counsellor unintentionally (or intentionally) occupies a superior position to the client. However hard the counsellor tries, however genuine the counsellor's intentions, it is quite difficult to discard the asymmetrical nature of client–counsellor relationships.

To a large extent the theoretical assumptions which underlie the nature of client centred counselling must be seen against the backdrop of the shared cultural ideology between the client and the counsellor/therapist.

Problems of transplanting client centred counselling/therapy

1 NON-HIERARCHICAL RELATIONSHIPS The idea that the relationship between the client and the counsellor must be based on a premise of

equality stems from the fundamental notion of Individualism, which is one of the distinguishing features of Western society. Individualism, among other things, implies the acceptance of an individual's uniqueness, a recognition of and a respect for the other person's individuality. Individualism also recognizes the individual's ability to pursue their own clearly defined goals, take responsibility for their actions, cope with their problems, take credit for their successes and accept blame for any failures encountered on the way.

When one turns to Indian culture, one finds that the concept of individualism has little meaning among the people of that culture. Indian society has always been and continues to be a community based society. People live in extended family networks, where relationships are maintained on a hierarchical basis. A community in India has several unique features. People within a group are united by a common caste rank. Caste itself operates on a ranking or a hierarchical system. Elders and persons in positions of authority, for example teachers, gurus etc., are accorded special status and are generally deferred to. On important issues, members of the family and one's *jati* (sub-community) may meet, and confer with one another and any decisions taken are often binding on the rest of the members within the community. Given the early socialization of Indians into a hierarchical social and familial structure, it would be difficult, if not impossible, for an Indian client to accept a counselling relationship based on the premise of equality. It is a situation in which the Indian client would feel extremely uncomfortable.

2 THE COUNSELLOR/THERAPIST AS THE EXPERT   The Indian client is likely to search for a therapist he/she can respect, look up to and defer to. To an Indian client, the counsellor or therapist is seen as a special person, as *the expert*, a person who is imbued with special powers, even in some instances with *psycho-magical powers*, which can be used to alleviate the client's personal and familial problems (Roland, 1988). For an Indian client to operate on terms of equality with his/her therapist/counsellors is totally alien to his/her way of thinking.

3 ACCEPTANCE OF PERSONAL RESPONSIBILITY   Again, while the philosophy of individualism permits an individual to take credit for his/her successes and accept blame for his/her failures, this attitude is also alien to an Indian way of thinking. A strong belief in a deterministic philosophy allows, for instance, a Muslim client to explain away failures and successes in terms of the Will of Allah, and for the Hindu, to the inexorable consequences of his/her karma. The acceptance of personal responsibility for the consequences of one's actions is not as straightforward a concept as would appear at first sight. It is in need of a careful analysis.

4 NON-DIRECTIVE/DIRECTIVE COUNSELLING   While some Western clients would be willing to attempt to arrive at an understanding of their inner conflicts and dilemmas with only minimal assistance from their therapists/counsellors, Indian clients would find it virtually impossible to follow such a lead. Because of their imbuing their therapist/ counsellor with superior powers bordering, in some cases, on the magical and mystical, they would expect to be guided and directed by them at every stage in their attempts at seeking a 'cure' to their psychological problems. This attitude seriously compromises the funda- mental assumption related to non-directive counselling/therapy.

5 EMOTIONALISM   It should also be recognized that Indian society, in contradistinction to Western society, operates on an emotional mode, whereas Western society operates on a cognitive mode. These different constructions of their private and social worlds stem from their inherit- ance of their different philosophical legacies. As a result, Westerners are able to engage in work-related contractual arrangements with their therapists/counsellors. A therapist is a person with whom one *works* in order to resolve a personal problem. Note the emphasis on the word 'work'. The relationship is contractual. Both the parties in the contract have specific obligations towards one another. The fact that the nature of the transaction between the therapist and the client is of an emotional nature does not alter the contractual arrangements.

Indians, on the other hand, operate in an emotional mode. Indian society therefore tends to be relation centred rather than work-and- activity centred. Work is often seen as a by-product of relationships. Consequently, Indians find it extremely difficult to enter into impersonal contractual arrangements. They look for a greater emotional connected- ness with their therapists, which would allow them to express their dependency needs. As Roland points out (1988: 32):

> In contrast to Western hierarchical relationships – which tend to be based on a fixed status and power relationship, governed by contractual agreements and an ideology of essential equality – Indian hierarchical relationships are oriented toward firmly internalized expectations in both superior and sub- ordinate for reciprocity for mutual obligations in a more closely emotionally connected relationship.

The few examples which have been offered demonstrate quite clearly that any attempt to impose the client centred therapeutic model on people from non-Western cultures, particularly those from the Indian subcontinent, is doomed to failure. Counsellors need to realize that knowledge of Indian culture and history and/or the ability to speak one of the scores of Indian languages is not the same thing as understanding how Indians function psychologically. Sadly, there are no instant recipes for understanding how people of other cultures construe their own private and social worlds, how they relate to themselves, to their kith and kin and to the members of the host community. To rely on superficial accounts related to the dietary practices of people of non-Western cultures (for example, Muslims eat beef, but not pork; Hindus may eat pork but do not eat beef; Jains eat neither), their religious beliefs (for example, Hinduism is a pantheistic religion; they worship several Gods), the languages they speak (Gujarati, Bengali, Urdu, Hindi, Punjabi etc.), the clothes they wear (the saris and shalwar kurtas of the women, the five k's worn by Sikhs), the customs they follow (for example, the Diwali festival of Hindus, the Ramadan practices of Muslims), the traditions they abide by, the rites and rituals they observe at christenings, engagements, weddings and funerals etc., may form the basis of a good beginning. These, however, are superficial observations; they do not help us to go beyond such superficialities. Such knowledge is certainly not enough for a Western counsellor to impose a client centred therapeutic model on those people.

An unintentional error which counsellors – and indeed the majority of Westerners all over the Western world – make is to be misled by the perceived Westernization of their Indian clients. Should they meet with an Indian who speaks English fluently and colloquially, one who dresses in a Western manner, is involved in a professional occupation, and for all appearances gives the impression of being a Westerner, that person is also assumed to be a Westerner. *The Indian is then imbued with a Western mind.* He/she is then divested of most, if not all, of his/her cultural inheritance.

Why this is done is in itself an interesting issue. Several speculative observations can be made. There is a widespread Eurocentric belief that all developing countries over time will be influenced by Western science, technology and know-how, to such an extent that they too, in the process, will become Westernized and indistinguishable from other Western countries. The West sets, so to speak, the gold standard, which developing nations attempt to achieve. If developing nations, and/or members of ethnic minorities living in Western nations, are all driven to become Westernized, there is hardly any point in trying to understand an Indian from his/her own unique cultural perspective. What Westerners find difficult to understand and consequently come to terms with is the fact that the psyche of the members of ethnic minorities (as indeed of every person) is made up of several layers, of which the Western persona is the most easily observable one. Such a persona no doubt is desirable. It dilutes, if not conceals, differences which would otherwise be difficult to accommodate in one's psychological schema. It facilitates intercultural relationships at a functional level, but beneath the easily acquired cosmetic Westernized persona is to be found a psyche whose roots can be traced back to one's own ancestral cultural upbringing, which exercises a profound influence on the individual in terms of the individuals' evaluations of themselves, their identity and their own unique world view.

It is evident that client centred therapy/counselling runs into serious problems not only among the indigenous members of Western society but more importantly among the members of ethnic minorities, particularly those from the Indian subcontinent. We have seen that it does not live up to its fundamental assumptions. There are within it serious inconsistencies which only further research ought to be able to clarify.

The main problem with client centred therapy/counselling – as indeed with all therapies – is the one of commensurability. Does it work? If so, how does it work? How do we know that it works? Vital though the issue is, most practitioners tend to shy away from it. This is a question which pleads for an answer. Just because a therapy is seen as being attractive or is seen as being politically correct, or is in keeping with current social trends, does not in itself merit its usage unless one can establish its validity as clearly, as comprehensively and as unequivocally as possible. To turn away from the notion of validity and even look upon it as obscene as some therapists do, is to adopt an ostrich-like attitude, which in the long run will harm the very clients we are meant to help.

Conclusion

Let me end my chapter with an illustration from a personal experience. It is not a case study in the strict sense of the word. Nor is it a summary of a counselling session. It has more to do with cross-cultural encounters and the voiced and unvoiced assumptions which we make (and occasionally act upon) when we relate to people of cultures other than our own. It is also concerned with the manner in which people define and perceive themselves and are perceived by others. Since the episode has a bearing on the problem of cross-cultural encounters and to a certain extent on cross-cultural counselling, it merits a brief discussion.

Several years ago, when I was single and lived in a flat in central London, I had appointed a sort of major-domo whose job it was to look after my flat, clean it, paint it, do my shopping, iron my shirts, answer my telephone in my absence, and so on. When in the mood, he even cooked a meal for me. He had keys to my flat, and he came and went as he pleased. I trusted him with my life.

During the five years that Bernie worked for me, he never once addressed me by my first name, and I never called him by his surname. (In fact, to this day, I regret to say, I do not know his surname.) Bernie, who belongs to what I can only describe as the 'old school', never took the liberty of sitting in my living room. Even when invited to do so, he always found an excuse not to sit in the living room. We always sat in the kitchen. It was obvious that he respected and adhered to the class boundaries which divided us. This, however, did not deter him from expressing his firm views on a variety of subjects, ranging from football, politics, immigration, to religion, science and life in general. Nor did it in anyway inhibit him from talking about his own personal problems related to his very recent separation from his wife, the ensuing legal battles over the equitable division of their assets and the custody of their two young daughters. However, Bernie was blessed with a cheerful disposition. And he was an incorrigible raconteur. It was nice having him around.

One day, out of the blue, Bernie paid me what he thought was a supreme compliment.

'You know, Dr Laungani, you are almost a true Brit! Almost one of us!'

'But not quite!' I replied, smiling.

'You're getting there.'

For a moment I thought he was pulling my leg. I looked at him, sitting on the kitchen stool, sipping his mug of coffee. He seemed dead serious. I was aware that he was paying me a genuine compliment. However, in his compliment lay several implicit Anglocentric cultural assumptions, which are:

1 Britain provided the gold standard for other cultures all over the world.
2 A desire to be British was the standard, the goal, to which all non-Britishers automatically aspired.
3 However hard one tried, one would never become a true Brit – whatever the term 'true Britisher' might mean.
4 Other forms of developments in other cultures did not merit serious consideration.

I felt it would have been too complicated to explain to him all the implications of his compliment. I felt too that the explanations might cause him some discomfort or even anguish. Not wishing to cause Bernie any distress, I merely smiled and replied, '*Vive la difference.*'

'You can't be serious,' he replied, remonstrating with me.

He, however, refused to let the matter drop. He insisted that I was almost like 'one of us', by which he meant, a 'true Brit', thereby coaxing me to get involved in an argument which I had had no intention of starting, let alone continuing.

I asked him to consider the idea that I might genuinely not wish to be like a true Brit – whatever that might mean. He was genuinely surprised at my remark and confessed after due thought that he found it difficult why anyone should not wish to be a true Brit.

Rather than pursue the point, I asked him to consider the idea that I might be quite content with my own personal identity which I had 'worked out' for myself over the years and (hopefully) would continue to live with until I died.

Bernie looked puzzled. 'Yes, but . . .' was the only objection he raised.

I asked him to consider that all identities – mine was no exception in that sense – consisted of multiple layers which were built up through familial, cultural, religious, educational, professional influences. Occasionally these influences cohered to create a holistic personality pattern within the individual, but, more often than not, it conflicted to create fractures within the human psyche. I asked him to consider the occasions when all of us have been totally bewildered by our own irrationalities, and by our own inability to understand our own actions. Although human beings prided themselves on being rational animals, no one was rational for 24 hours of the day.

'With me,' he replied self-deprecatingly, 'it is the other way round. I am often surprised by my occasional rationality.'

We laughed.

Didn't this suggest, I continued, that there are layers upon layers to our identities or personalities, which often remain unplumbed and unknown.

'You're right, you know,' he replied. 'Just when you think you know some one well . . .'

'You mean your wife?'

'Yes. And then suddenly, the ground under your feet gives way.'

'Crash, bang! Everything comes tumbling down. Right?'

'Right.' He then went on to discuss his marital problems, and after a long, circuitous route, returned to the theme of identity.

I asked Bernie if his wife were a true Brit.

He deliberated over my question and after a while said, 'Not after what she's gone and done to me. Buggered off with someone else.'

Since I already knew what she had done, I didn't pursue the point any further.

'She's English, isn't she?'

'Oh yes. She's Brit, alright, but not a true Brit.'

We both laughed at his subtle distinction. It seemed that Bernie was talking about two types of identities: *ascribed* and *achieved*. Being British was an ascribed identity, given to one at birth. This was not dissimilar to the caste into which a Hindu is born. When I asked him to explain what a true Brit was, he hesitated. He went round in circles, trying to find the right words or actions which would allow him to explain his own conceptions of a true Brit. He felt defeated by his inability to put into words what he felt with great intensity. I knew the feeling. I have experienced it many times myself. I waited. From what I could gather it seemed that a 'true Brit' identity had to be achieved by the performance of certain types of noble, courageous and virtuous deeds and actions, some of which involved keeping one's promises, not letting the 'side' down, doing what was considered to be noble and honourable, defending one's country, even laying down one's life for one's country, and so on.

I asked him if he could give me an example which would illustrate the identity of a true Brit. As an example, he chose to discuss his wife. (Although we were supposedly having a friendly, light-hearted discussion, he kept returning to the theme of his wife. It soon became obvious to me that he was using this occasion to express his feelings of anger, hostility, disappointment and bitterness towards his estranged wife.) His wife, he said, had never achieved the true-Brit identity, or if she had, she had lost it as a result of her actions which affected him and his children. In so far as his own assessment of *my* identity was concerned, he felt that I was getting there. I was on the way to acquiring a true-Brit identity. I wondered, smiling to myself, what further actions I would need to perform before I achieved the identity of a true Brit.

'What about all those with British passports?' I asked him. 'Aren't they Brits like you?'

'I don't think so.' He hesitated for a while and continued. 'It takes more to make a Brit than having a British passport. Anyone can hold a British passport!'

'I see.'

'A passport is just a travel document. Nothing to do with being a Brit.'

'If I get you right, what you're saying Bernie, is that Brits have to be born Brits.'

'Absolutely.'

'What about the Asians and the Afro-Caribbeans whose children are born here? Would you consider them to be Brits?'

'Well. But they are not true Brits.'

'But aren't all Brits true Brits?' I inquired.

'Not all. We'd have never lost the bleeding Empire otherwise, would we? No offence to you, Dr Laungani.'

'None taken. Let me get this right. What you're saying is this: One may be born a Brit. But that does not necessarily make the person a true Brit. To be a true Brit one has to acquire certain qualities, and behave in a certain manner.'

'Precisely! Have you read "If"? Years ago, I read it at school. It's stayed with me, ever since.'

'So did I,' I replied, surprised by his reference to Kipling's well-known poem. 'Is that what you mean by a true Brit?'

'Not quite, but more or less.'

'But tell me Bernie, if a Brit can stop being a true Brit, why can't a non-Brit ever be a true Brit?'

'You mean yourself?'

'No, not me. I was asking a general question.'

'I don't see why not. But it ain't easy, I tell you.'

Wanting to be a true Brit seemed like a spiritual quest.

I then urged him to consider the idea that human identity was too complex to be encapsulated or pinned down by resorting to nationalistic labels, such as one is a Brit (or a true Brit), one is an Indian, one is an Asian, one is an Afro-Caribbean, one is a Pakistani, or that one is white, one is brown, one is black, one is yellow, and so on.

'But don't we all do that?' he replied defensively.

'Yes I know. But they are just labels,' I replied.

'If you say so,' he answered vaguely.

Labels, I explained, were identification tags, best put on parcels – not on human beings. Labels, at best, might serve as reference points, but one would need to go beyond the labels, way way beyond the labels, if one wanted to understand one's own identity or that of one's fellow human beings. 'You're English. That's one label. You're British. That's a second label. You're white. That's a third label. You're male. A fourth label. You're a father. That's a fifth label. You come from a certain social class background. That's a sixth label. I am sure we could find several more labels to stick on you, if you wanted. What would all these labels tell us about you as a person? Practically nothing of any importance. If only it were that simple! Imagine a suitcase with labels of all the exotic places in the world stuck on it. All that the suitcase tells us is that the owner may perhaps have visited those exotic places. But it tells us nothing more about the owner. Not even whether he was rich or poor. For he could have been a merchant seaman.'

He made himself another cup of coffee, giving himself time to consider what I had said.

'But we all use labels, surely. All the time!'

'You're right. But because we all use labels, it doesn't make it right.' The use of labels on human beings, I pointed out to him, could also lead to disastrous consequences for individuals and for society as a whole. To bring home the point, I mentioned a few antisemitic, anti-Indian, anti-Pakistani labels which were fashionable in England today.

'But surely one can ignore them,' he replied defensively.

'I don't believe that necessarily helps the person who has been labelled. Labels create their own stigmas. The individual who is labelled is often helpless against the social stigmas which labels carry. It is society that needs to be changed. It is society that needs to stop using labels on others. So long as we continue to use labels on people, we will continue to create divisions in society.'

But Bernie wasn't going to surrender the argument that easily. Eager to have the last word, he replied, 'But there are labels and labels and labels. There is something quite special about being a true Brit, you know. It's only when you become one then you know what it's like being one!'

How could any one rise to that!

DISCUSSION ISSUES

In what ways do you either agree or disagree with Laungani's views on client centred counselling?

Indian society operates in an emotional mode whereas Western society operates in a cognitive mode. Discuss.

What theoretical assumptions does your approach to counselling have and how could these assumptions impact upon your counselling with ethnic minorities?

Professionally trained counsellors would not make mistakes similar to Bernie's. Discuss.

References and further reading

Bloom, A. (1987) *The Closing of the American Mind*. London: Penguin.

Doyal, L. and Harris, R. (1986) *Empiricism, Explanation and Rationality: an Introduction to the Philosophy of the Social Sciences*. London: Routledge.

Gellner, E. (1985) *Relativism and the Social Sciences*. Cambridge: Cambridge University Press.

Ivey, A.E., Ivey, M.B. and Simek-Morgan, L. (eds) (1993) *Counselling and Psychotherapy: a Multicultural Perspective*. Needham Heights, MA: Allyn & Bacon.

Lakatos, I. (1970) 'Falsification and the methodology of scientific research programmes', in I. Lakatos and A. Musgrave (eds), *Criticism and the Growth of Knowledge*. Cambridge: Cambridge University Press.

Laungani, P. (1992) *It Shouldn't Happen to a Patient: a Survivor's Guide to Fighting Life-Threatening Illness*. London: Whiting & Birch.

Laungani, P. (1993) 'Cultural differences in stress and its management', *Stress Medicine*, 9 (1): 37–43.

Laungani, P. (1994) 'Cultural differences in stress: India and England', *Counselling Psychology Review*, 9 (4): 25–37.

Laungani, P. (1995a) 'Can psychotherapy seriously damage your health', *Counselling, Journal of the British Association for Counselling*, 6 (2) (May): 110–15.

Laungani, P. (1995b) 'Stress in Eastern and Western cultures', in John Brebner, Esther Greenglass, Pittu Laungani and Ann O'Roark (eds) (series editors Charles D. Spielberger and Irwin G. Sarason), *Stress and Emotion*, vol. 15, Washington, DC: Taylor & Francis. pp. 265–80.

Laungani, P. (1996) 'Death in a Hindu family', in C.M. Parkes, P. Laungani and W. Young (eds), *Death and Bereavement Across Cultures*. London: Routledge.

Laungani, P. (1997) 'Mental illness in India and Britain: theory and practice', *Medicine and Law*, 16: 509–40.

Musgrove, F. (1982) *Education and Anthropology: Other Cultures and the Teacher*. Chichester: Wiley.

Parkes, C.M., Laungani, P. and Young, B. (1996) *Death and Bereavement Across Cultures*. London: Routledge.

Popper, K. (1972) *Objective Knowledge: an Evolutionary Approach*. Oxford: Clarendon Press.

Rogers, C. (1961) *On Becoming a Person*. Boston, MA: Houghton-Mifflin.

Rogers, C. (1970) *On Encounter Groups*. New York: HarperCollins.

Rogers, C. (1972) *Becoming Partners*. New York: Delta.

Roland, A. (1988) *In Search of Self in India and in Japan: Toward a Cross-Cultural Psychology*, Princeton, NJ: Princeton University Press.

Sachdev, D. (1992) 'Effects of psychocultural factors on the socialisation of British born Indian children and indigenous British children in England'. Unpublished doctoral dissertation, South Bank University, London.

Sookhoo, D. (1995) 'A comparative study of the health beliefs and health practices of British whites and Asian adults with and without myocardial infarction'. Paper read at the 53rd Annual Convention of the International Council of Psychologists, Taipei, Taiwan.

Williams, B. (1985) *Ethics and the Limits of Philosophy*. London: Fontana.

Ziman, J. (1978) *Reliable Knowledge: an Exploration of the Grounds for Belief in Science*. Cambridge: Cambridge University Press.

7

IN SEARCH OF EFFECTIVE
COUNSELLING ACROSS CULTURES

Stephen Palmer

The research into effective counselling is full of contradictions. Often a range of questions are frequently asked by inexperienced and experienced practitioners alike. For example, are all approaches equal in effectiveness? Are techniques more important than the therapeutic relationship? Should counsellors put every client into the same therapeutic strait-jacket? Should counsellors be flexible in the application of their approach? Are counsellor attitudes more important than the therapeutic approach when considering outcomes? This turmoil has been reflected in recent books on comparative psychotherapy such as *Which Psychotherapy?* (Feltham, 1997) in which leading exponents were asked a number of questions (backcover):

- which approaches they consider to be ineffective, misleading or dangerous,
- which approaches seem to be more promising or effective,
- why their approach is more effective or comprehensive and why it may be more suited to certain clients or client problems,
- how they account for research which suggests that no one approach seems more effective than any other.

Although this book is a fascinating read and I would thoroughly recommend it to counsellors wanting to gain more insight into this subject, it becomes apparent that leading exponents of therapy have difficulty agreeing with each other on many relevant factors. This may make my task in writing this chapter rather difficult to say the least.

There is even less research about effective counselling across cultures in Britain (Jewel, 1994). This chapter attempts to cover some of these issues and give a consensual opinion of what is best practice by noting what a number of practitioners have found helpful and effective. Ridley and associates (1997: 141) suggest that 'Effective intervention with racial and ethnic minority clients requires that counselors look beyond the universal perspective. A more advantageous approach involves counseling minority clients idiographically.' This chapter concludes by examining the idiographic approach to counselling.

What is counselling?

It may be useful to focus on a current definition of counselling taking a cross-cultural perspective to aid our understanding of its very nature. In the *Dictionary of Counselling* counselling is defined thus (Feltham and Dryden, 1993: 40):

> a principled relationship characterized by the application of one or more psychological theories and a recognized set of communication skills, modified by experience, intuition and other interpersonal factors, to clients' intimate concerns, problems or aspirations.

This explanation appears straightforward. Counselling is seen as 'principled', in other words an ethical endeavour with strict boundaries (Feltham, 1995). Obviously, in practice, whether the psychological theories underpinning the counselling practice help or hinder the 'principled relationship' is possibly debatable. In addition, are these theories more applicable to people of European descent or can they apply equally to all races? London (1964: 33) made the following observation: 'however interesting, plausible and appealing a theory may be, it is techniques, not theories, that are actually used on people'. Therefore from one perspective it is even possible to consider that the psychological theories could be redundant.

Are the 'recognized set of communication skills' suitable to all cultures? Let us take just one example. Each culture tends to have its own specific repertoire of behaviours which do not necessarily cross cultures, such as non-verbal communication. Observe tourists from different cultures conversing with each other. Even if they are talking to a person from an adjacent country in Europe, difficulties can arise if both cultures operate on a different body distance. Ullmann and Krasner (1975) emphasize that each culture develops its own norms for expected social role behaviours and determines which behaviours are called 'abnormal'. Therefore each cross-cultural counsellor would need to pay attention to the social meaning and context of presenting problems or intimate concerns (Higginbotham and Tanaka-Matsumi, 1991).

Feltham and Dryden continue (1993: 40):

> Its predominant ethos is one of facilitation rather than of advice-giving or coercion. It may be of very brief or long duration, take place in an organizational or private practice setting and may or may not overlap with practical, medical and other matters of personal welfare.

You may ask where did the notion of 'facilitation rather than advice-giving' arise? This was probably a direct influence of Carl Rogers (1951) and the client centred philosophy on the field of counselling. This approach reflected white American culture, values and aspirations, and now in Britain it is enshrined in the British Association for Counselling's Code of Ethics and Practice for counsellors as below (BAC, 1996):

Article 3.1
The overall aim of counselling is to provide an opportunity for the client to work towards living in a more satisfying and resourceful way. The term 'counselling' includes work with individuals, pairs or groups of people often, but not always, referred to as 'clients'. The objectives of particular counselling relationships will vary according to the client's needs. Counselling may be concerned with developmental issues, addressing and resolving specific problems, making decisions, coping with crisis, developing personal insight and knowledge, working through feelings of inner conflict or improving relationships with others. The counsellor's role is to facilitate the client's work in ways which respect the client's values, personal resources and capacity for self-determination.

This description of counselling is reasonably flexible. However, it is interesting in that counselling is one profession that does not apparently offer clients advice. Does your surveyor, estate agent, accountant, physician, surgeon, occupational therapist, dentist or whatever offer advice or facilitation? In most cases we would expect advice. Yet many clients' expectations are probably similar to the *Oxford English Dictionary* definition (Simpson and Weiner, 1989): 'the giving of advice on personal, social, psychological, etc., problems'. Counsellors can overcome this 'minor' issue by being non-directive or by providing information as opposed to giving advice. If we asked clients whether their counsellor offered advice or provided information I wonder how they would respond. I suspect they would perceive providing information as offering advice. I am lingering on this issue because some non-Western forms of therapy tend to take a directive and instructive approach (see Chapter 6). Walsh (1995: 388) goes further and suggests that, 'instruction and assistance from a skilled helper is regarded as essential in all Asian practices, which are never entirely solitary'. Other researchers have suggested the use of more directive counselling styles for a range of ethnic minority groups (e.g. Berman, 1979; Draguns, 1981; Exum and Lau, 1988; Sue and Sue, 1990).

Transcultural counselling

The term 'transcultural counselling' has become popular in Britain amongst counsellors since the publication of d'Ardenne and Mahtani's (1989) excellent book *Transcultural Counselling in Action*. They chose the term 'trans' as opposed to 'inter' or 'cross' cultural counselling as they wanted to emphasize the active and reciprocal process that is involved in counselling (1989: 5). Their approach to transcultural counselling included a number of components (1989: 6):

- counsellors' sensitivity to cultural variations and the cultural bias of their own approach;
- counsellors' grasp of cultural knowledge of their clients;
- counsellors' ability and commitment to develop an approach to counselling that reflects the cultural needs of their clients;
- counsellors' ability to face increased complexity in working across cultures.

In addition, they asserted that there were three significant areas in any counselling relationship that were especially important in a transcultural relationship: the establishment of boundaries; transference and counter-transference issues; and recognition that anyone seeking counselling is in transition. Their approach was underpinned by a number of assumptions (1989: 12–13):

- All cultural groups have an equal right to benefit from counselling in our society.
- The majority culture is hostile to people from other cultures (for example, counsellors blaming their clients' cultures for their problems).
- In order for all members of society to have equal access to coun-selling, majority counsellors will need to acknowledge their own ethnocentricity.
- Class and gender interact with culture, and also have an effect upon counselling outcome.

Their approach is practice-based and suitable for clients from all cultures. They do not 'prescribe rules for specific cultures' (1989: 13). In the next section we consider what makes up effective counselling.

Effective counselling?

If we consider two forms of therapy that are often considered as diametrically opposite in their basic approach to helping clients then we can perhaps start to infer the nature of effective counselling. In one study, Raskin (1974) compared the practice of Carl Rogers, the founder of client centred therapy, with that of Albert Ellis, the founder of rational emotive therapy (RET), later renamed as rational emotive behaviour therapy (REBT) (Ellis, 1994). Twelve therapist variables were rated by 83 therapist judges. They observed the following: Ellis was rated high on the Therapist-directed and Cognitive dimensions. Rogers was rated high on Congruence, Ability to inspire confidence, Empathy and Unconditional positive regard. Ellis was rated low on Unconditional positive regard, while Rogers was rated low on the Therapist-directed dimension.

Raskin and Rogers (1995: 132) found the following differences between the two forms of therapy:

1 Unlike RET, the person-centered approach greatly values the therapeutic relationship.
2 Rational-emotive therapists provide much direction, while the person-centered approach encourages the client to determine direction.
3 Rational-emotive therapists work hard to point out deficiencies in their clients' thought processes; person-centered therapists accept and respect their clients' ways of thinking and perceiving.
4 Person-centered therapy characteristically leads to actions chosen by the client; rational-emotive methods include 'homework' assignments by the therapist.
5 The person-centered therapist will relate to the client on a feeling level and in a respectful and accepting way; the rational-emotive therapist will be inclined to interrupt this affective process to point out the irrational harm that the client may be doing to self and interpersonal relationships.

Apart from being a human being and sitting in the same room as the client, some of the key observable strategies and interventions used by person centred and rational-emotive therapists are clearly different.

It may be useful to compare person centred therapy with another approach. Meador and Rogers (1984: 146) distinguished person centred therapy from psychoanalysis in a number of ways:

In psychoanalysis the analyst aims to interpret connections between the past and the present for the patient. In person-centered therapy, the therapist facilitates the client's discoveries of the meanings of his or her own current inner experiencing. The psychoanalyst takes the role of a teacher in interpreting insights to the patient and encouraging the development of a transference relationship, a relationship based on the neurosis of the patient. The person-centered therapist presents him- or herself as honestly and transparently as possible and attempts to establish a relationship in which he or she is authentically caring and listening. In person-centered therapy, transference relationships may begin, but they do not become full-blown. . . . Person-centered therapists tend to avoid evaluation. They do not interpret for clients, do not question in a probing manner, and do not reassure or criticize clients. Person-centered therapists have not found the transference relationships, central to psychoanalysis, a necessary part of a client's growth or change.

As with REBT, again it appears that person centred therapy differs from psychoanalysis in its overall strategies and interventions. Where does this leave us? We have three major forms of therapy which are still being practised by many counsellors and psychotherapists in the Western world. Perhaps we should consider the research findings. Luborsky and associates (1975) claimed that no single treatment is more effective than any other. They called this the 'Dodo Bird' verdict – everyone has won and all must have prizes! In a study by Smith and associates (1980) a similar conclusion was drawn. Assuming the studies are not seriously flawed, we could infer that person centred therapy, rational emotive behaviour therapy and psychoanalysis have equal outcomes even though the therapies are actually practised quite differently.

This leaves us with a conundrum. If these three therapies use different strategies, relationship styles, techniques and interventions, yet all are equally effective (depending upon different criteria), putting common sense aside, it becomes difficult to conclude what are the essential ingredients of effective counselling. The only key common factor that immediately springs to mind is another person (the counsellor) with a psychological theory underpinning his or her practice, with an apparent interest in the client or his or her problem(s). The counsellor may or may not even use basic counselling skills, such as reflecting, paraphrasing, summarizing and immediacy. However, we should bear in mind that some researchers have discussed the limitations of studies based on meta-analysis (see Wilson, 1985; Wilson and Rachman, 1983). Taking a cross-cultural perspective, would an Indian guru agree with either Rogers or Ellis on a list of therapeutically crucial components (see Draguns, 1996: 4)? Would an Indian guru agree with our general descriptions or definitions of counselling?

By the 1970s there was considerable evidence which linked the provision of the person centred conditions, that is, congruence, empathy and unconditional positive regard, with positive therapy outcome (Bergin and Garfield, 1971). More recently, the original conclusions have been challenged (Stubbs and Bozarth, 1994). Interestingly, self-help books such as *Living with Fear* (Marks, 1980) can provide useful bibliotherapy. The author, Issac Marks, has suggested that patients on waiting lists have cured themselves of phobias after reading and applying the behavioural techniques from his book. More recently, CD-ROM computer therapy has been used to help clients deal with depression and anxiety. This raises another question. Can a book or computer provide the core conditions of congruence, empathy and unconditional positive regard which apparently are essential for effective therapy? Do self-help books and computer programs facilitate, offer advice or provide information? I pose these questions as devil's advocate, however, not intending to berate any particular form of counselling or therapy.

Barkham (1996: 53) states: 'While the facilitative conditions have been viewed as a possible mechanism of change, the therapeutic alliance is best viewed as a mechanism which enables the client to remain in and comply with treatment.' Perhaps this opinion, which highlights the importance of the therapeutic alliance, takes us a little closer in our search. Horvath and Symonds (1991) undertook a meta-analytic review of 24 studies and concluded that the alliance was positively related to therapeutic outcome. We could conclude that for effective counselling both the facilitative conditions and a good therapeutic alliance are beneficial (see Fischer et al., 1998).

Let us attempt to resolve the issue of effectiveness by focusing on a specific problem such as post-traumatic stress disorder (PTSD). Foa and associates (1991) compared three treatment groups: stress inoculation training (SIT) (see Resick et al., 1988), exposure (see Richards et al., 1994) and non-directive counselling. Richards (1996: 79) summarized the results:

1 All three treatments reduced non-specific distress such as depression and anxiety.
2 Specific PTSD symptoms were only treated successfully by exposure or SIT, not by supportive counselling.
3 Immediately post-treatment (4.5 weeks after starting), SIT produced the most consistent gains.
4 At follow-up, 3.5 months later, the exposure group continued to improve, whereas the SIT group lost some of their gains. At this point, exposure was superior to SIT.

Richards (1996: 79) concludes that 'this seems to provide us with the clearest evidence that exposure to traumatic memories and avoided situations, key areas of PTSD dysfunction, is the treatment strategy of choice for PTSD. It also confirms Duckworth and Charlesworth's (1988) view that supportive counselling is only of general, not specific, use in PTSD treatment.' Therefore, we can assume that particular techniques or approaches are effective for specific problems. Of course, more research is needed to show that these interventions can be applied across *all* cultures or with *all* minority groups (see Marsella et al., 1996). Fortunately, Westermeyer (1995) reports that the situation regarding research is improving.

When we examine other cultures we may find that the therapies used for dealing with anxiety related disorders are similar to Western cognitive behavioural strategies. A review of published literature does, in fact, uncover a number of options. For example, if we focus on Japan we discover a form of therapy called '*Morita*' which uses cognitive reattribution and behavioural exposure techniques to help clients overcome anxiety, phobias, a dislike of bodily symptoms and perfectionism. The therapy programme has four main components: acceptance, reattribution, dereflection and active engagement (see Walsh, 1995). Much published literature exists on the efficacy of Morita Therapy (see Ishiyama, 1986). This suggests that some other cultures may also be willing to use more directive methods which may be an anathema to many counsellors practising in Britain. This is an important factor that counsellors may need to be aware of if they wish to be effective when working in multicultural settings.

If we ignore the therapeutic approach or techniques for the moment, there is little research to show that Accredited Counsellors, Registered Psychotherapists or Chartered Psychologists are any more effective than beginner or trainee counsellors. Of course, a lack of research does not necessarily imply that all counsellors, whether experienced or inexperienced, qualified or unqualified, are equal in their therapeutic effectiveness. Common sense tells us that fully trained counsellors 'should' be more effective. In fact a recent study demonstrated that an experienced supervisor of cognitive behaviour therapy was slightly more effective than his/her supervisees (Stokes et al., 1996). Interestingly, research has not confirmed that either recognition or advanced qualifications lead to less therapist abuse of clients. In fact, the converse has been shown in the United States of America for similar professions (see Szymanska and Palmer, 1997 for a general discussion of this subject).

So where does this leave us? Whilst the jury is still out regarding the relative effectiveness of approaches or the experience of the counsellor, it appears that certain strategies or techniques may prove beneficial for specific problems and disorders. For example, exposure techniques, both *in vivo* or imaginal, have been effective with anxiety related disorders such as PTSD and phobias. The distinction between Rogers's and Ellis's practice discussed earlier highlights that various core conditions or skills are not necessarily important for client change and perhaps the key issue is a counsellor who is willing to listen to and help a client, in whatever way, to deal with his or her problem(s). By focusing on the commonalities we may discover further clues in the search for effective counselling. Raskin and Rogers (1995: 133) suggested that both Rogers and Ellis shared a number of important beliefs and values:

1 A great optimism that people can change, even when they are deeply disturbed.
2 A perception that individuals are often unnecessarily self-critical, and that negative self-attitudes can become positive.
3 A willingness to put forth great effort to try to help people, both through individual therapy and through professional therapy and non-technical writing.
4 A willingness to demonstrate their methods publicly.
5 A respect for science and research.

They suggested that similar commonalities and differences could be found when Rogers was compared to other cognitive therapists, such as Aaron Beck. If the above commonalities are the important ingredient of effective counselling, then the next question we are left with is whether these are of benefit to ethnic minority client groups, especially as they are practised within a Westerncentric therapeutic framework?

Webb Johnson and Nadirshaw (1993: 6) suggest that at present 'there are no well-established theoretical models of transcultural therapy to substitute for traditional approaches'. They assert that with clients of South Asian origin, the therapist variables are probably more important in the process and outcome of therapy than particular schools of therapy. The variables include (1993: 26–7):

- The therapist's credibility in the client's mind.
- The therapist's ability to let the client dictate the goals and purpose of the therapy.
- The therapist's ability to convince the client that he/she is understood.
- The therapist's ability to communicate effectively with the client – for example, by listening actively and showing empathy and unconditional positive regard.
- The therapist's ability to show genuine respect for his/her client's cultural values and to refrain from imposing his/her own frame of reference on the client's experiences and behaviour.
- The therapist's assumptions and values concerning the experiences of people from the ethnic communities.
- The therapist's ability to address and confront his/her own stereotypical/prejudiced views and racist assumptions.
- The therapist's awareness of how his/her own cultural values can be imposed, perhaps unconsciously, on the client and can affect the interpretation of the client's experiences: for example, a white female therapist's prejudice towards an Asian female client's problems relating to her arranged marriage.
- The therapist's ability to increase his/her awareness of the cultural, religious, social and political factors which impact upon the lives of members of the ethnic communities.
- The therapist's ability to become acquainted with the strengths of the client and to treat the client as an individual.

Challenging assumptions

It has been suggested that 'assumptions and beliefs held by mainly white, mainstream therapists and counsellors' should be challenged (Nadirshaw, 1992: 257). It may be useful to consider some of these assumptions which could interfere with effective cross-cultural counselling (Nadirshaw, 1992: 258–9).

   i) Certain ethnic minority groups (e.g. Asians) are psychologically more robust than the indigenous population and do not require 'verbal therapies'.

ii) Black communities (Asians, Afro-Carribeans) represent homogenous groups, sharing a common culture and heritage, without acknowledging the diversity that exists within each of these groups.

iii) Minority communities want directive (medical) treatment rather than non-directive therapy; they want to be told what to do.

iv) They are aware of therapy and other mental health services, know how to access it but they 'care for their own' and 'keep the problem' in-house.

v) The client's problem (distress/discomfort) is located within the person rather than seen as an emotional reaction to the external hostile sociopolitical and economic factors that impinge on the black client's life, leading to discrimination and disadvantage.

vi) The therapist is 'the expert', with the black client being unable to define their own situation, or the methods to achieve the goals for successful resolution of the problem.

vii) The process of therapy is of an unbiased and objective nature and that it is conducted in a non-judgemental manner.

viii) The client's values, attitudes and ways of behaving have to be changed, altered or modified rather than the therapist who bring their own values, beliefs, prejudices into the therapeutic/counselling situation.

ix) All the problems/difficulties experienced are related to the cultural and ethnic background of the client. Conversely, the 'culture-blind' approach, i.e. not acknowledging the role of culture and ethnic background in mental health, could also be used.

x) The therapist has to be a 'culture expert' for the therapeutic alliance to be effective in leading to a successful outcome.

xi) If client and therapist come from the same cultural background, they are assumed to be sharing a common framework for understanding the problem.

Although these assumptions could be challenged during counsellor training, so far in Britain few courses give cultural issues more than a cursory mention. In fact, many counselling courses do not cover these issues at all. Therefore, counsellors interested in learning more about cross-cultural or transcultural counselling either have to attend specific workshops/courses/conferences or read appropriate literature. However, this subject has been rather marginalized and consequently few books appertaining to cross-cultural or transcultural counselling in Britain have been published. Thus counsellors are sometimes faced with having to reflect on their own practice by themselves, with interested colleagues or their supervisors, who may not be adequately trained in this area.

Guidelines for counselling across cultures

Let us consider the latest guidelines taken from the *Handbook of Counselling*, which focused on counselling within Britain. There Lago and

Thompson (adapted 1997: 293–8) gave 17 'tentative' guidelines for counsellor practice.

1 Attempt to gain an awareness and knowledge of your own culture and cultural style, race and racial origins.

2 Specifically, attempt to gain more understanding of the historical and contemporary relationship that has existed and presently exists between your own race and that of your clients.

3 Develop a 'structural awareness' of society, including the effects of history and the mechanisms of oppression and systems of discrimination that operate in society.

4 Attempt to gain knowledge of the client's culture, cultural style, race and racial origins (avoiding simplistic beliefs and views based on inadequate, biased, or limited accounts).

5 Hold in mind that any breakdown in communication may be attributable to the dynamic process between you.

6 Be aware of (and beware) your assumptions, stereotypes and immediate judgements.

7 Remember that many concepts like truth, honesty, intent, politeness, self-disclosure and so on are culturally bound.

8 The dominant manner through which all counsellors operate is one that is underpinned by attention-giving and active listening to the client.

9 Be alert to your usage of language.

10 Pay attention also to paralinguistic phenomena such as sighs, intonation, grunts, expression and silences, for they also can ensure that real communication does not occur.

11 A more open and accepting approach to many models of counselling and helping is required within this sphere. (Remember also that this statement implicitly incorporates non-Eurocentric models of helping.)

12 Monitor your own attitudes during the interview, especially in relation to feelings of superiority or power over the client (associated with the areas of racism and oppression).

13 There are circumstances in which it will be appropriate for white and black counsellors, in being sensitive to the issues or racism, to explicitly acknowledge and explore this topic within the counselling process.

14 We would encourage counsellors to proceed cautiously and be in favour of minimum contact rather than long-term work (as the latter may have a poor prospective outcome).

15 Generate possible sources of referral to helpers or counsellors of the same race/culture as the client.

16 Similarly, attempt to locate a suitable consultant who has experience of or is the same race as the client, if the client becomes a medium- to long-term one.

17 Explore the experience of consulting racially different people with your own personal difficulties or for therapy, in order to gain insight into what it is you are attempting with your racially different clients.

These guidelines are explored in greater depth elsewhere (Lago and Thompson, 1996, 1997). Counsellors can use the guidelines as a checklist and for regular self-audits to ensure that they are maintaining good practice. Supervisors of counsellors who work in multicultural settings can raise some of these issues during supervision sessions.

Counselling idiographically

Let us start with the proposition that each client is a unique individual with a combination of different aspects and characteristics. Even identical twins brought up in the same family will have had different experiences which may have affected them. Each twin may require a different style of counselling for maximum effectiveness. Idiographic counselling attempts to cater for each client's uniqueness by counsellors examining their clients' personal experiences and problems which then guides the entire process of counselling (Ridley, 1995). Assumptions will not be made prematurely about either assessment and the subsequent therapy without first meeting the client and ascertaining their goals (if any). Therefore it may contrast with others who are prepared to state (Noonan, 1983: ix):

> Nearly everyone who comes to see us brings a reality problem to be sorted out and an unconscious to be explored, an anxiety to be relieved and a phantasy to be untangled, an acute need to be helped and a transference relationship to be tested out.

Of course, understandably this possibly reflects Noonan's psychodynamic stance which underpins her practice.

Ridley (1995: 82–5) has developed five principles which he believes will help counsellors acquire a therapeutic mindset that enables them to counsel ethnic minority clients more effectively:

1 Every client should be understood from his or her unique frame of reference.
2 Nomothetic, normative information does not always fit a particular client.
3 People are a dynamic blend of multiple roles and identities.
4 The idiographic perspective is compatible with the biopsychosocial model of mental health.
5 The idiographic perspective is transtheoretical.

Understanding clients from their own unique frame of reference is based on the work of Rogers and his concept of empathy. Raskin and Rogers (1995: 142) describe it as:

an active, immediate, continuous process. The counselor makes a maximum effort to get within and live the attitudes expressed instead of observing them, diagnosing them, or thinking of ways to make the process go faster. The accuracy of the therapist's empathic understanding has often been emphasized, but more important is the therapist's interest in appreciating the world of the client and offering such understanding with the willingness to be corrected.

Recently the term 'cultural empathy' has been used to describe the ability of counsellors to understand and communicate the concerns of clients from their cultural perspective (Ridley, 1995; Ridley and Lingle, 1996; Ridley et al., 1994). Cultural empathy has two dimensions: understanding and communication. To understand a client involves really grasping their idiographic meaning which necessitates the counsellor not allowing any cultural bias to interfere with their perceptions. Communication involves the ability to demonstrate to the client that the counsellor has understood the client's idiographic experience. Also the counsellor ensures that he or she is using language that is meaningful to the client (Ridley, 1995).

A nomothetic perspective focuses on the distinguishing characteristics of a group to which a person belongs. Although this may be useful, the counsellor can overlook important aspects or characteristics about any individual within the group. In counselling the idiographic perspective avoids this particular problem. Ridley (1995) suggests that counsellors need to look at group norms as long as they do not necessarily expect to understand clients without first exploring their 'frame of reference'.

Each person is a member of overlapping groups with many roles and identities. To help the counsellor to understand the client, these will need to be explored. (Idiographic role maps can be used to plot these many roles, thereby helping the counsellor to imagine what it is like to be their client. See Chapter 8, p. 183 for a completed idiographic role map.)

The biopsychosocial model of mental health attempts to understand individuals by examining their interpersonal and social competence, physical health and psychological and emotional wellbeing. It is a health promotion model which focuses on changing behaviours to prevent or alleviate disease. Stressors, harmful behaviours/lifestyles and illnesses can be targeted for change (Krantz et al., 1985). Ridley (1995: 51) asserts that the biopsychosocial model is not 'inherently racist', assuming that it is applied correctly and therefore is suitable for 'treating minority clients'.

Counsellors employing a transtheoretical approach do not stick rigidly to any one therapeutic orientation or theory. Assuming that the counsellors are adequately skilled, they will select and use whatever approach or technique will help clients deal with their presenting problem(s) or current situation. Sue (1977) suggests that equitable therapy or treatment may be discriminatory whereas the idiographic approach supports the concept of differential but non-discriminatory treatment (Ridley, 1995).

Ridley (1995: 88–102) suggests twelve actions to help in counselling ethnic minority clients idiographically:

1 Develop cultural self-awareness.
2 Avoid value imposition.
3 Accept your naïvete as a multicultural counsellor.
4 Show cultural empathy.
5 Incorporate cultural considerations into counselling.
6 Do not stereotype.
7 Weigh and determine the relative importance of the client's primary cultural roles.
8 Do not blame the victim.
9 Remain flexible in your selection of interventions.
10 Examine your counselling theories for bias.
11 Build on the client's strengths.
12 Do not protect clients from emotional pain.

Although these actions are self-explanatory, it may be useful to look at a real example where the counsellor is adapting her approach and interventions to the needs of the client. In the following case study Gita Patel is counselling a young refugee attending The Refugee Project in London (Patel, 1997: 30):

One young man of 16 had arrived in this country [England] alone after he witnessed his mother's death. He was uncertain whether his father was dead or alive. At the start of the counselling he was very unsettled, could not acknowledge or talk about his mother, almost acting as though she were still alive. His main use of the session was to talk about his school and his home and his social life. The only reason he came to counselling was because of his terrible nightmares which he talked about in a distant way but he said coming to counselling stopped the nightmares, so he would continue to see me. At times it felt like he was avoiding any talk about his real issues and wanted to 'be positive' about everything.

After 6 months the client received his permanent stay in the UK, got into college and found his own place to live. The counselling sessions changed completely. He began to talk about his parents and the pain of losing them, finally able to grieve over his losses. The transient nature of his existence in Britain and his instability had made this young man well-defended against any real emotions as he was working hard to survive in an unpredictable situation. Once he knew his life was more stable, he could afford to let himself feel some of his anxieties and worries. An approach that did not see his issues in the context of his seeking asylum may have decided that he was not suitable for counselling or therapy.

It is possible that if Patel had focused on the client's 'real issues' at the beginning of counselling, the client would not have been able to cope with the high levels of anxiety that the issues may have triggered. This could have seriously affected his ability to cope in an already difficult situation as a refugee. Perhaps a sensible avoidance by the client at that time. In fact, I suspect that premature discussion of the 'real issues' would have increased the likelihood of attrition occurring and one of the client's major emotional supports would have been lost.

Jewel (1994), Palmer (1997), Ponterotto (1987) and Ridley (1984, 1995) recommend multimodal therapy as a flexible approach suitable for treating ethnic minority clients. The multimodal approach (Lazarus, 1989) rests on the assumption that unless seven discrete but interactive modalities are assessed, treatment will probably overlook significant concerns. The modalities are: Behaviour, Affective responses, Sensory reactions, Images, Cognitions, Interpersonal relationships and the need for Drugs and other biological interventions (Lazarus, 1995). Lazarus believes that the entire range of personality is comprised within these seven modalities. The first letters of each modality produce an easy to recall acronym, BASIC ID. The approach is technically eclectic as it uses techniques taken from many different psychological theories and systems, without necessarily being concerned with the validity of the theoretical principles that underpin the different approaches from which it takes its techniques. The techniques are applied systematically, based on data from client qualities, specific techniques and the counsellor's clinical skills (Palmer and Dryden, 1995). Multimodal counsellors 'are not confined to interventions that may be inappropriate or unhelpful. Instead, they can select interventions addressing the needs of clients in each modality' (Ridley, 1995: 97).

Counsellors wishing to take an idiographic approach will be placing high demands upon themselves as they will need a broad repertoire of therapeutic responses and have to pay close attention to the cultural cues sent and received by the client (see Ridley et al., 1997).

Multicultural training

Before we conclude the chapter it may be worth briefly considering issues around training. If we assume that the educative process should help trainees to become more effective as counsellors then we need to look at both training and the trainer. A number of interesting and challenging papers appeared in a special issue of *The Counseling Psychologist* on multicultural counselling training (see Kiselica, 1998; Lark and Paul, 1998; Ponterotto, 1998; Rooney et al., 1998). Their findings are worth considering and will be discussed below.

In the USA, compared to Britain, a greater emphasis is placed on multicultural training to help practitioners become more competent when working with ethnic minority individuals. In fact, 89 per cent of the doctoral programmes in counselling psychology included a course on multiculturalism (Ponterotto, in press – cited in Kiselica, 1998).

Kiselica (1998) asserts that the multicultural movement has developed several models of multicultural training (e.g. Pedersen, 1988; Sue and Sue, 1990). Kiselica suggests that the models were designed to promote (1998: 6):

(a) self-knowledge, especially an awareness of one's own cultural biases;
(b) knowledge about the status and cultures of different cultural groups;
(c) skills to make culturally appropriate interventions, including a readiness to use alternative counseling strategies that better match the cultures of clients than do traditional counseling strategies; and
(d) actual experiences in counseling culturally different clients.

Kiselica adds that these components are not sufficient in themselves to help trainees to process the 'intensely personal experiences and changes that are prompted by multicultural training and counseling' (p. 6). He suggests that due to the possible 'painful self-discovery' trainees should be provided with a highly supportive environment to enable the safe processing of these experiences.

Rooney and associates (1998) believed that Kiselica made a useful recommendation when he discussed the importance of instructors' self-disclosure regarding how they have been affected by racism. Rooney gave an example of how an instructor had started a multicultural course by stating, 'I am racist, I am sexist, I am homophobic; this is my inheritance for growing up in America.' His willingness to share his own experiences and struggles contributed to the group discussions. Lark and Paul (1998: 41) both viewed Kiselica's article as a 'significant contribution to the literature on multicultural training for White students in counseling psychology' and extended his article with stories illustrating the importance of multicultural mentoring by their doctoral chairs. Ponterotto (1998) concluded that their doctoral chairs were at a higher stage of racial and multicultural identity development than they were and served as a role model for identity development. However, Ponterotto questioned whether a higher level of development would generally be the norm when comparing faculty members with students. I would concur with this, as from my personal experience I have been aware of Directors of Training who believe that some ethnic minority students are 'difficult' when, in my opinion, it has been the trainer/supervisor who has been difficult and unaware of the different cultural issues involved.

So what are the characteristics of the ideal trainer? Ponterotto integrated the views of the other authors of the special edition and presented a general profile of multiculturally competent trainers and mentors (adapted 1998: 49–50):

1 are in, and have been in, the process of examining their own racial identity and developing a multicultural identity. I use Rooney et al.'s

(1998) eloquent depiction of a multiculturalist to define my perception of a multicultural identity: 'The multiculturalist adopts into his or her person a lifestyle that incorporates not only increased knowledge about new ideas and perspectives but also strives to experience new and diverse contacts with those who are culturally different' (p. 31).

2   realize that they have 'not arrived' in a place of complete multicultural identity and that their growth and role modeling is a lifelong process.

3   have got in touch with their own experiences of being oppressed on some level (e.g. as persons of color, gays or lesbians, women, persons with a disability, short or 'overweight' people, etc.).

4   understand the dynamics of oppression and have struggled and come to grips with (on some level) their participation in oppression and privilege (as Whites and men) or in internalized racism, sexism, or homophobia (as people of color, women, and gay and lesbian persons).

5   openly self-disclose and model (as did Kiselica and Lark and Paul's doctoral chair) their experiences, frustrations, and joys in developing multicultural awareness and insight.

6   share with students where they currently are with regard to their own identity development, what questions they are currently pondering, and what their present goals are for continuing multicultural development.

7   encourage and in fact lead students, both inside and outside the class-room, to explore their own racial, gender, and sexual orientation attitudes and serve as multicultural mentors to students and advisees.

8   give students 'permission' to make 'cultural mistakes' and to embarrass themselves with lack of knowledge or experience, and they encourage risk taking in terms of discussing and processing multicultural and self-identity issues.

9   facilitate an atmosphere in the class that is safe, respectful, and confi-dential, thus providing the anchor needed for risk taking and self-exploration.

10   are courageous and competent in dealing with strong emotions and help students process evocative reactions to multicultural issues.

11   can effectively deal with and process the more painful and frustrating aspects of training, for example, when working with non-response and/ or resistant trainees and providing necessary but perhaps unwelcome feedback to students.

12   have excellent group process skills, and can facilitate ongoing discussion, set limits, mediate interactions, intervene to support a student who has become vulnerable through revealing self-disclosure.

13   are supportive and empathic toward students and encourage students to reflect on, observe, and take responsibility for their attitudes and behaviour.

14   shape an environment characterized by inquiry, observation, and self-analysis rather than one characterized by blame and fault finding.

15   allow students multiple routes of expression – logs, journals, portfolios, diaries, small group discussions and so forth.

16   have a multicultural orientation toward life and the profession and role model this to students; display multicultural awareness not just in the multicultural counselling class, but in all course work, staff meetings, and so forth.

Of course, this list is the possible ideal to strive for and trainers and mentors should not become too despondent if they discover that, like their trainees, they are fallible human beings too. But perhaps a personal and shared recognition of their fallibility and the strong desire to continue their multicultural development is an appropriate goal.

Conclusion

This chapter has covered a range of issues focusing on the nature of counselling, effective counselling and effective counselling across cultures. As there was no simple formula or answer to the question 'What is effective counselling across cultures?', we considered a range of suggestions from a number of practitioners focusing on attitudes, assumptions and skills. One of the themes to arise from Ridley's discourse is that multimodal therapy is flexible in its choice of interventions and may be a suitable approach to use with ethnic minority clients (Ponterotto, 1987; Ridley, 1995). However, as the literature in Britain is somewhat underrepresented in this area of work, Chapter 8 highlights how I have applied multimodal therapy to ethnic minority clients and gives an in-depth account of this idiographic approach.

DISCUSSION ISSUES

What is effective counselling?

What assumptions do you hold that still need challenging?

In what way is cultural empathy different from empathy? Is it different?

What are the advantages and disadvantages of idiographic counselling?

References

BAC (British Association for Counselling) (1996) Code of Ethics and Practice for Counsellors, rev. edn. Rugby: BAC.

Barkham, M. (1996) 'Quantitative research on psychotherapeutic interventions: methodological issues and substantive findings across three research generations', in R. Woolfe and W. Dryden (eds), Handbook of Counselling Psychology. London: Sage.

Bergin, A.E. and Garfield, S.L. (eds) (1971) Handbook of Psychotherapy and Behavior Change: an Empirical Analysis. New York: Wiley.

Berman, J. (1979) 'Counselling skills used by black and white male and female counsellors', *Journal of Counseling Psychology*, 26: 81–4.

D'Ardenne, P. and Mahtani, A. (1989) *Transcultural Counselling in Action.* London: Sage.

Duckworth, D.H. and Charlesworth, A. (1988) 'The human side of disaster', *Policing*, 4: 194–210.

Draguns, J.G. (1981) 'Counseling across cultures: common themes and distinct approaches', in P.B. Pedersen, J. Draguns, W. Lonner and J. Trimble (eds), *Counseling Across Cultures*, rev. edn. Honolulu: University of Hawaii Press.

Draguns, J.G. (1996) 'Humanly universal and culturally distinctive: charting the course of cultural counselling', in P.B. Pedersen, J.G. Draguns, W.J. Lonner and J.E. Trimble (eds), *Counseling Across Cultures*, 4th edn. Thousand Oaks, CA: Sage.

Ellis, A. (1994) *Reason and Emotion in Psychotherapy.* New York: Carol Publishing.

Exum, H.A. and Lau, G.Y. (1988) 'Counseling style preference of Chinese college students', *Journal of Multicultural Counseling and Development*, 16: 84–92.

Feltham, C. (1995) *What is Counselling?* London: Sage.

Feltham, C. (ed.) (1997) *Which Psychotherapy?* London: Sage.

Feltham, C. and Dryden, W. (1993) *Dictionary of Counselling.* London: Whurr.

Fischer, A.R., Jome, L.M. and Atkinson, D.R. (1998) 'Reconceptualizing multicultural counseling: universal healing conditions in a culturally specific context', *The Counseling Psychologist*, 26 (4): 525–88.

Foa, E.B., Rothbaum, B.O., Riggs, D.S. and Murdock, T.B. (1991) 'Treatment of post-traumatic stress disorder in rape victims: a comparison between cognitive-behavioural procedures and counselling', *Journal of Consulting and Clinical Psychology*, 59: 715–23.

Higginbotham, H.N. and Tanaka-Matsumi, J. (1991) 'Cross-cultural application of behavior therapy', *Behaviour Change*, 8: 35–42.

Horvath, A.O. and Symonds, D.B. (1991) 'Relation between working alliance and outcome in psychotherapy', *Journal of Counseling Psychology*, 38: 139–49.

Ishiyama, F. (1986) 'Morita therapy', *Psychotherapy*, 23: 375–80.

Jewel, P. (1994) 'Multicultural counselling research: an evaluation with proposals for future research', *Counselling Psychology Review*, 9 (2): 17–34.

Kiselica, M.S. (1998) 'Preparing Anglos for the challenges and joys of multiculturalism', *The Counseling Psychologist*, 26 (1): 5–21.

Krantz, D.S., Grunberg, N.E. and Baum, A. (1985) 'Health psychology', *Annual Review of Psychology*, 36: 346–83.

Lago, C. and Thompson, J. (1996) *Race, Culture and Counselling.* Buckingham: Open University Press.

Lago, C. and Thompson, J. (1997) 'Counselling and race', in S. Palmer (ed.) and G. McMahon (assoc. ed.), *Handbook of Counselling.* London: Routledge.

Lark, J.S. and Paul, B.D. (1998) 'Beyond multicultural training: mentoring stories from two white American doctoral students', *The Counseling Psychologist*, 26 (1): 33–42.

Lazarus, A.A. (1989) *The Practice of Multimodal Therapy.* Baltimore, MD: The Johns Hopkins University Press.

Lazarus, A.A. (1995) 'Foreword', in S. Palmer and W. Dryden, *Counselling for Stress Problems.* London: Sage.

London, P. (1964) *The Modes and Morals of Psychotherapy.* New York: Holt, Rinehart & Winston.

Luborsky, L., Singer, B. and Luborsky, L. (1975) 'Comparative studies of psychotherapies: is it true that everyone has won and all must have prizes?', *Archives of General Psychiatry*, 32: 995–1008.

Marks, I. (1980) *Living with Fear*. New York: McGraw-Hill.

Marsella, A.J., Friedman, M.J., Gerrity, G.T. and Scurfield, R. (eds) (1996) *Ethnocultural Aspects of Post-Traumatic Stress Disorders: Issues, Research, and Clinical Applications*. Washington, DC: American Psychological Association.

Meador, B.D. and Rogers, C.R. (1984) 'Person-centered therapy', in R.J. Corsini (ed.), *Current Psychotherapies*, 3rd edn. Itasca, IL: F.E. Peacock.

Nadirshaw, Z. (1992) 'Therapeutic practice in multi-racial Britain', *Counselling Psychology Quarterly*, 5 (3): 257–61.

Noonan, E. (1983) *Counselling Young People*. London: Methuen.

Palmer, S. (1997) 'A multimodal approach with ethnic minorities'. Paper given at the First International Counselling Psychology Conference, held by the British Psychological Society, Division of Counselling Psychology, at Stratford-upon-Avon, 1997.

Palmer, S. and Dryden, W. (1995) *Counselling for Stress Problems*. London: Sage.

Patel, G. (1997) 'Nafsiyat Intercultural Therapy Centre: developing counselling and therapy for young refugees', *RACE Journal*, 14 (Autumn): 30–1.

Pedersen, P. (1988) *A Handbook for Developing Multicultural Awareness*. Alexandria, VA: American Association for Counseling and Development.

Ponterotto, J.G. (1987) 'Counseling Mexican Americans: a multimodal approach', *Journal of Counseling and Development*, 65 (6): 308–12.

Ponterotto, J.G. (1998) 'Charting a course for research in multicultural counseling training', *The Counseling Psychologist*, 26 (1): 43–68.

Raskin, N.J. (1974) *Studies of Psychotherapeutic Orientation: Ideology and Practice*. Research Monograph No. 1. Orlando, FL: American Academy of Psychotherapists.

Raskin, N.J. and Rogers, C.R. (1995) 'Person-centered therapy', in R.J. Corsini and D. Wedding (eds), *Current Psychotherapies*, 5th edn. Itasca, IL: F.E. Peacock.

Resick, P.A., Jordan, C.G., Girrelli, S.A., Hutter, C.K. and Marhoefer-Dvorack, S. (1988) 'A comparative outcome study of behavioural group therapy for sexual assault victims', *Behaviour Therapy*, 19: 385–401.

Richards, D.A. (1996) 'Traumatic stress at work: a public health model', in S. Palmer and W. Dryden (eds), *Stress Management and Counselling: Theory, Practice, Research and Methodology*. London: Cassell.

Richards, D.A., Lovell, K. and Marks, I.M. (1994) 'Post-traumatic stress disorder: evaluation of a behavioural treatment programme', *Journal of Traumatic Stress*, 7 (4): 669–80.

Ridley, C.R. (1984) 'Clinical treatment of the nondisclosing black client: a therapeutic paradox', *American Psychologist*, 39 (11): 1234–44.

Ridley, C.R. (1995) *Overcoming Unintentional Racism in Counseling and Therapy: a Practitioner's Guide to Intentional Intervention*. Thousand Oaks, CA: Sage.

Ridley, C.R. and Lingle, D.W. (1996) 'Cultural empathy in multicultural counselling: a multidimensional process model', in P.B. Pedersen, J.G. Draguns, W.J. Lonner and J.E. Trimble (eds), *Counseling Across Cultures*, 4th edn. Thousand Oaks, CA: Sage.

Ridley, C.R., Espelage, D.L. and Rubinstein, K.J. (1997) 'Course development in multicultural counseling', in D.B. Pope-Davis and H.L.K. Coleman (eds),

Multicultural Counseling Competencies: Assessment, Education and Training, and Supervision. Thousand Oaks, CA: Sage.

Ridley, C.R., Mendoza, D. and Kanitz, B. (1994) 'Multicultural training: reexamination, operationalization, and integration', *The Counseling Psychologist*, 22 (2): 227–89.

Rogers, C.R. (1951) *Client-centred Therapy*. London: Constable.

Rooney, S.C., Flores, L.Y. and Mercier, C.A. (1998) 'Making multicultural education effective for everyone', *The Counseling Psychologist*, 26 (1): 22–32.

Simpson, J.A. and Weiner, E.S.C. (eds) (1989) *Oxford English Dictionary*, 2nd edn. Oxford: Oxford University Press.

Smith, M.L., Glass, G. and Miller, T. (1980) *The Benefits of Psychotherapy*. Baltimore, MD: The Johns Hopkins University Press.

Stokes, P., Blore, D. and Meats, P. (1996) 'Behavioural psychotherapy by trainee psychotherapists: does it work and is it cost effective?', *Behavioural and Cognitive Psychotherapy*, 24 (2): 185–8.

Stubbs, J.P. and Bozarth, J.D. (1994) 'The dodo bird revisited: a qualitative study of psychotherapy efficacy research', *Journal of Applied and Preventive Psychology*, 3: 109–120.

Sue, D.W. (1977) 'Counseling the culturally different: a conceptual analysis', *Personnel and Guidance Journal*, 55 (7): 422–5.

Sue, D.W. and Sue, D. (1990) *Counseling the Culturally Different: Theory and Practice*, 2nd edn. New York: Wiley.

Szymanska, K. and Palmer, S. (1997) 'Counsellor–client exploitation', in S. Palmer (ed.) and G. McMahon (assoc. ed.), *Handbook of Counselling*. London: Routledge.

Ullmann, L.P. and Krasner, L. (1975) *A Psychological Approach to Abnormal Behavior*, 2nd edn. Englewood Cliffs, NJ: Prentice-Hall.

Walsh, R. (1995) 'Asian psychotherapies', in R.J. Corsini and D. Wedding, *Current Psychotherapies*. Itasca, IL: F.E. Peacock.

Webb Johnson, A. and Nadirshaw, Z. (1993) 'Good practice in transcultural counselling: an Asian perspective', *British Journal of Guidance and Counselling*, 21 (1): 20–9.

Westermeyer, J. (1995) 'Cross-cultural Care for PTSD: research, training, and service needs for the future', in G.S. Everly, Jr and J.M. Lating (eds), *Psychotraumatology*. New York: Plenum Press.

Wilson, G.T. (1985) 'Limitations of meta-analysis in the evaluation of the effects of psychological therapy', *Clinical Psychology Review*, 5: 35–47.

Wilson, G.T. and Rachman, S. (1983) 'Meta-analysis and evaluation of psychotherapy outcome: limitations and liabilities', *Journal of Consulting and Clinical Psychology*, 51: 54–64.

8

DEVELOPING AN INDIVIDUAL COUNSELLING PROGRAMME: A MULTIMODAL PERSPECTIVE

Stephen Palmer

Some years ago I became disillusioned with the 'apparent' inflexibility of the popular therapeutic approaches. I believed in many cases a major problem was that the client had to fit the therapy. Gradually, I became more convinced that the therapy should fit the client and not vice versa.

I asked a number of questions:

- Were counsellors actually rigidly sticking to their advocated model of counselling?
- Did behaviour therapists only pay attention to behaviour?
- Did person centred counsellors stay non-directive with all clients on all issues?
- Did psychodynamic counsellors only focus on the past to help clients deal with current problems?
- Did rational emotive behaviour therapists dispute clients' beliefs insensitively even when 'helping' a person overcome a recent bereavement?
- Did counsellors adapt their approach depending upon each client?
- Did counsellors automatically pay due attention to clients' social and cultural contexts?
- Did counsellors take into account the environmental constraints that affect many clients?
- Did counsellors demonstrate authority and expertise when necessary with particular client groups?
- Did counsellors undertake a thorough assessment of each client? If not, why not and what occasions did they choose not to?
- Did counsellors actually negotiate the counselling programme with the client?

These were just a few of the questions I asked. On talking to colleagues and students, it became apparent that many of them, but not all, in some circumstances applied their approach reasonably flexibly if they found that it was not working with a particular client. However, the published literature did not necessarily reflect their modifications. There were few guidelines on how to adapt their approach to individual clients. Others did not alter their approach; therefore, if a client asked for or blatantly needed, for example, a problem focused approach, the counsellor still adhered to his or her non-directive methods. In addition, I was not convinced that the Eurocentric models of counselling used by myself and others readily adjusted to the individuals from ethnic minority groups whom I saw for counselling.

I spent time researching different forms of counselling to find one which attempted to:

1   Fit the therapy to the client and *not* vice versa.
2   Was flexible, but still underpinned by research.
3   Took account of the wide range of clients I regularly saw in counselling, in particular in London.
4   Took a holistic approach to the person, including social, cultural and interpersonal aspects.
5   Could be applied to individual, family, group, community arenas.
6   Would include both directive and non-directive methods without being in conflict with the model.
7   Seriously considered each client as unique.

After some research, I began to realize that multimodal therapy might just match my requirements. I started to use the assessment template devised by Arnold Lazarus (1981, 1989) in which seven discrete but interactive dimensions or modalities are routinely examined. The modalities are: Behaviour, Affect, Sensation, Imagery, Cognition, Inter-personal, Drugs/biology. The helpful acronym BASIC ID arises from the first letter of each one (Palmer and Lazarus, 1995). Arnold Lazarus asserted that the entire human personality could be included within the seven modalities. I tentatively applied this approach to a range of different client groups and found it sufficiently flexible to use with most clients, including individuals from ethnic minorities suffering from stress (see Palmer, 1992; Palmer and Dryden, 1991). The approach certainly considered each client as unique with a combination of qualities and characteristics with a different story to tell. By focusing in on the clients' personal experiences the approach takes an idiographic perspective which has been argued as 'the most advantageous approach to counselling minority clients' (Ridley, 1995: 81). In addition, multi-modal therapy employs a systematic assessment procedure which over-comes the more usual wild and undisciplined approach of many eclectic practitioners.

The multimodal framework is underpinned by a broad social and cognitive learning theory (Bandura, 1969, 1977, 1986; Rotter, 1954), whilst also drawing on group and communications theory (Watzlawick et al., 1974) and general system theory (Bertalanffy, 1974; Buckley, 1967). However, as far as I was concerned, probably one of the most important aspects of the multimodal approach was that the therapist could choose not to apply these theories obsessively to each client (also see Jewel, 1994). Sometimes 'no therapy' is prescribed. For example, on one occasion, Arnold Lazarus advised a client to 'Use the money that you would have spent on therapy to have someone clean your house, have your hair done, and take tennis lessons. You will still have some money left over to meet friends for coffee or a snack. Be sure to engage in these activities on four different days each week, and after doing this for two months, please call and let us know if you are enjoying life more, if you feel less tense, less anxious and less depressed' (Lazarus, 1995: 327). Not surprisingly, this resulted in an amelioration of the client's problems.

In multimodal therapy the counsellor examines the interpersonal, sensory and biological dimensions which are often either underplayed or overlooked by some therapeutic approaches. I saw the interpersonal modality as one area which could focus on the social and cultural contexts that affect clients. Also, I had found that some clients would focus on one or two particular modalities such as the sensory and biological modalities when they were describing symptoms that reflected depression or anxiety. Therefore, the client's symptoms and problems could easily fit within the multimodal assessment procedure.

One of the aspects which caught my imagination was that 'multimodal therapy' *per se* does *not* exist, as multimodal counsellors, as technical eclectics, draw from as many other approaches or systems as necessary. To be accurate, there is a multimodal assessment format and a multimodal framework (see Lazarus, 1989, 1997; Palmer and Dryden, 1995). The comprehensive assessment and extensive framework enables counsellors to choose, with negotiation with their clients, the most appropriate counselling programme (see Palmer, 1997a). I vaguely hoped, possibly naïvely, that this would avoid any Eurocentric bias as I could adapt the approach to fit within a client's own belief and cultural system. Therefore, depending upon clients' cultural expectations, if they needed a 'listening ear' I would take a non-directive approach; if the client needed or expected a directive approach then this would also be offered. I would choose to demonstrate expertise if this was a major factor in building up trust.

A structured counselling programme would be available if this would put the client at his or her ease. In fact, Sue (1981) suggested that unstructured counselling can trigger anxiety in ethnic minority clients which could interfere with the counselling process.

From the multimodal perspective, a good relationship, a constructive working alliance and adequate rapport are usually necessary but often insufficient for effective therapy (Fay and Lazarus, 1993; Lazarus and Lazarus, 1991a). The counsellor–client relationship is considered as the soil that enables the techniques to take root. The experienced multi-modal counsellor hopes to offer a lot more by assessing and treating the client's BASIC ID, endeavouring to 'leave no stone (or modality) unturned' (Palmer, 1997a).

Assessment procedures

During the first counselling session the multimodal counsellor derives 14 determinations (based on the 12 determinations of Lazarus, 1987; adapted Palmer and Dryden, 1995: 19):

1 Are there signs of 'psychosis'?
2 Are there signs of organicity, organic pathology or any disturbed motor activity?
3 Is there evidence of depression, or suicidal or homicidal tendencies?
4 What are the persisting complaints and their main precipitating events?
5 What appear to be some important antecedent factors?
6 Who or what seems to be maintaining the client's overt and covert problems?
7 What does the client wish to derive from therapy or training?
8 Are there clear indications or contraindications for the adoption of a particular therapeutic style (for example, is there a preference for a directive or a non-directive style)?
9 Are there any indications as to whether it would be in the client's best interests to be seen individually, as part of a dyad, triad, family unit and/or in a group?
10 Can a mutually satisfying relationship ensue, or should the client be referred elsewhere?
11 Has the client previous experience of therapy or relevant training? If yes, what was the outcome: was it positive, negative or neutral experience and why?
12 Why is the client seeking therapy at this time and why not last week, last month or last year?
13 What are some of the client's positive attributes and strengths?
14 What are some of the client's resources (for example, cultural, social, family, employment, health care, religious, financial, education)?

In the beginning phase of counselling the multimodal counsellor is collecting information and looking for underlying themes and problems. Moreover, the counsellor determines whether a judicious referral may be necessary to a medical practitioner or psychiatrist if the client presents problems of an organic or psychiatric nature. A referral may also be recommended if a productive match between the counsellor and client is not possible. As more data is gathered it may become apparent that the client would benefit from, for example, group anxiety management, couples therapy or group therapy. This issue would then be discussed with the client. Counsellors working within a multicultural setting should expect that clients may bring members of the family or community elders to the first and sometimes subsequent counselling sessions. If the counsellors find this unacceptable then they will need to assess whether the true source of this problem rests with them and not necessarily their clients and their social and cultural milieu.

The multimodal counsellor usually examines each modality in a thorough, systematic manner. Nevertheless, the counsellor needs to take a flexible approach to avoid overwhelming the client with too many questions too soon. Some clients could easily feel interrogated or undermined by questions which could appear intrusive. However, it is worth noting that some clients would expect a counsellor to ask wide ranging questions about their problem and to them this would indicate that the counsellor was being professional and taking a real interest in their difficulties. If members of their family or community have accompanied them to the counselling session then the counsellor may also glean useful information from these additional sources. Obviously, the issue of confidentiality can be very challenging for inexperienced counsellors working in this type of context. The counsellor will need to have some clear idea on how this can be dealt with should these circumstances arise.

Some of the questions frequently used in assessment are those below (adapted Palmer, 1997b).

- **Behaviour**
  What would you like to start or stop doing?
  What behaviours are preventing you from being happy?
  What do you avoid doing?
  What skills would you like to develop further?
  When do you procrastinate?
  Are 'significant others' doing things you would like to do?
  What is preventing you from doing things that you want to do?
  How does your behaviour affect your relationships (or emotions, or images, or sensations, or thoughts, or health)?

- **Affect**
  What are your most predominant emotions?
  What appears to trigger these negative emotions (for example, particular images, cognitions, interpersonal conflicts)?
  What do you: cry/laugh about?
  What do you: get angry/anxious/depressed/sad/guilty/jealous/hurt/envious about?

How do your emotions affect your relationships (or behaviour, or images, or sensations, or thoughts, or health)?

- **Sensation**
  What unpleasant sensations do you suffer from, if any (for example, chronic pain, tremors, tics, tension, lightheadedness etc.)?
  What do you like to: taste/see/touch/hear/smell?
  What do you dislike: tasting/seeing/touching/hearing/smelling?
  How do you feel emotionally about any of your sensations?
  How do your sensations affect your relationships (or behaviour, or images, or thoughts, or health)?

- **Imagery**
  Can you describe your self-image (or body-image)?
  What images do you have that you like/dislike?
  When you have these negative images, do you feel less or more depressed (or anxious, or guilty etc.)?
  Describe any recurrent: daydreams/dreams/nightmares you may have?
  Describe any pleasant/unpleasant flashbacks (or memories) you may have?
  Can you picture any scene that you find relaxing?
  What do you picture yourself doing in the immediate future (and/or six months', and/or one year's, and/or two years', and/or five years', and/or ten years' etc. time)?
  In moments of solitude, do you picture any particular event from your past or have any fantasy about your future?
  How do these images affect your emotions (or behaviour, or thoughts, or sensations, or relationships, or health)?

- **Cognition**
  If you could use one word to describe yourself, what would it be?
  If you could use one word to describe your main current problem what would it be?
  What are your main musts, shoulds, oughts, have/got tos?
  What are your main wants, wishes, desires and preferences?
  What are your main values you believe are important?
  What are your main beliefs you believe are important?
  In key areas of your life what basic philosophy do you hold?
  What perfectionist beliefs do you hold?
  What are your major intellectual interests?
  What are the main cultural/societal beliefs you strongly hold?
  How do your thoughts and beliefs affect your emotions (or behaviour, or sensations, or relationships)?

- **Interpersonal**
  What expectations of others do you have?
  What expectations do you think they have of you?
  What expectations do you believe society has of you?
  What expectations do you believe your culture has of you?
  How assertive (or aggressive, or passive) are you?
  When are you most likely to be assertive (or aggressive, or passive)?
  What people are important in your life?
  What people have been important in your life?
  Who has been the most significant person in your life?
  How do the significant people in your life affect you (for example, emotionally, practically etc.)?
  How do you affect the significant people in your life?
  What social situations do you prefer (and/or avoid)?
  To what extent are you either highly gregarious or a loner?

- **Drugs/biology**
  What are your main concerns about your health?
  Are you on medication?
  Do you take drugs (and/or smoke)?
  Do you regularly use alternative/complementary medicine? (In what way to you benefit?)
  Have you ever undergone major surgery?
  How much alcohol do you drink in a week?
  Can you describe your typical diet?
  Have you tried to lose weight? (Were you successful?)
  What type of exercise do you do?
  Do you have any problems sleeping? If so, what problems?
  Are you interested in improving your general health?
  Do you believe that if you are taking regular exercise and eating a balanced diet you will feel better about yourself?
  Have significant others set you a good/poor health-related role model?

Selective use of these questions helps the multimodal counsellor to assess the client's entire BASIC ID. In many cases clients only need an in-depth assessment of key modalities in which they are experiencing difficulties, for example, a client suffering from a simple phobia. Most counsellors would first discuss the presenting problems or issues, for example, 'You said that your wife makes you feel guilty. How exactly does she do this?' 'When do your migraines appear to occur?' When focusing on a particular problem, the counsellor may rapidly traverse the entire BASIC ID to ensure that the relationship between each modality is noted, for example, when feeling anxious (Affect) the client may be demanding perfection from herself (Cognition) and in her mind's eye have a picture of herself failing to give a good presentation

(Imagery). In addition, a multimodal counsellor discerns which specific modalities are being discussed and which are being overlooked or avoided, otherwise useful information may be missed.

Ponterotto (1987) added another modality for investigation which he called 'Interaction with Oppressive Environment'. Assessment of this modality can be useful when counselling ethnic minority clients for a number of reasons:

(a)   the counsellor acknowledges the oppressive environment;
(b)   it helps the counsellor to understand the difficulties the client may be encountering on a regular basis;
(c)   depending upon the circumstances, the counsellor and client can develop a plan of action to deal with the oppressive environment.

An in-depth BASIC ID and life history assessment can be undertaken by asking the client to complete the Multimodal Life History Inventory (MLHI) as a homework assignment (Lazarus and Lazarus, 1991b). This 15-page questionnaire helps the counsellor and client to assess the problems and develop the counselling programme without too much time being taken up in the counselling session. However, it has to be used with caution as a reasonable grasp of English is required. Therefore its use may be contraindicated with clients suffering from dyslexia or those with a poor understanding of written English. In my experience many clients whose first language is not English do encounter diffi-culties. The MLHI asks many questions that may not be directly related to the client's presenting problem. Thus the counsellor needs to assess whether the client will find it unnecessarily intrusive and subsequently counterproductive to the therapeutic alliance.

I have found it useful to write up a problem list in the first or second counselling session. Initially, I normally listen to the client tell me his or her problems and difficulties. I then explain that we may find it helpful if I write up their problems on a whiteboard or flipchart focusing on seven specific areas which will hopefully ensure that I have not overlooked any relevant aspect. With their agreement I examine each BASIC ID modality in turn, usually starting with Behaviour.

Table 8.1 illustrates a Modality Profile which lists the problems of Paola. She is Italian, lives in England and is married to a white English male. They have two children who see themselves as English. She works part-time as a bank clerk. When writing up a Modality Profile with the client, I usually avoid using psychobabble, therefore 'Affect' becomes 'Emotion' or 'Feelings' and 'Cognitions' becomes 'Thoughts/beliefs'. The following dialogue illustrates how the subject can be introduced in the counselling session.

Stephen: We may find it useful if we write up on the whiteboard some of the problems you have just mentioned. In my experience, it would ensure that I have not overlooked any important issues that you want to cover. Is that okay?

Paola: It sounds a good idea.

Stephen: Perhaps we could just focus on a number of the behavioural problems you raised. [*Counsellor writes 'Behaviour' on the whiteboard.*] These are literally anything you actually 'do' or 'avoid doing'. You mentioned binge eating. [*Counsellor writes 'Binge eating' on the whiteboard.*] Any other behavioural problems?

Paola: My procrastination and poor time management go together! [*Laughs*] [*Counsellor writes them on the whiteboard.*]

Stephen: Any others?

Paola: No. I think these are my main problems.

Stephen: Let's now focus on the emotions you mentioned. [*Counsellor writes 'Emotion' on the whiteboard.*]

Paola: I get anxious at work about meeting important deadlines.

Stephen: I suppose if we were being really accurate you are anxious about *not* meeting important deadlines! Let's suppose that I could guarantee that you could reach your important deadline, would you be anxious then? [*Counsellor refining the presenting problem.*]

Paola: No. You're right. [*Counsellor writes redefined problem on the whiteboard.*]

The assessment continues in a similar manner covering all of the modalities. It is recommended that the counsellor leaves sufficient space on the whiteboard (or flipchart) for the inclusion of additional issues if they arise during the session. At the end of the counselling session, the counsellor writes up the Modality Profile and in the next session can provide the client with a photocopy.

Interaction between modalities

Notice the interaction between the different modalities on Paola's problem Modality Profile. For example, when she is anxious (Affect) about deadlines, she procrastinates and applies poor time management (Behaviour), she has palpitations and is shaky (Sensations), has images about making a fool of herself (Imagery), holds beliefs that she 'must perform well' (Cognitions), and possibly gives herself migraines (Drugs/biology). In the counselling sessions, the counsellor will probably show the client how the different modalities interact and thereby increase her levels of anxiety which then interferes with her ability to perform.

We will refer back to Paola's Modality Profile in the section on 'From assessment to an individual counselling programme'.

Role map

I recommend the use of a simple role map to remind the counsellor of the client's idiographic centre which focuses on his or her different cultural roles (see Ridley, 1995). Figure 8.1 is Paola's role map. It illustrates Paola's various roles which contribute to the total picture. Ridley

Table 8.1 *Paola's Modality Profile*

Modality	Problem
Behaviour	Binge eats Procrastinates Poor time management
Emotion (Affect)	Anxiety about not meeting important deadlines Shame after binge eating Depressed about missing her parents and family Feels guilty after speaking to mother
Sensations	Palpitations and shaky when anxious Empty feeling before binge eating
Imagery	Images of making a fool of herself at work Images of losing control
Thoughts/beliefs (Cognitions)	I must perform well I must not let my parents down otherwise I'm worthless We should be together as a family I can't stand difficulties
Interpersonal	Rows with husband and children Passive with work colleagues and boss Allows mother to manipulate her
Drugs/biology	High blood pressure Migraines when under pressure

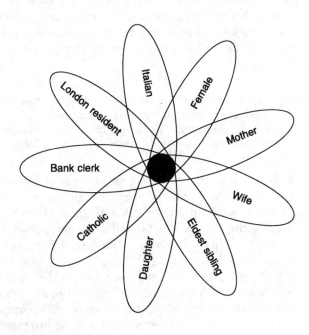

Figure 8.1 *Paola's role map*

(1995) suggests that counsellors should explore the client's unique frame of reference based upon conjoint membership in these roles. He suggests that to obtain an insightful look at the client, counsellors need to focus their attention on the centre of the diagram – in Paola's case her uniqueness as a person having nine cultural roles. Ridley (1995) suggests that viewed from this perspective, the client's idiographic experience – in our example, Paola – sets her apart from every other Italian, female, mother, wife, daughter, eldest sibling, Catholic, bank clerk and resident of London, England. Every role should not be ignored as each contributes to understanding Paola.

The relationship and therapeutic approach

Even before the initial counselling or assessment session, if at all possible, it is important to put clients at their ease. When they make the first contact with the counselling centre they are sent information about the counsellor, the approach and any fees. If they are keen to read about the approach or techniques in depth then we may recommend suitable bibliotherapy (e.g. Palmer and Strickland, 1996). Also we offer them the opportunity to read a checklist covering relevant issues that they may wish to consider about counselling, such as discussing their goals and expectations of therapy with their counsellor (see Box 1).

In the early counselling sessions the counsellor closely observes the client's reaction to his or her strategies, interventions and comments. This helps the counsellor to determine the most appropriate interpersonal approach to take. This was summarized by Palmer and Dryden as below (1995: 24).

1   Monitor the client's response to directive and non-directive interventions.
2   Discover whether the client responds well to humour.
3   Decide whether the client prefers a formal or informal relationship.
4   Establish how the client responds to counsellor self-disclosure.

It is hypothesized that the matching of counsellor behaviour with client expectations will aid the development of a good therapeutic alliance and help to build up trust. This may have other benefits too, such as decreasing the rate of attrition (that is, the premature termination of therapy). Arnold Lazarus describes the counsellor who attempts to decide the relationship of choice as an 'authentic chameleon' (Lazarus, 1993). The counsellor shows different aspects of him- or herself to the client that helps the relationship, such as the use of humour, being formal or informal, willing to share experiences (if appropriate) as well as the use of directive and non-directive counselling interventions and skills.

Box 1

Issues for the client to consider in counselling or psychotherapy

1 Here is a list of topics or questions you may wish to raise when attending your first counselling (assessment) session:

(a) Check that your counsellor has relevant qualifications and experience in the field of counselling/psychotherapy.

(b) Ask about the type of approach the counsellor uses, and how it relates to your problem.

(c) Ask if the counsellor is in supervision (most professional bodies consider supervision to be mandatory; see footnote).

(d) Ask whether the counsellor or the counselling agency is a member of a professional body and abides by a code of ethics. If possible, obtain a copy of the code.

(e) Discuss your goals/expectations of counselling.

(f) Ask about the fees if any (if your income is low, check if the counsellor operates on a sliding scale) and discuss the frequency and estimated duration of counselling.

(g) Arrange regular review sessions with your counsellor to evaluate your progress.

(h) Do not enter into a long term counselling contract unless you are satisfied that this is necessary and beneficial to you.

If you do not have a chance to discuss the above points during your first session discuss them at the next possible opportunity.

General Issues

2 Counsellor self-disclosure can sometimes be therapeutically useful. However, if the sessions are dominated by the counsellor discussing his/her own problems at length, raise this issue in the counselling session.

3 If at any time you feel discounted, undermined or manipulated within the session, discuss this with the counsellor. It is easier to resolve issues as and when they arise.

4 Do not accept significant gifts from your counsellor. This does not apply to relevant therapeutic material.

5 Do not accept social invitations from your counsellor. For example, dining in a restaurant or going for a drink. However, this does not apply to relevant therapeutic assignments such as being accompanied by your counsellor into a situation to help you overcome a phobia.

6 If your counsellor proposes a change in venue for the counselling sessions without good reason do not agree. For example, from a centre to the counsellor's own home.

7 Research has shown that it is not beneficial for clients to have sexual contact with their counsellor. Professional bodies in the field of counselling and psychotherapy consider that it is unethical for counsellors or therapists to engage in sexual activity with current clients.

8 If you have any doubts about the counselling you are receiving then discuss them with your counsellor. If you are still uncertain, seek advice, perhaps from a friend, your doctor, your local Citizens Advice Bureau, the professional body your counsellor belongs to or the counselling agency that may employ your counsellor.

9 You have the right to terminate counselling whenever you choose.

Footnote: Counselling supervision is a formal arrangement where counsellors discuss their counselling in a confidential setting on a regular basis with one or more professional counsellors.

Source: adapted from Palmer and Szymanska, 1994

Even the appearance of the counsellor may also be of vital importance in relationship building. Clients of different age groups from diverse social and cultural backgrounds have different expectations of helping professionals. If I may possibly overgeneralize just for a moment, in my experience as a male counsellor, the referrals I have from industry tend to expect me to be dressed in a suit or a jacket. However, this more formal clothing may prove anxiety-provoking for many adolescents who associate them with authority figures (Palmer and Dryden, 1995). The latter may be put at their ease more readily by the counsellor wearing informal attire.

In addition to focusing on the seven BASIC ID modalities, the Multimodal Life History Inventory explores the client's expectations of counselling which helps to guide the counsellor in matching the counselling programme and his or her interpersonal approach with these expectations. For example, one of my clients', Alpana, responded to the 'Expectations Regarding Therapy' section of the MLHI in the following manner:

Q: In a few words, what do you think therapy is all about?
A: Receiving guidance and advice about my problems.
Q: How long do you think your therapy should last?
A: As short as possible.
Q: What personal qualities do you think the ideal therapist should possess?
A: Absolutely trustworthy and able to keep confidences.

This suggested that she would prefer an active–directive approach focusing on her particular problems. I thought that it would be a good idea to confirm this during the counselling session. Also I was concerned that she thought that I could give her 'advice'. We explored these two issues:

Stephen: Am I right in thinking that you would like us to remain problem focused and arrive at a number of possible solutions to dealing with your problems?
Alpana: Yes. I would be very pleased if you could tell me how to deal with my problems.
Stephen: I'm not sure whether it's a good idea for me to tell you exactly how to deal with your problems as it may not help you in the future to stand on your own two feet. But I can help you to explore different options and choose which solution may have the most beneficial outcome. With my help we can literally consider their 'pros' and 'cons' and arrive at a possible answer.
Alpana: As long as we can come up with some options, that's fine with me.

I then went on to discuss the length of counselling:

Stephen: Generally I find that if we just focus on the type of problems you have presented, about six sessions will be sufficient. In session six we could review how you are progressing and if you need any more sessions we could extend your counselling. Does that sound acceptable?

Alpana: Yes. I hope that I don't really need six sessions.

Stephen: If you find that the problems have been resolved, of course, we could finish counselling even before the sixth session. That would be fine with me.

Triseliotis (1986: 213) observed that clients from China and the Indian subcontinent prefer 'a logical, rational, structured counselling approach'. In my experience, this could also include receiving advice. However, it is important not to make assumptions like these as such overgeneralizations may not apply to the client you are meeting for the first time whatever his or her social or cultural background. When taking an idiographic approach it is recommended that you clarify these issues with the client and modify your approach accordingly. Discussing the preferred approach, in particular, 'advice' with Alpana was potentially a risk that could have led to attrition occurring. As this was her second session I had some idea of her views. If I had predicted that she would have responded negatively to my reframing of her need for 'advice' I would have avoided the issue in this session and perhaps seriously considered using 'directives'. It is worth considering that Alpana could have perceived me as unskilled if I did not offer appropriate 'advice' or take an authoritative approach.

From assessment to an individual counselling programme

The 'main hypothesized ingredients of change' in multimodal counselling are as follows (adapted Dryden and Lazarus, 1991: 132).

- Behaviour: positive reinforcement; negative reinforcement; penalties; rewards; counter-conditioning; extinction.
- Affect: admitting and accepting feelings; abreaction.
- Sensation: tension release; sensory pleasuring.
- Imagery: coping images; changes in self-image.
- Cognition: greater awareness; cognitive restructuring.
- Interpersonal: non-judgemental acceptance; modelling; dispersing unhealthy collusions.
- Drugs/biology: better nutrition and exercise; substance abuse cessation; psychotropic medication when indicated.

Table 8.2 summarizes the most commonly used techniques and interventions in multimodal counselling (Palmer, 1997a: 58). These techniques are selected by negotiation with the client. It is important to remember that the counsellor attempts to fit the therapy to the client and not vice versa. Therefore, if an Asian or Chinese client believes that meditation, massage, yoga or herbal medicine may help him or her to deal with stress, then a judicious referral to a qualified practitioner

Table 8.2 *Frequently used techniques/interventions in multimodal therapy and training*

Modality	Techniques/interventions
Behaviour	Behaviour rehearsal
	Empty chair
	Exposure programme
	Fixed role therapy
	Modelling
	Paradoxical intention
	Psychodrama
	Reinforcement programmes
	Response prevention/cost
	Risk-taking exercises
	Self-monitoring and recording
	Stimulus control
	Shame-attacking
Affect	Anger expression
	Anxiety/anger management
	Feeling-identification
Sensation	Biofeedback
	Hypnosis
	Meditation
	Relaxation training
	Sensate focus training
	Threshold training
Imagery	Anti-future shock imagery
	Associated imagery
	Aversive imagery
	Coping imagery
	Implosion and imaginal exposure
	Positive imagery
	Rational emotive imagery
	Time projection imagery
Cognition	Bibliotherapy
	Challenging faulty inferences
	Cognitive rehearsal
	Coping statements
	Correcting misconceptions
	Disputing self-defeating beliefs/schema
	Focusing
	Positive self-statements
	Problem solving training
	Rational proselytizing
	Self-acceptance training
	Thought stopping
Interpersonal	Assertion training
	Communication training
	Contracting
	Fixed role therapy
	Friendship/intimacy training
	Graded sexual approaches

continued

Table 8.2   (*cont.*)

Modality	Techniques/interventions
	Paradoxical intentions
	Role play
	Social skills training
Drugs/biology	Alcohol reduction programme
	Life style changes, e.g. exercise, nutrition etc.
	Referral to physicians or other specialists
	Stop smoking programme
	Weight reduction and maintenance programme

Source: Adapted from Palmer (1996).

would be seriously considered as a primary intervention or as an adjunct to counselling. Therefore this would not necessarily prevent the multimodal counsellor from still seeing the client.

For further in-depth information about these techniques, including indications and contraindications, I refer the reader to *Counselling for Stress Problems* (Palmer and Dryden, 1995).

Completed Modality Profile

In an earlier section I illustrated Paola's problem Modality Profile (see Table 8.1). In fact it was incomplete, as it only showed her problem list broken down into the BASIC ID modalities. This illustrated the assessment stage. The next stage is to move from assessment to developing the counselling programme. In the counselling session the full Modality Profile would be developed with the cooperation of the client. It would include strategies, techniques and interventions that the client was willing to use. Although the counsellor may demonstrate his or her expertise by suggesting useful interventions and explaining the rationale for their application, clients will often have their own ideas which could be included on the profile. In my clinical experience clients will frequently recommend coping strategies such as time management, exercise, assertiveness training, massage, improved nutrition, yoga, hypnosis and relaxation to help them deal with stress. Lazarus (1973) discovered that if client expectations are met, then this will usually lead to a better outcome. Surprisingly, he demonstrated that if clients believe that hypnosis will help, then this method was more effective than another technique named 'relaxation' even though the latter was still essentially the same hypnosis intervention. I have also reported a similar experience with a client (see Palmer, 1993; Palmer and Dryden, 1995: 28–9).

I have found it useful if clients have undertaken relevant bibliotherapy, which includes how different techniques can be applied. The self-help book *Stress Management: a Quick Guide* (Palmer and Strickland, 1996) describes in clear and uncomplicated English the most frequently used techniques.

Table 8.3 is Paola's full Modality Profile. Once the Modality Profile is devised the client and counsellor mutually agree which intervention to use first. Notice that in Paola's Modality Profile, relaxation training occurs three times. This would be a relatively easy place to start the counselling programme as Paola would be able to listen to a relaxation tape daily. Another initial assignment could be to read a section on thinking errors and thinking skills in a self-help book such as *Stress Management: a Quick Guide* (Palmer and Strickland, 1996). She could then keep a note in her diary of the thinking errors she makes in the course of the day, with a special focus on her interactions with her family and her work colleagues.

It is usually a good idea to review therapeutic progress every five or six sessions. The Modality Profile aids this review and is updated as problems are overcome and added to as new information is obtained. Near the end of the counselling programme, the counselling sessions are spaced out to encourage the client to deal with problems as they arise on their own, with the goal of reaching total independence of the counsellor. Clients may return for 'booster sessions' after a longer period of time, such as 6–12 months. This helps to reduce the idea that they have been abandoned, which can occur in a minority of cases.

Second-order Modality Profile

A Second-order Modality Profile assessment is undertaken if a client is experiencing difficulty overcoming a particular problem and the selected strategies applied have been unsuccessful. For example, if Paola continued to experience high blood pressure then the new profile would focus specifically on all issues possibly connected with high blood pressure, for example, rows, cognitions that exacerbate stress such as 'I must perform well' and cultural beliefs about family solidarity etc. In cases where a client has a medical condition it is important for the counsellor to liaise with the client's physician. This will need the client's formal permission. I have found it useful to send a copy of an article that explains the approach I'm using to the physician. This helps him or her to understand the therapy and often the physician is surprised that a comprehensive approach is being suggested. With medical conditions it is imperative that the physician agrees with the programme in case of later complications. If stress-reducing techniques such as relaxation, meditation or cognitive reframing are successful, often the level of medication for various disorders needs to be decreased. Again this will need the physician's approval and guidance.

Table 8.4 illustrates a Second-order Modality Profile for a client with high blood pressure (Palmer and Dryden, 1995: 164). This profile illustrates how an assessment across all of the modalities is necessary to develop a comprehensive intervention strategy.

Table 8.3 *Paola's full Modality Profile*

Modality	Problem	Counselling programme
Behaviour	Binge eats	Stimulus control; find triggers
	Procrastinates	Dispute self-defeating thinking
	Poor time management	Time management and assertion skills bibliotherapy
Emotion	Anxiety about not meeting important deadlines	Anxiety management; dispute beliefs; rational coping statements
	Shame after binge eating	Self-acceptance training
	Depressed about missing her parents and family	Counsellor support and rational discussion
	Feels guilty after speaking to mother	Self-acceptance training and coping statements
Sensations	Palpitations and shaky when anxious	Relaxation training; positive imagery
	Empty feeling before binge eating	Focus on self-defeating beliefs; assess for low frustration tolerance
Imagery	Images of making a fool of herself at work	Coping imagery; time projection imagery
	Images of losing control	Coping imagery
Thoughts/ beliefs	I must perform well	Dispute self-defeating beliefs
	I must not let my parents down otherwise I'm worthless	Develop forceful coping statements; self-acceptance training
	We should be together as a family	Examine belief; bibliotherapy
	I can't stand difficulties	Increase tolerance levels to difficulties
Interpersonal	Rows with husband and children	Time-limited communication; dispute unhelpful beliefs; coping imagery
	Passive with work colleagues and boss	Assertiveness training
	Allows mother to manipulate her	Assertiveness and communications skills; focus on underlying beliefs which trigger her guilt and depression
Drugs/ biology	High blood pressure	Liaise with physician; possible medication; relaxation training; bibliotherapy
	Migraines when under pressure	Dispute self-defeating beliefs; relaxation training; biofeedback

Other strategies

Bridging

Many clients have preferred modalities which they may use to communicate with the counsellor, for example talking about pictures or images. Multimodal counsellors will intentionally use a 'bridging' procedure to initially 'key into' the client's preferred modality, before gently

Table 8.4   *Second-order BASIC ID for an individual with high blood pressure*

Modality	Problem	Counselling programme
Behaviour	Type A behaviour	Behavioural education, e.g. undertake one task at a time; leave more time to do tasks; only take on tasks within job remit; leave time for relaxation. Dispute self-defeating beliefs which are responsible for hostility and 'hurry up' behaviours
	Smokes 30 cigarettes a day	Stop-smoking programme
Affect	Feels very angry when work targets not achieved	Anger management
Sensation	Physically tense	Relaxation exercises and biofeedback, e.g. biodots
Imagery	Picture of self failing at tasks	Coping imagery
Cognition	I/others must perform well; if I fail to reach my targets then I am a failure and I am worthless and deserve to be punished	Disputation of stress-inducing beliefs Coping statements on cards
Interpersonal	Aggressive with staff	Assertiveness training
	Acts impatiently with staff	Dispute belief that 'I can't stand being kept waiting'
Drugs/ biology	High blood pressure	Blood pressure reduction programme; drug treatment if necessary. Liaise with medical specialist and general practitioner
	Poor diet	Nutritional education, e.g. decrease intake of saturated fats, consume fish three times a week, decrease salt intake, increase fibre intake, eat lean meat
	Drinks 32 units of alcohol a week	Reduce alcohol intake to 12 units a week
	2 stone overweight	Weight reduction and graded exercise programme

Source: Adapted from Palmer and Dryden (1995).

exploring a modality that the client may be intentionally or unintentionally avoiding, such as the affect/emotions (Lazarus, 1987). Bridging is undertaken if the avoided modality may be clinically useful to examine.

Tracking

'Tracking' is another procedure often used in multimodal therapy in which the 'firing order' of the different modalities is noted for a specific problem (Lazarus, 1981, 1989). For example, one client first had the cognition, 'I can't stand giving presentations', closely followed by an image of an audience laughing at him, and then physical sensations of anxiety. This would occur within 5 seconds and the client would then behaviourally attempt to escape from the situation by refusing the invitation to speak at a conference. This was a C–I–S–B sequence. The client was instructed to match the firing order of the modalities with a C–I–S–B sequence of interventions, thus ensuring a quick reduction of the stress response.

Structural Profiles

In longer term therapy, Structural Profiles are drawn to elicit additional clinical information (see Figure 8.2; Palmer, 1997b: 155). This is obtained by either asking clients to complete page 14 of the Multimodal Life History Inventory or by asking them to rate subjectively, on a score of 1–7, how they perceive themselves in relation to the different modalities. Typical assessment questions are (adapted Lazarus and Lazarus, 1991b):

- Behaviour: How much of a doer are you?
- Affect: How emotional are you?
- Sensation: How 'tuned in' are you to your bodily sensations?
- Imagery: How much are you into mental images or pictures?
- Cognition: How much of a 'thinker' are you?
- Interpersonal: How much of a 'social being' are you?
- Drugs/biology: To what extent are you health conscious?

If we consider the example in Figure 8.2, Kate perceives herself as a 'thinker' and a 'doer' as she rated herself at 7 on both the cognitive and behaviour modalities respectively. Her low interpersonal score of 2 was due to her perceiving herself as a 'loner'. Once the Structural Profile had been discussed with Kate, then a 'desired' Structural Profile was developed. Kate was asked in what way she would like to modify her profile during the course of therapy (Palmer, 1997b: 154–5):

Counsellor: Kate, now you have seen your profile [pointing to the profile], it may be a good idea to consider each of the seven areas again and decide whether you would like to change them during the course of therapy. What do you think?

Kate: Yeah. Sounds good.

Counsellor: Let's start at the biological factors. You have rated yourself at 3. Is this an area for change?

Kate: You bet. I really want to start taking regular exercise and stop smoking. In fact I know I should eat more fruit too!

Counsellor: What would be your desired score [points to the 3 on the Structural Profile bar chart]?

Kate: I reckon I could achieve 6. I reckon 7 will be unrealistic.

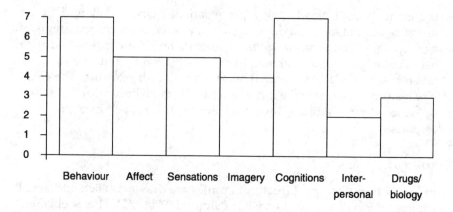

Figure 8.2   *Kate's structural profile*

Counsellor: Can we make this more specific. You would like to stop smoking. Correct?

Kate: Yes.

Counsellor: What exercise do you want to do and how often?

Kate: I want to work-out at the gym three times a week. My flatmate is already going. I can join her.

Counsellor: You mentioned fruit. What about us looking at your diet and seeing how it could be improved. I've got a number of guides and leaflets on this subject that may help.

Kate: Sounds fine.

This procedure is repeated for each modality and the new desired scores are transferred to a Desired Structural Profile (see Figure 8.3). The counsellor ensures that a record of each specific goal or target is noted. If there is sufficient room then each goal is written directly onto the profile or if not, written in the client's records. The client is given a copy for his or her own records and as a reminder of what he or she would like to achieve during counselling. This helps to keep clients working towards their goals.

In my clinical experience in many cases clients are keen to improve their Drugs/biology modality as they believe that if they are physically feeling fine then they will feel emotionally better and be more able to deal with other problems. However, the other modality scores do not necessarily reflect an area that needs change if they are either low or high. For example, a client may be happy being 'tuned in' to her bodily sensations (for example, sensory pleasures such as food and sex) and having a subjective score of 7, whereas another client may decide that a score of 7 indicates that she is too focused on negative bodily sensations (for example, palpitations) and would strongly prefer a score of 3. In Kate's case, in discussion with her counsellor, she soon realized that

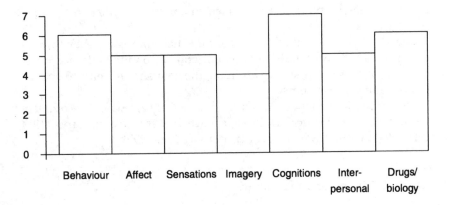

Figure 8.3   *Kate's desired structural profile*

being a loner (interpersonal score of 2) did not help her deal with occupational stress as she avoided seeking social support when facing major workplace problems. She decided that this would be a good area for improvement (Palmer, 1997b: 156). However, many other clients prefer to keep a low interpersonal score. It is important to remember that these are subjective scores that can help the counselling process and are usually unique to each client, especially in relation to the desired goals.

If the counsellor has contracted with the client regularly to review his or her therapeutic progress, then comparing the actual Structural Profile and the desired Structural Profile can form part of that review. At this stage clients will often want to revise their desired Structural Profiles. Sometimes they realize that their targets or goals were set too low. As they achieve success in specific areas, with increased confidence, they then want to deal with more difficult issues such as binge eating or being assertive with their partner.

Counsellors who undertake marital or couples counselling have found that using Structural Profiles can provide valuable information (Lazarus, 1989). In addition, the profiles can be compared in the session and used to highlight difficulties that a couple may be experiencing. For example, if one partner has a low behaviour rating, while the other partner has a high rating, they may perceive each other as a 'headless chicken' and 'couch potato' respectively. This may lead to conflict and resentment. The counsellor can compare and contrast the different profiles and discuss them with both partners (see Palmer and Dryden, 1995).

Herman (1992, 1994; Herman et al., 1995) has undertaken extensive research into Structural Profiles. He has found that when counsellors and clients have wide differences on their Structural Profiles, therapeutic outcomes are unfavourably affected (Herman, 1991). This indicates that it could be used to match client to counsellor in a counselling centre.

Further research could be undertaken to confirm whether this method could work cross-culturally.

The strategies described in this section help the counsellor to tailor the approach to each individual client and unconditionally accept the uniqueness of each person. In addition, they enhance the effectiveness of a counselling programme.

For further information on Multimodal Therapy, I would recommend the literature that describes the approach in depth (see Lazarus, 1981, 1989, 1997; Palmer, 1997b; Palmer and Dryden, 1995).

'Overcoming apparent resistance'

Multimodal counsellors are trained not to assume immediately that clients are 'resistant' if they do not wish to undertake an agreed task, such as a role play exercise. Counsellors are encouraged to understand why the client is reluctant to do the task and examine whether they are expecting too much too soon and/or whether or not they have inadequately prepared the client. For example, an in vivo exposure programme may have been recommended by the counsellor to help the client deal with agoraphobia. However, this may prove to be an overwhelming exercise for the client as it can trigger very high levels of anxiety. The client could have been more adequately prepared to undertake an exposure programme after first practising coping imagery and a breathing technique. The motto for the counsellor to remember would be 'challenging but not overwhelming' (see Palmer and Dryden, 1995). By preparing the client in this systematic manner, he or she is more likely to undertake the assignment and attrition is less likely to occur.

Strategies and techniques such as Second-order Modality Profiles, Bridging and Tracking can all be used to overcome apparent resistance.

To reduce the rate of attrition and aid the therapeutic alliance, multimodal counsellors are encouraged to consider five key factors when deciding how to respond and what techniques to use with each unique client in therapy (see Palmer, 1997a,c):

1   Client qualities.
2   Counsellor qualities.
3   Counsellor skills.
4   Therapeutic alliance.
5   Technique specificity.

These five interacting factors may determine the therapeutic relationship and the choice of interventions. Careful consideration should be given to each of them during the course of therapy. The interaction of the client–counsellor qualities may determine therapeutic outcome. For example, if the client is passive, slow talking and takes time to think ideas through, whereas the counsellor is very active–directive, fast talking and quick thinking, the latter's approach will discourage the client from speaking and talking in the session. As the client retreats into his or her proverbial shell, the counsellor may respond by becoming more active–directive, which in turn encourages the client to become even more passive. In this example, it would be preferable for the counsellor to adjust his or her interpersonal style and become less active–directive to encourage the client to participate in the counselling process. Another example would be that a client is likely to realize quickly that a counsellor is prejudiced and intolerant of others' opinions. The client is likely to start feeling rejected if his or her comments are dismissed. This could lead to unnecessary attrition.

The counsellor may have knowledge of a wide range of techniques, interventions and skills but be unable to demonstrate or apply them in therapy. Therefore the strategies selected for a client's counselling programme may also be determined (and limited) by the counsellor's therapeutic skills or skills deficits. However, with appropriate training and supervision these types of problems may be overcome.

The therapeutic alliance is underpinned by many different factors. Some clients expect counsellors to demonstrate their expertise whereas others may just want a listening ear. Some clients want a clear explanation of how the therapy works and can be applied to their problems. Others want support through a difficult period. It is the counsellor's responsibility to help build up and maintain a satisfactory therapeutic alliance by adjusting his or her interpersonal style and interventions pitched at the correct level for a particular client. This is often by a process of trial and error, although as discussed previously, counsellors can ask their clients what exactly they expect from the counsellor and the therapy. The building up of trust is not always easy and the counsellor may have to demonstrate certain behaviours, skills and attitudes to aid this process. If the counsellor asks the client to undertake overwhelming assignments, this could very easily damage a good working relationship.

When attempting to select the correct intervention or technique for a specific problem, guided by the latest research findings, the counsellor needs to ask a number of reflective questions:

1 Have I assessed the client/problem correctly? Have I identified the antecedents or maintaining factors correctly?
2 Does the research indicate that this is the correct intervention/technique for this particular problem or disorder?
3 Even if the intervention/technique has been shown to be the most effective one to use for this specific problem, will it trigger too high a level of anxiety for this client? If it does, should I use a less anxiety provoking intervention/technique?

4 Does the client understand the rationale for this intervention/ technique?
5 Does the client trust my therapeutic judgement?
6 Am I sufficiently skilled to undertake or demonstrate this intervention, technique or skill? If not, should I choose a different method, obtain more training, seek relevant supervision, or refer the client elsewhere?
7 Am I expecting too much change, too soon?
8 Would this intervention/technique suit the client's personality?
9 Does this intervention/technique help the client to achieve his or her goals?
10 Are there any indications or contraindications for the use of this intervention/technique with this particular client?

If a therapeutic impasse appears to have been reached, then the counsellor can ask him or herself the following questions in addition to the previous questions (see Palmer and Dryden, 1995: 39):

11 Is there a client–counsellor mismatch? Is a referral necessary?
12 Is the client ashamed to express emotion or disclose personal information about him/herself or their family in the counselling session?
13 Is the client avoiding certain issues because they are so painful even to think about or discuss?
14 Is a significant other(s) interfering or undermining the client's goals of counselling?
15 Was the homework assignment perceived by the client as relevant?
16 If the client does not wish to undertake the homework assignment what is holding him/her back or preventing him/her from doing it? Can this barrier be circumnavigated?
17 If the client improves and overcomes his/her target problems would this detrimentally affect relationships with significant others as perceived by the client?
18 Does the client trust me? Do I need to work on strengthening the therapeutic alliance before we tackle more difficult issues?

These issues can also be considered during supervision when difficulties arise.

When counselling cross-culturally, Ridley (1995: 135–6) suggests that counsellors should not react defensively to so-called 'resistant' clients. He gives a number of useful examples of counsellor defensiveness with minority clients which I would recommend that counsellors could monitor in themselves.

- Talking excessively about racial issues.
- Avoiding discussions about racial issues.

- Making treatment expectations of minority clients unnecessarily easy.
- Making treatment expectations of minority clients unnecessarily stringent.
- Using minority expressions and idioms inappropriately to gain acceptance.
- Emphasizing one's friendship with other members of the client's race.
- Claiming one's impartiality.
- Overemphasizing one's support of minority causes.
- Not examining one's reactions to client resistance.
- Failing to channel client resistance into an asset rather than a liability.

If counsellors record their counselling sessions for supervision purposes they and their supervisors are in a good position carefully to examine their responses to so-called 'resistant' clients.

Conclusion

Multimodal counselling is an approach that takes Paul's (1967: 11) mandate very seriously: 'What treatment, by whom, is most effective for this individual with that specific problem and under which set of circumstances?'. But, in addition to applying the strategies or techniques of choice, as discussed earlier, the multimodal counsellor also attempts to be an authentic chameleon who also considers the relationships of choice (Lazarus, 1993). As I have stated elsewhere (Palmer, 1997b: 164):

> In the first therapy session the multimodal therapist may tentatively experiment with different styles of interaction with the client to discover the interpersonal approach that may benefit the therapeutic relationship. Decisions are made on when and how to be directive, non-directive, supportive, cold, warm, reflective, gentle, tough, formal, informal or humorous. Would the client prefer the therapist to take the stance of a coach or trainer rather than that of a warm, empathic counsellor. These issues are all considered important in forming a good therapeutic alliance with the client (Bordin, 1979).

The counsellor avoids placing clients on a Procrustean bed and treating them alike but will look for a broad, tailor-made combination of effective techniques and strategies to bring to bear upon the problem. The methods are carefully applied within an appropriate context and delivered in a manner or style that is most likely to have a positive impact and a good long-term outcome (Palmer, 1997c).

In conclusion, by taking a flexible, idiographic perspective, multi-modal counselling can be used successfully with many ethnic minority clients, including those experiencing extreme difficulties (see Slowinski, 1985).

DISCUSSION ISSUES

What are the advantages and disadvantages of using multimodal therapy with ethnic minority clients?

What demands does multimodal therapy place on the counsellor?

Is multimodal therapy truly idiographic? Discuss.

How does a multimodal counsellor view the so-called 'resistant' client? In what way is this view helpful to the therapeutic alliance?

References

Bandura, A. (1969) *Principles of Behaviour Modification*. New York: Holt, Rinehart & Winston.

Bandura, A. (1977) *Social Learning Theory*. Englewood Cliffs, NJ: Prentice-Hall.

Bandura, A. (1986) *Social Foundations of Thought and Action: a Social Cognitive Theory*. Englewood Cliffs, NJ: Prentice-Hall.

Bertalanffy, L. von (1974) 'General systems theory', in S. Arieti (ed.), *American Handbook of Psychiatry*, vol. 1. New York: Basic Books.

Bordin, E.S. (1979) 'The generalizability of the psychoanalytic concept of the working alliance', *Psychotherapy: Theory, Research and Practice*, 16 (3): 252–60.

Buckley, W. (1967) *Modern Systems Research for the Behavioral Scientist*. Chicago, IL: Aldine.

Dryden, W. and Lazarus, A.A. (1991) *A Dialogue with Arnold Lazarus: 'It Depends'*. Milton Keynes: Open University Press.

Fay, A. and Lazarus, A.A. (1993) 'On necessity and sufficiency in psycho-therapy', *Psychotherapy in Private Practice*, 12: 33–9.

Herman, S.M. (1991) 'Client-therapist similarity on the Multimodal Structural Profile Inventory as predictive of psychotherapy outcome', *Psychotherapy Bulletin*, 26: 26–7.

Herman, S.M. (1992) 'Predicting psychotherapists' treatment theories by Multimodal Structural Profile Inventories: an exploratory study'. *Psychotherapy in Private Practice*, 11: 85–100.

Herman, S.M. (1994) 'The diagnostic utility of the Multimodal Structural Profile Inventory', *Psychotherapy in Private Practice*, 13: 55–62.

Herman, S.M., Cave, S., Kooreman, H.E., Miller, J.M. and Jones, L.L. (1995) 'Predicting clients' perceptions of their symptomatology by multimodal structural profile inventory responses', *Psychotherapy in Private Practice*, 14: 23–33.

Jewel, P. (1994) 'Multicultural counselling research: an evaluation with proposals for future research', *Counselling Psychology Review*, 9 (2): 17–34.

Lazarus, A.A. (1973) 'Multimodal behavior therapy: treating the BASIC ID', *Journal of Nervous and Mental Disease*, 156: 404–11.

Lazarus, A.A. (1981) *The Practice of Multimodal Therapy*. New York: McGraw-Hill.

Lazarus, A.A. (1987) 'The multimodal approach with adult outpatients', in N.S. Jacobson (ed.), *Psychotherapists in Clinical Practice*. New York: Guilford Press.

Lazarus, A.A. (1989) *The Practice of Multimodal Therapy*. Baltimore, MD: The Johns Hopkins University Press.

Lazarus, A.A. (1993) 'Tailoring the therapeutic relationships or being an authentic chameleon', *Psychotherapy*, 30: 404–7.

Lazarus, A.A. (1995) 'Multimodal therapy', in R.J. Corsini and D. Wedding (eds), *Current Psychotherapies*, 5th edn. Itasca, IL: W.E. Peacock.

Lazarus, A.A. (1997) *Brief but Comprehensive Psychotherapy*. New York: Springer.

Lazarus, A.A. and Lazarus, C.N. (1991a) 'Let us not forsake the individual nor ignore the data: a response to Bozarth', *Journal of Counseling and Development*, 69: 463–5.

Lazarus, A.A. and Lazarus, C.N. (1991b) *Multimodal Life History Inventory*. Champaign, IL: Research Press.

Palmer, S. (1992) 'Multimodal assessment and therapy: a systematic, technically eclectic approach to counselling, psychotherapy and stress management', *Counselling*, 3 (4): 220–4.

Palmer, S. (1993) *Multimodal Techniques: Relaxation and Hypnosis*. London: Centre for Multimodal Therapy.

Palmer, S. (1996) 'The multimodal approach: theory, assessment, techniques and interventions', in S. Palmer and W. Dryden (eds), *Stress Management and Counselling: Theory, Practice, Research and Methodology*. London: Cassell.

Palmer, S. (1997a) 'Multimodal therapy', in C. Feltham (ed.), *Which Psychotherapy?* London: Sage.

Palmer, S. (1997b) 'Modality assessment', in S. Palmer and G. McMahon (eds), *Client Assessment*. London: Sage.

Palmer, S. (1997c) 'A multimodal approach with ethnic minorities'. Paper given at the First International Counselling Psychology Conference, British Psychological Society, Division of Counselling Psychology, Stratford-upon-Avon, 1997.

Palmer, S. and Dryden, W. (1991) 'A multimodal approach to stress management', *Stress News*, 3 (1): 2–10.

Palmer, S. and Dryden, W. (1995) *Counselling for Stress Problems*. London: Sage.

Palmer, S. and Lazarus, A.A. (1995) 'In the counsellor's chair. Stephen Palmer interviews Arnold Lazarus', *Counselling*, 6 (4): 271–3.

Palmer, S. and Strickland, L. (1996) *Stress Management: a Quick Guide*. Dunstable: Folens.

Palmer, S. and Szymanska, K. (1994) 'How to avoid being exploited in counselling and psychotherapy', *Counselling, Journal of the British Association for Counselling*, 5 (1): 24.

Paul, G.L. (1967) 'Strategy of outcome research in psychotherapy', *Journal of Consulting Psychology*, 331: 109–18.

Ponterotto, J.G. (1987) 'Counseling Mexican Americans: a multimodal approach', *Journal of Counseling and Development*, 65 (6): 308–12.

Ridley, C.R. (1995) *Overcoming Unintentional Racism in Counseling and Therapy*. Thousand Oaks, CA: Sage.

Rotter, J.B. (1954) *Social Learning and Clinical Psychology*. Englewood Cliffs, NJ: Prentice-Hall.

Slowinski, J.W. (1985) 'Three multimodal case studies: two recalcitrant "Ghetto Clients" and a case of posttraumatic stress', in A.A. Lazarus (ed.), *Casebook of Multimodal Therapy*. New York: Guilford Press.

Sue, D.W. (1981) *Counseling the Culturally Different: Theory and Practice*. New York: Wiley.

Triseliotis, J. (1986) 'Transcultural social work', in J. Cox (ed.), *Transcultural Psychiatry*. London: Croom Helm.

Watzlawick, P., Weakland, J. and Fisch, F. (1974) *Change: Principles of Problem Formation and Problem Resolution*. New York: Norton.

AFTERWORD

This edited book has contained eight chapters focusing on a range of important issues when counselling in a multicultural society, including culture, identity, racism, assessment, culture centred counselling, effective counselling and an idiographic approach to counselling. Although this book was not intended to be a comprehensive handbook, the subjects covered may help counsellors intending to work in multicultural settings to gain an insight into some of the key areas that need to be addressed. Experienced counsellors could view the book as part of continuing professional development, whether or not they agree with some of the views of the authors. We decided to include a chapter giving the multimodal perspective as this approach is not well known in Britain, unlike the USA.

Appendix 1

RECOMMENDED READING

We provide below a recommended reading list to highlight some of the books that we have found useful in increasing our understanding of counselling in a multicultural society. Although some of the books focus on counselling ethnic minority groups in America, in our opinion they also raise interesting issues that are relevant to cross-cultural counselling in Britain. In addition, we have included publications that may help the reader to study in more depth some of the subjects and issues covered in this book. For the reader's convenience, we have given the title of the book first.

Against Therapy, by J. Masson, 1989. London: Collins.

Aliens and Alienists: Ethnic Minorities and Psychiatry, 3rd edn, by R. Littlewood and M. Lipsedge, 1997. London: Routledge.

Applied Cross-cultural Psychology, edited by R.W. Brislin, 1990. Newbury Park, CA: Sage.

Assessing and Treating Culturally Diverse Clients, by F.A. Paniagua, 1994. Thousand Oaks, CA: Sage.

Challenges to Counselling and Psychotherapy by A. Howard, 1996. London: Macmillan.

Client Assessment, edited by S. Palmer and G. McMahon, 1997. London: Sage.

Clinical Guidelines in Cross-cultural Mental Health, by L. Comas-Diaz and E.E.H. Griffith, 1988. New York: Wiley.

Counselling Across Cultures, 4th edn, edited by P.B. Pedersen, J.G. Draguns, W.J. Lonner and J.E. Trimble, 1996. Thousand Oaks, CA: Sage.

Counselling the Culturally Different: Theory and Practice, by D.W. Sue, 1981. New York: Wiley.

Counselling for Stress Problems, by S. Palmer and W. Dryden, 1995. London: Sage.

Culture-centred Counselling and Interviewing Skills, by P. Pedersen and A.E. Ivey, 1993. Westpoint, CT: Greenwood/Praeger.

Cultures of Healing, by R.T. Fancher, 1995. San Francisco: W.H. Freeman & Co.

Death and Bereavement Across Cultures, edited by C.M. Parkes, P. Laungani and B. Young, 1996. London: Routledge.

The Decline and Fall of the Freudian Empire, by H.H. Eysenck, 1985. London: Methuen.

Eastern and Western Approaches to Healing: Ancient Wisdom and Modern Knowledge, by A. Sheikh and K.S. Sheikh, 1989. New York: Wiley.

Effective Psychotherapy, edited by A.S. Gurman and A.M. Razin, 1977. New York: Pergamon Press.

The Effects of Psychotherapy, by H.H. Eysenck, 1966. New York: International Science Press.

A Guide to Treatments that Work, by P.E. Nathan and J.M. Gorman, 1997. New York: Oxford University Press.

Handbook of Counselling, edited by S. Palmer and G. McMahon, 1997. London: Routledge.

Handbook of Cross-cultural Counselling and Therapy, edited by P. Pedersen, 1987. London: Praeger.

Handbook of Culture and Mental Illness: an International Perspective, edited by I. Al-Issa, 1995. Madison, CT: International University Press.

Handbook of Multicultural Counselling, edited by J.G. Ponterotto, J.M. Casas, L.A. Suzuki and C.M. Alexander, 1995. London: Sage.

In Search of Self in India and Japan: Toward a Cross-cultural Psychology, by A. Roland, 1988. Princeton, NJ: Princeton University Press.

Mental Health, Race and Culture, by S. Fernando, 1991. London: Macmillan/MIND.

Minority Children and Adolescents in Therapy, by M.K. Ho, 1992. London: Sage.

Overcoming Unintentional Racism in Counseling and Therapy, by C.R. Ridley, 1995. Thousand Oaks, CA: Sage.

The Practice of Multimodal Therapy, by A.A. Lazarus, 1989. Baltimore, MD: Johns Hopkins University Press.

Psychology and Culture, edited by W.J. and R.S. Malpass, 1994. Boston, MA: Allyn and Bacon.

Race, Culture and Counselling, by C. Lago and J. Thompson, 1996. Buckingham: Open University Press.

Race, Culture and Difference, by J. Donald and A. Rattansi, 1992. London: Sage/Open University.

Shamans, Mystics and Doctors, by S. Kakar, 1982. New York: Knopf.

Social Foundations of Thought and Action: a Social Cognitive Theory, by A. Bandura, 1986. Englewood Cliffs, NJ: Prentice-Hall.

Third World Challenge to Psychiatry, by N.H. Higginbotham, 1984. Honolulu: University Press of Hawaii.

Transcultural Counselling in Action, by P. d'Ardenne and A. Mahtani, 1989. London: Sage.

Transcultural Counselling, by Z. Eleftheriadou, 1994. London: Central Publishing House.

Appendix 2

CROSS-CULTURAL COUNSELLING AND PSYCHOTHERAPY CENTRES AND OTHER RELEVANT ORGANIZATIONS

Compiled by Zack Eleftheriadou

African Caribbean Mental Health Association
35 Electric Avenue
London SW9

Asian Family Counselling Service
74 The Avenue
West Ealing
London W13 8LB

British Psychological Society
Race and Culture Special Interest Group
The Chair
St. Andrews House
48 Princess Road East
Leicester LE1 7DR

British Refugee Council
3–9 Bondway
London SW8 1SJ

Daryeelka Maanka: Somali
MIND
3 Merchant Street
London E3 4LY
(0181) 981 7979

Hammersmith Counselling Centre
182 Hammersmith Road
London W6 7DJ

King's Fund
11–13 Cavendish Square
London W1M 0AN
Tel. (0171) 307 2400

Nafsiyat Intercultural Therapy Centre
278 Seven Sisters Road
Finsbury Park
London N4

The RACE Division
British Association for Counselling
1 Regent Place
Rugby
Warwickshire CV21 2PJ

Somali Community Association in Tower Hamlets
2 Zanginll House
Carr Street
London E14

Tower Hamlets MIND
Open House Community Project
Tidey Street
London E3
(Projects for Afro-Caribbean and Bangladeshi clients)

Transcultural Psychiatry Society (UK)
The Secretary
Sue Anson, Senior Social Worker
Ashworth Hospital Authority
Bronte House
Parkbourn
Maghull
Liverpool L31 1HW

Transcultural Psychiatry Society Unit
Lyndfield Mount Hospital
Heights Lane
Bradford BD9 6DP

Women and Medical Practice
40 Turnpike Lane
London N8 0PS

INDEX